100 THINGS
VIRGINIA FANS
SHOULD KNOW & DO
BEFORE THEY DIE

Brian Leung

TRIUMPH
BOOKS

Library of Congress Cataloging-in-Publication Data

Names: Leung, Brian J., author.
Title: 100 things Virginia fans should know & do before they die / Brian J. Leung.
Other titles: One hundred things Virginia fans should know and do before they die
Description: Chicago, Illinois : Triumph Books, [2016]
Identifiers: LCCN 2016011977 | ISBN 9781629371740 (paperback)
Subjects: LCSH: University of Virginia—Football—History. | Virginia Cavaliers (Football team)—Miscellanea. | University of Virginia—Basketball—History. | Virginia Cavaliers (Basketball team)—Miscellanea. | BISAC: SPORTS & RECREATION / Football. | TRAVEL / United States / South / South Atlantic (DC, DE, FL, GA, MD, NC, SC, VA, WV).
Classification: LCC GV958.U5864 L48 2016 | DDC 796.04309755/481—dc23 LC record available at https://lccn.loc.gov/2016011977

This book is available in quantity at special discounts for your group or organization. For further information, contact:
    Triumph Books LLC
    814 North Franklin Street
    Chicago, Illinois 60610
    (312) 337-0747
    www.triumphbooks.com

Printed in U.S.A.
ISBN: 978-1-62937-174-0
Design by Patricia Frey
Photos courtesy of AP Images unless otherwise indicated

To the memory of Grandma, who didn't know English and didn't care about Virginia sports, but nonetheless would have loved to see me finish this.

Contents

Foreword

When I arrived at the University of Virginia to coach the men's basketball team in 1974, the university was a sleeping giant with a strong regional academic reputation and a proud history. At times to outsiders like me, preserving that history seemed to be more important than ensuring that the university's future was even brighter than the past. The sleeping giant, however, was already responding positively to the significant presence that four full classes of undergraduate women would soon have on the Grounds as well as having the opportunity to cheer for a genuine basketball hero in Barry Parkhill.

During our first 16 seasons in the ACC from 1955 to 1970, no Virginia team had posted a winning season. Parkhill and his teammates provided back-to-back winning seasons in 1971 (15–11) and 1972 (21–7), and Barry was named ACC Basketball Player of the Year and ACC Athlete of the Year. Those two winning seasons plus the 1976 ACC Tournament championship—with Wally Walker being named the tournament's Most Valuable Player—ignited a fanbase that would later provide the enthusiasm and energy to help UVA play a major role at the highest competitive levels of intercollegiate athletic success.

Recruits responded positively to the newfound success of Virginia basketball. The signing of Jeff Jones, Jeff Lamp, Lee Raker, Ralph Sampson, and the dynamic duo of Ricky Stokes and Othell Wilson drew a great deal of attention. And those players helped put outstanding teams on the floor, resulting in an amazing five-year run that included the 1980 NIT Championship, 1981 Final Four, 1982 Sweet 16, 1983 Elite Eight, and 1984 Final Four.

Virginia high school standouts like Sampson, Stokes, and Wilson were important to the admissions office's efforts to attract a diverse student body while the success of Virginia basketball on the court and the resulting media attention made the University of Virginia a household name.

The athletic success of the late 1970s also provided athletic director Gene Corrigan with an opportunity to submit a draft of what would become known as the "Corrigan Report." Under the leadership of president Frank Hereford, the Corrigan Report became the blueprint for the role that athletic success should play in the university's aspirations to become a national leadership university and, ultimately, the powerhouse international leadership university that we know today.

The Corrigan Report's recommendations also acknowledged the need for more scholarships for the Olympic sports, more academic and other support for all student-athletes, as well as the need for first-class training and playing facilities for all sports. It is hard to imagine, but without the Corrigan Report, none of the premier facilities we enjoy today would be on Grounds. During my time as Virginia's athletic director in the 1990s, it became apparent that our facilities were still behind our ACC peers. Of particular concern were the football stadium, University Hall, and the baseball stadium.

The great on-field success of football coach George Welsh and the generosity of former UVA football player Carl Smith and his wife, Hunter, created the Carl Smith Center, home of David Harrison Field at Scott Stadium. As soon as that project was completed, the planning and fund-raising for the John Paul Jones Arena and Davenport Field began, and the construction and/or renovation of facilities have continued. Virginia athletics currently stands toe to toe with those intercollegiate institutions competing at the highest level. Director of athletics Craig Littlepage and his staff are dedicated to providing facilities that will allow each sport to compete for ACC and national championships.

The success of each program today builds on what all of us, as members of the university community, have done in the past. *100 Things Virginia Fans Should Know & Do Before They Die* serves as a great resource for looking back at the people and moments that have gotten us this far.

—Terry Holland
Virginia basketball coach (1974–90)
Virginia athletic director (1994–2001)

1 Ralph Sampson

Just before the start of the 1979–80 college basketball season, Virginia had won a long, competitive battle with Kentucky, North Carolina, Virginia Tech, and about 50 other colleges for Ralph Sampson, the 7'4" center who had won just about every high school accolade there was to win. "Is one player strong enough to lift a team to the top of the college basketball world?" Ken Rappoport wrote for the AP. "Perhaps—if his name is Sampson."

Rappoport's words may have been a little harsh on the rest of the team. Virginia's 1979–80 team returned three starters from a squad that went 19–10 and participated in the NIT the year prior. One of those starters included Jeff Lamp, who was the ACC's scoring leader at 22.9 points per game.

From his first day on the court as a Cavalier, Sampson proved he was worth the hype of the tremendous recruiting efforts put on by Virginia and other schools while he was still in high school, and Virginia head coach Terry Holland was not shy about the expectations he had with Sampson. "What we're thinking about now is winning the NCAA title," he said shortly after Sampson announced his decision to attend Virginia. "That has to be our goal."

The goal would never be realized during Sampson's time, but the big man, whom his teammates began calling "Stick" because of Sampson's thin frame and stature, would still take the Cavaliers to uncharted territory during his four years. In Sampson's freshman year, he played in all 34 games, averaging 14.9 points, 11.2 rebounds, and 4.6 blocks per game. After jumping out with 12 wins in the first 13 games, the Cavaliers were ranked No. 8 in the country—just the first time since the 1971–72 season that Virginia was able to crack the Top 10. A rocky February finish sent the Cavaliers to the NIT, where Virginia would capture their first ever NIT championship. For his efforts Sampson was awarded ACC Rookie of the Year honors.

Sampson continued to push the team his sophomore year, the most successful season for the Cavaliers in Virginia history. Ranked in the Top 10 the entire season, Virginia climbed its way to its first No. 1 ranking after a 23–0 start to the season, a feat that remains unmatched for Virginia. The Cavaliers upended Villanova, No. 15 Tennessee, and No. 16 BYU en route to the program's first ever Final Four appearance, where they lost to No. 6 North Carolina, a team Virginia had beaten twice earlier in the season, and Sampson's first shot at a national championship would slip through his fingers.

Virginia would open Sampson's junior season with a No. 7 preseason ranking. The Hoos won 27 of their first 28 games, losing only to top-ranked North Carolina. Unfortunately, Virginia would eventually fall in the second round of the NCAA Tournament.

All the pieces looked to be in place for a deep NCAA Tournament run for Sampson's senior season. Virginia was ranked No. 1 in the preseason and had an All-Star cast of Craig Robinson, Tim Mullen, Ralph Sampson, Rick Carlisle, and Othell Wilson as its starters with support coming from Jim Miller, Ricky Stokes, and Kenton Edelin. Sampson's senior season was a roller coaster that saw what many dubbed the "Game of the Decade," a showdown featuring Ralph Sampson's No. 1 Virginia taking down Patrick Ewing's No. 3 Georgetown. Two weeks later the team hit a low as the country saw No. 1 Virginia fall to unranked, unheralded Chaminade 77–72 in what many dubbed the "Upset of the Century."

Heading into the ACC and NCAA Tournaments, the team felt more prepared than ever to make a deep run and capture a championship. "Everything we have done," Holland told *The New York Times* in 1983, "has been predicated on preparing this team

Virginia center Ralph Sampson holds the Wooden Award after he earns Player of the Year honors in 1982.

BRIAN LEUNG

for the NCAA Tournament, even if it meant losing games. We did not worry about even a regular season championship. Our goals are much longer range than that. The only thing left for this team is to win a national championship."

It was a goal that would never be achieved. Virginia would be denied both an ACC title and another NCAA Final Four appearance at the hands of North Carolina State, who defeated Virginia 81–78 and 63–62, respectively. Sampson would graduate from Virginia without any ACC or NCAA hardware.

That's not to say he didn't pick up a few accolades along the way. Sampson was a three-time ACC Player of the Year. He was also a three-time National Player of the Year, one of only two individuals to have that claim; UCLA's Bill Walton was the other. The Houston Rockets selected Sampson as the overall No. 1 pick in the 1983 NBA Draft. In the NBA he was named the Rookie of the Year in 1984 and made four NBA All-Star games, earning NBA All-Star Game MVP honors in 1985.

The Times article also recalls a story about Sampson, which spoke to his personality. Just a few days before the NCAA Tournament, he and some old friends were gathered at a restaurant recounting stories from the past year. "You know who has good cheerleaders?" Sampson asked his friends. "Utah. We said, 'We've got to meet these girls.' So we're in the lobby of the hotel, and they want to take a picture, and I said, 'You want to take a picture? Come on.'" As the cheerleaders gathered around him, Sampson pulled teammates Othell Wilson and Doug Newburg into the picture as well.

A team player from start to finish, Sampson had been looking for girlfriends for Wilson and Newburg. It was Newburg who got a Utah cheerleader's address.

An injury in the 1986–87 NBA season cut his promising career short, though Sampson would stay in the league until 1991. Sampson was not inducted into the College Basketball Hall of

4

Fame until 2011, five years after it was founded. His No. 50 jersey has been retired at Virginia. "He changed the whole game, the whole game," said former Duke forward and current ESPN analyst Jay Bilas. "It was like playing against your dad in the driveway. You had no shot. I held him to 36 points and thought I did a pretty good job."

2 1995 Florida State Game

They're gonna say no! They're gonna say no! Virginia won the football game!

With those words Virginia football radio play-by-play announcer Warren Swain exemplified the sheer emotion behind the Cavaliers' biggest win ever.

On November 2, 1995, the Florida State Seminoles were the No. 2 team in the country at 7–0 and in their fourth season as members of the Atlantic Coast Conference. They'd never lost an ACC game, going 29–0 in conference play since the 1992 season. Virginia was 6–3 and ranked No. 24 with their three losses coming by a combined seven points. Two of those losses came by one point on the final plays of the games at Michigan and Texas.

An over-capacity crowd 44,300 made for a raucous atmosphere. Two decades later longtime ESPN sideline reporter Dr. Jerry Punch recalled that it was a setting comparable to football powers like Nebraska and Alabama.

Virginia and Florida State went back and forth over the first portion of the game. The Cavaliers twice answered Seminoles touchdowns with one of their own, and both involved legendary running back Tiki Barber. The first came on a long end-around run, and the other was a short pass from quarterback Mike Groh. Virginia took a 17–14 lead on a Rafael Garcia field goal early in the second quarter on a drive set up by a blocked James Farrior punt.

A memorable 72-yard touchdown pass later in the second quarter from Groh to Pete Allen would end up being Virginia's final touchdown of the game. Allen made the catch over FSU defensive back Samari Rolle, who fell down while trying to make the play. As Rolle tried to get up, he inadvertently tripped up teammate Sean Hamlet, who also fell to the turf. With 15 yards of space between Allen and the nearest Seminole, Allen strode into the end zone comfortably for the score.

It didn't take long for the Seminoles to respond, as Florida State quarterback Danny Kanell threw a 38-yard touchdown strike to E.G. Green just 52 seconds after Virginia's big play to cut the Cavaliers' lead to 24–21.

Virginia closed out the half with a field goal, held the Seminoles scoreless in the third quarter while securing a field goal of their own, and struck first in the fourth quarter with yet another field goal. Florida State's potent offense found no answers until 6:13 remaining in the game when the Seminoles found the end zone to bring the game to 33–28 in favor of Virginia.

With less than three minutes on the clock and a chance for Florida State to drive for the win, Kanell launched a long pass down the middle of the field. Virginia's Percy Ellsworth made an athletic grab at the Cavaliers' 45-yard line and returned the interception about five yards before sliding to ensure that the pick wouldn't be negated by a turnover. The Scott Stadium crowd went berserk as the potential for a program-defining win shifted to a probability in a flash.

Virginia, however, didn't make this one easy on their fans. Their ensuing drive quickly stalled after three plays, and FSU was given one last chance to make the miracle happen. With 21 seconds left and fans congregating at the bottom of the hill on the east side of the stadium ready to storm the field, Kanell completed a pass that went for more than 30 yards and got the Seminoles to the Virginia 12. A penalty for having 12 men on the field against UVA moved Florida State inside the seven-yard line with nine seconds left. The Virginia defense almost sacked Kanell, but he threw it away just in time to leave four seconds left on the clock. That gave FSU one last play to move the ball just six yards into the end zone.

Virginia fans began to storm the opposite end of the field, thinking the game was over. But they were quickly told, with the assistance of the Virginia bench, to get off the field so the game could be finished. When they did, the final play began with a direct snap to legendary FSU running back Warrick Dunn, who danced around and through the line. Finding a seam, he lunged toward the goal line. For a brief moment—loss then a heartbeat—the world stood still for Virginia fans. Did Dunn, or more importantly, did the football break the plane of the end zone? Virginia's Anthony Poindexter and Adrian Burnim were there to make the tackle, but were their efforts enough? The ESPN commentators called the touchdown but quickly realized that the Cavaliers had done what many though was impossible.

Pointdexter and Burnim had stopped Dunn just inches shy of the goal line. Virginia just handed Florida State its first ever ACC loss.

To this day Warrick Dunn swears the ball passed the line.

Thousands of fans rushed the field in a fit of exuberance, having witnessed what they thought was a minor miracle. In the process FSU became the highest ranked team that Virginia had ever defeated. Rugby Road was alive all through the night as the town celebrated an occasion that is still talked about more than 20 years later.

3 2014 ACC Tournament Champions

With what sounded like the entire Charlottesville area in attendance at the ACC Tournament, Joe Harris and the Virginia Cavaliers came together in mid-March of 2014 in Greensboro, North Carolina, to engineer perhaps the most magical weekend in the previous 38 years of UVA athletics.

For 19 years the UVA basketball team hadn't even reached the semifinals of the ACC Tournament. Whether it was for a chance to keep NCAA Tournament hopes alive or a chance at a higher seed in the NCAA Tournament, Virginia simply couldn't get over that hump. After a reasonably comfortable win in the quarterfinals against Florida State, the Hoos, the top seed in the tournament for the first time since 1981, got the first monkey off their back to reach the semifinals.

The Cavaliers had last reached the finals of the tournament in 1994, when they fell to North Carolina. Before reaching the finals this year, though, they would have to face Pittsburgh, a team the Cavaliers had barely escaped earlier in the season, needing Malcolm Brogdon to hit a three for the win with virtually no time left on the clock.

In the semifinal neither Pitt nor Virginia was able to create much separation throughout. Stout defensive play, which featured a famous triple-block from Virginia's Anthony Gill, Justin Anderson, and Darion Atkins, staked the Cavaliers to a 47–44 lead with two minutes left. Pitt's Josh Newkirk missed what would have been a game-tying three, and a big-time layup from Brogdon with a minute left made it 49–44 in the Hoos' favor. With time running out and Pitt not going away, Gill hit two clutch foul shots with 8.5 seconds left to make the score 51–48. Pitt's James Robinson pulled up for a three from the corner with about three seconds left, but the 6'6" Anderson got a fingertip on the ball, and it went well short and into the arms of Gill. A Pitt foul and an intentionally missed Virginia free throw later, and the Cavaliers had finally fought their way back into the ACC finals to face Duke.

For Duke it may have just been another game for yet another ACC title, but for Virginia this was a big opportunity to cement this year's team in the history books. For both teams their brightest stars came out to shine. Duke's Jabari Parker, who would be the second overall selection in the 2014 NBA Draft three months later, scored a team-high 23 points. Brogdon also led the Cavaliers with 23, going 7-of-17 from the floor. But it was senior Joe Harris who earned sweet redemption for the Cavaliers, who had lost to Duke earlier in the year 69–65.

Harris made a driving layup and was fouled with 7:42 left. The normally reserved guard pumped his fist and shouted as the play directed the lead—and seemingly the momentum—back to the Cavaliers. A Parker turnover created by Akil Mitchell getting his hands dirty in the low post led to a fast break opportunity for Virginia. Just shy of the center line, London Perrantes spotted an open Harris calling for the ball from the left wing. Perrantes sent a behind-the-head pass to Harris, who turned toward the basket and fired in one smooth motion.

A flawless arc took the ball through the bottom of the net, and with two minutes left, the Virginia bench erupted as the Hoos gained a 64–57 lead, which would prove too great for Duke to overcome. The shot that had gone against Virginia in so many ways over the intervening years since UVA's first conference title in 1976 was true, and the Cavaliers immediately sensed a championship. The killer instinct that was a trademark of that team was displayed, as a defensive stop on the other end further drove a stake into Duke's hopes.

After a Brogdon layup, the Hoos made six of their final eight free throws to ice the win. Duke coach Mike Krzyzewski decided to stop fouling with 15 seconds left—a sight that Virginia's loyal fans had been aching to see. Justin Anderson and Joe Harris embraced in victory, Bennett and Krzyzewski shook hands, confetti flew, and both Greensboro and Charlottesville swelled with euphoria. At 3:12 PM on March 16, 2014, Virginia players, administrators, coaches, and fans could savor victory in a way that had eluded them for 38 long years. UVA had lost the ACC title game in 1977, 1982, 1983, 1990, and 1994.

Harris would be named tournament MVP. He was just the second Virginia player, along with Wally Walker, to receive the honor, and Brogdon, Gill, and Mitchell would appear on either the first or second All-Tournament team.

4 The 1990 Game vs. Georgia Tech

Coming off an ACC Co-Championship and a 10–3 season in 1989, the 1990 Virginia Cavaliers picked up exactly where they left off. Ranked No. 15 to start the season, the first time the Cavaliers had been ranked preseason, Virginia rattled off seven straight wins. In a season where the top team in the land consistently struggled to hold on to its No. 1 ranking, Virginia climbed the rankings to the top. By the time they were facing No. 16 Georgia Tech (6–0–1), the Cavaliers were in their third straight week at the top of the college football world.

The big contributing names on Virginia's roster that season included junior quarterback Shawn Moore, junior wide receiver Herman Moore (no relation), sophomore defensive end Chris Slade, and sophomore running back Terry Kirby. Tight end Bruce McGonnigal, also a critical part of Virginia's dangerous offense, had ruptured his spleen and was not able to play.

Georgia Tech's playmakers included quarterback Shawn Jones, running back William Bell, linebacker Calvin Tiggle, and the unexpected hero, kicker Scott Sisson.

It was homecoming weekend for Virginia. The night before the game, vandals broke into Scott Stadium and burned a portion of the turf. The morning of the game, the Georgia Tech athletic director called his head coach, Bobby Ross, saying that the game may get canceled due to the turf conditions. However, the Virginia grounds crew was able to patch up the burned portion using leftover artificial turf from Virginia's baseball infield.

The Virginia offense was as advertised, scoring on each of their first five possessions of the game to take a 28–14 lead going into the half. Shawn Moore had run the ball in for touchdowns of one yard, one yard, and six yards. Two field goals by Virginia kicker Jake McInerney and a Moore-to-Moore connection for a two-point conversion helped give Virginia its healthy halftime lead.

In the second half, Georgia Tech quarterback Jones and the rest of the Yellow Jackets' offense exposed Virginia's defense from every angle. The Jackets scored on five of their six second-half possessions. With back-to-back touchdowns, Georgia Tech tied the game at 28 points apiece. From there, it just became a shootout between the teams. "It was almost like a track race," Jones said after the game. "I said all week it was going to be like this. They kept scoring, so we had to keep scoring."

"I just kept thinking, *Why are we making so many careless mistakes? Why are we helping them out?*" said cornerback Tony Covington, who was forced out of the game with an ankle injury. "I couldn't figure it out."

After exchanging a pair of touchdowns, including a 63-yard pass from Shawn Moore to Herman Moore, Georgia Tech took a 38–35 lead on a 32-yard field goal by Sisson. With just 2:44 to play, Virginia thought they would regain the lead on a 1-yard pass from Shawn Moore to tight end Aaron Mundy for the touchdown.

The play was called back, and Virginia was charged five yards on an illegal formation with only six players on the line of scrimmage.

Virginia's third-down pass to Herman Moore was deflected, leaving Virginia with the decision of either going for a chip of a field goal in hopes of getting the ball back or trying to win the game on fourth and goal from the 6-yard line. Virginia opted for the field goal and tied the game at 38. "I still don't think that you try for a touchdown," head coach George Welsh said after the game. "My God, what are the chances of that? I would never do it differently. There were two-and-a-half minutes. That's still enough time."

"I wanted to go ahead and go for it," Herman Moore said, "because you're giving the ball back to an offense that was moving the ball up the field the whole game. I have confidence in our offense, but I'm not the coach."

Georgia Tech drove 56 yards down the field in just five plays to set Sisson up for what would be a game-winning field goal that sailed straight through the uprights with just seven seconds left on the clock.

Virginia had one last chance to win the game. Shawn Moore heaved a Hail Mary into a crowd, and it would ultimately get intercepted by the Yellow Jackets. Georgia Tech had done it. They had taken down the No. 1-ranked, previously undefeated Virginia Cavaliers.

Both Shawn and Herman Moore had career days. Shawn Moore completed 18-of-28 passes for a Virginia single-game record of 344 yards. Herman Moore caught nine passes for a career-best 234 yards. "This loss hurts a lot because we worked so hard up to this point," Herman Moore said after the game. "It's devastating in the emotional aspect, but we've got to bounce back."

Virginia bounced back to defeat North Carolina the following week, but they would go on to lose the final three games of the season, against Maryland, Virginia Tech, and No. 10 Tennessee in the Sugar Bowl. With Shawn Moore still injured with a dislocated thumb, the Cavaliers would fall in their New Year's Day bowl but would finish the season ranked No. 23 in the final AP poll.

Georgia Tech, on the other hand, would win the remainder of their games, including a Citrus Bowl win over No. 19 Nebraska. They edged out Colorado by a single point from voters in the final UPI poll of the season to claim the UPI national championship. Colorado finished No. 1 in the AP poll. It would be another 18 years before Georgia Tech would be able to beat Virginia at Scott Stadium.

5 1981 Final Four

The Virginia Cavaliers got their first taste of a championship at the conclusion of the 1979–80 season when freshman phenomenon Ralph Sampson led the Hoos to a National Invitational Tournament championship with a 58–55 win against Minnesota. But it wasn't the championship they were hoping for.

When Sampson committed to Virginia, head coach Terry Holland was not shy about the team's goals for the next four years. "What we're thinking about now is winning the NCAA title," Holland said. "That has to be our goal."

As the 1980–81 season began, Virginia fans had to love what they were seeing. The Cavaliers were ranked No. 8 in the preseason and returning four of the previous year's starters in Sampson, forward Lee Raker, guard Jeff Lamp—a first-team All-ACC selection—and guard Jeff Jones. The media was also in a frenzy over Virginia. Whether it was *Sports Illustrated* covers or national television commercials, the hype machine for Virginia was working overtime. At one point *People* magazine reached out to the university requesting a photo shoot of Sampson standing with his head through a basketball hoop. That, however, was too much. "We said, 'No, we're not going that far,' and our guys rallied around Ralph and tried to protect him from the press," Holland recalled in a *UVA Magazine* article. "It worked to our advantage in a way because no one had to feel jealous of the publicity."

The season opened with a bang for the Cavaliers, who darted out to a 23–0 start on the season and a No. 1 ranking before finally losing their first game to No. 11 Notre Dame in a one-point contest. Over the first 23 games, only four opponents had managed to finish within five points.

When Virginia's ACC title run was cut short in a blowout loss to No. 20 Maryland in the ACC Tournament, all eyes turned to the NCAA Tournament with a 25–3 record.

Virginia rolled their way through the Eastern Regional championships, earning a spot in the Final Four in Philadelphia by taking down Villanova 54–50, No. 15 Tennessee 62–48, and No. 16 BYU 74–60. On deck for the Hoos was a familiar foe, the North Carolina Tar Heels, who were the Western Regional champions. In the regular season, Virginia had twice beaten North Carolina already, a 63–57 victory against the No. 16 Tar Heels at home followed by an 80–79 overtime win at Chapel Hill against the No. 11 team. Both wins were memorable to the fans, players, and coaches. Decades later Miami Hurricanes coach Jim Larrañaga, who was a Virginia assistant at the time, recalled the games fondly. "I remember [the game at Chapel Hill] being like a highlight reel. One great play after the other—Ralph was great, Jeff Lamp, Ricky Stokes, Othell Wilson, and UNC's players—Al Wood, James Worthy, and Sam Perkins—were all fantastic that night. It was an OT game and a one-point victory for us."

Many in the local and national media viewed Virginia as the favorite in the tournament, as Sampson had the ability on defense to limit opposing offenses to only one shot per possession while

Virginia's National Championships

Though Virginia missed out on a chance to bring home a national championship in basketball at the 1981 Final Four, the Cavalier trophy case isn't exactly hurting for hardware. In all, Virginia has brought home 24 NCAA team championships across a combined eight different sports:

baseball (one): 2015
boxing (one): 1938
women's cross country (two): 1981, 1982
men's lacrosse (five): 1972, 1999, 2003, 2006, 2011
women's lacrosse (three): 1991, 1993, 2004
women's rowing (two): 2010, 2012
men's soccer (seven): 1989, 1991, 1992, 1993, 1994, 2009, 2014
men's tennis (three): 2013, 2015, 2016

In addition to the 24 team titles, the Cavaliers have won 44 individual championships: men's tennis (six), women's tennis (two), track and field (10), cross country (one), men's golf (one), boxing (six), swimming (nine), and rowing (nine). These don't include other national titles that are not officially NCAA titles.

creating shots for teammates on offense. "If you choose to play him, he gets open shots for teammates," North Carolina head coach Dean Smith said leading up to the game. "If you don't play him, he can kill you. And he holds you to one shot, and most good teams need those second shots."

"We didn't come here with the idea of losing," said UNC forward Al Wood, who would be drafted No. 4 overall in the 1981 NBA Draft. "They beat us twice, but we could have won either with just a few turnarounds. You don't want a team to beat you three times in one season."

During the third meeting, neither team was able to gain traction during the first half, which had seven ties and six lead changes and ended in a 27-all deadlock. Virginia struck first in the second half on a Jeff Lamp driving layup followed by Sampson hitting one of two free throws (one of only two free throws he would miss that game) to take a 30–27 lead just 1:17 into the second half. Virginia looked like a team that had come out red hot in the second half.

But North Carolina would not be denied. Carolina guard Jimmy Black was awarded a goaltending call on Sampson and followed it up with an 18-foot jumper to give Carolina its first lead of the half. Freshman center Sam Perkins completed a three-point play, and Sampson committed another goaltend on Black, and suddenly the Tar Heels had gone on a nine-point run to open up the game 36–30.

Virginia answered with a 7–1 run of its own to tie the game at 37 points apiece with 13:02 remaining in the game in what looked to be a repeat of a tightly contested first half.

Over the next three minutes and change, though, North Carolina would open up a scoring battery, going on an 11-point scoring spree to take a 48–37 lead that would never dwindle back down to fewer than six points.

North Carolina's Al Wood scored a career-high 39 points in the winning effort for the Tar Heels. Perkins, who played a full 40 minutes for the Tar Heels, was able to match Sampson's points and rebounds totals at 11 and nine, respectively. North Carolina would lose in the national championship game to Indiana.

For Virginia Jeff Lamp had kept the Hoos in the game with 18 points. Raker followed up with 13, while Sampson and Jones each put up 11 points. The 1981 team remains perhaps the best and most successful team in Virginia basketball history. Sampson and Lamp were each named first-team All-ACC players and first-team All-Americans.

From that team seven players would eventually be drafted to the NBA. Lamp was drafted by the Portland Trail Blazers that year in the first round as the 15th overall pick while Raker was drafted in the fourth round by the San Diego Clippers, and Lewis Latimore was picked in the seventh round by the Milwaukee Bucks. In

1982 Jones was picked in the fourth round by the Indiana Pacers. In 1983 Sampson was selected as the overall No. 1 pick by the Houston Rockets, while Craig Robinson went in the third round to the Boston Celtics. Othell Wilson was drafted in the second round of the 1984 NBA Draft by the Golden State Warriors.

Virginia didn't get the national championship they dreamed of that year. Still, for a program that did not have the illustrious basketball history that a school like North Carolina did, the 1981 team came together as a family in a way that could only happen through its tremendous successes. "I can tell you that we had a great time with those kids in 1980–81," Holland recalled. "We were always pulling practical jokes on each other, coaches on the players, and vice versa. I had a gorilla costume that I brought out every Halloween to scare the women's basketball team and then come up with something to deal with our varsity team as well. We had a lot of fun together."

6 Breaking the Clemson Streak

The 1990 football season was arguably the greatest season in Virginia history, the peak of which was the Cavaliers' first and only No. 1 ranking in the country. Coming off an ACC co-championship the year prior, Virginia fans, students, and alumni had a hunch that it would be a special year, and they had their first taste of that in early September. On September 8, 1990, the ninth-ranked Clemson Tigers were traveling to Charlottesville to face the No. 14 Virginia Cavaliers. The two teams were no strangers. Since 1955 Virginia and Clemson had met 29 times.

In 29 tries Virginia had never beaten Clemson.

Over the course of the first four decades between the two teams, the Tigers had had their way with the Cavaliers. Although some contests were close, others were embarrassing. There were shutouts—seven of them, and the worst of which were 55–0 in 1984, 48–0 in 1982, and 47–0 in 1959. Fans of either team didn't even need to specify which series they were talking about when they simply referenced, "the Streak." In fact the series was so one-sided that the colorful Clemson coach Frank Howard once said, "Virginia? That's the white meat of our schedule."

No matter how good Virginia was—and to be fair, Virginia wasn't very good for the decades leading up to this game—it seemed that Clemson would always have their number. Nothing, it seemed, could push Virginia over that hump.

The 1990 season, however, felt different. Just the week prior, Virginia traveled to Kansas and handily defeated the Jayhawks 59–10. On both sides of the ball, Virginia seemed stacked with talent. At quarterback was senior captain Shawn Moore, who was in his third year as starter. Moore had won over the Virginia fanbase by showing that he could do anything he wanted with the ball—pass it short, air it out long, or keep it on the ground, and gain extra yardage himself.

On the receiving end of Shawn Moore's lasers was junior wide receiver Herman Moore (no relation). Herman Moore was coming off the 1989 season in which he was averaging just more than 23 yards per reception and scoring 10 touchdowns. Rounding out the offense for the Cavaliers was sophomore running back Terry Kirby, who would go on to set a couple of records during his time at Virginia, including rushing yards in a season and career rushing yards.

On the other side of the ball was sophomore linebacker Chris Slade, a future consensus first-team All-American and eventual Pro Bowl selection with the New England Patriots.

With this lineup Virginia fans felt as good as they possibly could going into the game. "The atmosphere built that whole summer," 1990 Virginia graduate Myron Ripley, who was working in the press box as a student at the time, said of the game. "Everyone knew we were good with Shawn, Kirby, Herman, Slade, etc. People were scared in one way to talk about it. Heck, at 29 games it seemed like [the streak] would never end. That year folks sort of knew we had a damn good chance. But still there was tension."

In front of an over-capacity Scott Stadium, Virginia went to work on what they knew would be their best shot at beating Clemson in four decades. The first quarter went almost exactly as scripted. Though Virginia was unable to find the end zone, the defense had held, and the Tigers also found themselves scoreless.

The Tigers would strike first in the second quarter behind a 25-yard run by Clemson quarterback DeChane Cameron, who escaped from two tackles en route to the end zone.

With only 3:26 to go in the half, Virginia's Jake McInerny connected on a 38-yard field goal. A couple minutes later, Slade broke through the offensive line and sacked the Clemson quarterback, forcing a momentum-shifting turnover that the Cavs would recover and convert into a field goal. Virginia would head into the locker room down only a point at the half.

The second half was all Virginia. Kirby used his strength and speed to punch his way to a touchdown just 3:43 into the third quarter. McInerny made Virginia's 133rd consecutive extra point—a streak going back to 1985—to give the Cavaliers a 13–7 lead that would not go back Clemson's way.

Clemson would be forced to punt on their following possession. Virginia's Jason Wallace would take the booming 55-yard punt at Virginia's own 15-yard line and return it 79 yards to Clemson's 7-yard line to set up the Cavaliers for another touchdown. Two plays and a false start later, Shawn Moore connected with Herman Moore on a 12-yard pass that had the 6'5" receiver leaping high into the air to pull down the ball and give Virginia what would become a 20–7 lead. At the time Herman Moore was the reigning ACC indoor high jump champion with over a seven-foot high jump and he needed just about every inch of that vertical to make that play.

The stadium was electric. Orange pom-poms riddled the air as the Cavaliers faithful began allowing themselves to believe that the Streak could be broken. Drive after drive, Clemson found themselves unable to overcome a staunch Virginia defense that refused to undermine what the offense had been able to accomplish all night.

With 48 seconds remaining in the game, fans began streaming over the walls of Scott Stadium ready to take the field. The Clemson equipment staff, knowing what was to come, began rolling their carts off the field. In fact so many fans had prematurely entered the field that those remaining in their seats started chanting, "Get off the field," as one of the goalposts was torn down completely with players still on the field trying to finish the game. Associate athletic director Jim West was cited in *The Cavalier Daily* as saying that the premature field charging, which resulted in a 10-minute delay, might have translated into a university forfeiture if it had not been contained.

As the final second ticked off and Clemson threw one last incompletion, the hoards of Virginia fans stormed Scott Stadium and covered the AstroTurf in a matter of seconds. The 1990 team had accomplished two things that no other Virginia team before them had been able to—beating Clemson and beating a top 10 team.

7 Hoos No. 1?

What if I told you that a team that had only two winning years in 29 seasons would take just two under a new head coach to get to a winning season—and just seven years after that to be ranked No. 1

in the nation? It almost sounds like an *ESPN 30 for 30*, but for the 1990 Virginia football team, it was the reality.

When George Welsh arrived in Charlottesville as head coach for the 1982 season, Virginia football was in shambles. The Cavaliers had gone 1–10 and winless in the ACC the prior year. In fact Virginia hadn't had a winning ACC record since 1968. But by 1983 Welsh had begun to transform the program. In 1983 the Cavaliers notched a winning 6–5 season and by 1984 they had gone 8–2–2 with a victorious trip to the Peach Bowl, the first ever bowl bid for the program. Welsh continued to lead the Cavaliers to winning seasons in four of the five next seasons, including a 10–3 record in 1989, when the Cavaliers were named ACC co-champions with a 6–1 conference record.

The players, the fans, the alumni…everyone knew as the 1990 season began that it would be special. Ranked No. 15 in the pre-season and having defeated Clemson for the first time in school history, Virginia opened the season with a perfect 5–0 record that included the program's first ever win against Clemson.

On October 13, 1990, the undefeated and No. 2 ranked Cavaliers dispatched a helpless North Carolina State team 31–0.

Later that evening No. 1 Michigan would be taking on Michigan State. Michigan had just reached the top ranking that week after Notre Dame, ranked No. 1 the week before, was upset by Stanford. Michigan's time atop the rankings would be short, as the Wolverines fell 28–27 to the rival Spartans. With Oklahoma's loss to Texas that same weekend, it was all but guaranteed that Virginia would rise to the top spot. "I was in the Cavalier Inn with my parents watching Michigan State beat Michigan," defensive end Chris Slade recalled in a 2010 *Daily Press* article, "and I remember jumping up and down excited like we had just won a game ourselves. I was probably more excited about [Michigan] losing than I was about us beating N.C. State earlier that day because I knew we were going to be the No. 1 team in the country."

When the AP Top 25 came out the next week, Virginia—with a perfect 6–0 record—could call itself king. The Cavaliers had received 38 of the possible 60 first-place votes to finish ahead of Miami (15 first-place votes), Tennessee (No. 2), and Nebraska (No. 3). The only other ACC team in the top 20 was undefeated Georgia Tech at No. 11. "I thought it was deserved," cornerback Jason Wallace recalled in 2010 about Virginia's No. 1 status. "It was something we were very proud of. That group of seniors— man, we put in some work to get the program to that point," Wallace said. "We didn't have any guys with big heads. We were just a bunch of good guys having a good time."

Slade recalled his excitement to see Monday's newspapers. "That was the first time I actually ran to the library," he said. "You went to the Corner, and they were already printing T-shirts: 'Look Hoos No. 1!'"

It was a new position for Virginia to be in. Student morale about the football team was astronomically high. Media, both local and national, flooded Charlottesville. "From like that Monday to Thursday, everyone was on an emotional high," Slade said. "The whole town was buzzing, and you had all the national media showing up to practice."

"I think I did interviews every day," Wallace said, "not just for one reporter but for tens of TV cameras."

Virginia would defeat Wake Forest 49–14 the following week, thereby retaining their No. 1 ranking, something that proved difficult for teams to do that season. The Cavaliers would drop a fateful contest two weeks later, following a bye week, to No. 16-ranked Georgia Tech. The Yellow Jackets would remain undefeated on the season with an 11–0–1 record, tying North Carolina, and would finish as the UPI national champion. (Colorado finished No. 1 in the AP Poll.)

Virginia would lose their last three games to close out the season ranked No. 23 in the AP Poll. But for three glorious weeks,

Virginia had stood atop the college football world for the first time in program history. No Cavaliers team since has been able to match this feat.

8 Tony Bennett

When the Dave Leitao era came to a close on March 16, 2009, the once-proud Virginia basketball program found itself at a crossroads. The Cavaliers' worst season in 41 years ended with a predictable loss to Boston College in the first round of the ACC Tournament. Leitao was fired the Monday after the game, and the search began for the man who Virginia fans hoped would be the savior of the program.

Wahoo fans were hoping for Tubby Smith, a national champion coach at Kentucky who resigned in 2007 to take over the reins of a less stressful Minnesota program. However, two weeks after Leitao's departure, *The Daily Progress* broke the story that a somewhat unheralded—if only for his overall lack of name recognition among the fanbase compared to his accolades—coach was coming to Charlottesville instead.

Thirty-nine-year-old Tony Bennett had just finished his third year at Washington State. Since taking over from his famous father, Dick, he'd guided the Cougars to top three finishes in the Pac-10 and the Sweet 16 in each of his first two years and was named both the Naismith and AP National Coach of the Year in 2007. A former player himself, a knee injury had derailed Bennett's NBA career, but the all-time record holder for three-point shooting percentage in college basketball was eager to go into coaching.

Those who followed the goings-on of the game outside of the Charlottesville and ACC circles knew that Bennett was a solid, if not showy, hire. But for those among the fanbase who tended only to know the more marquee names in the college coaching ranks, the choice by Virginia athletics director Craig Littlepage was uninspiring. Virginia legend Wally Walker told the *Daily Progress* after the hire, "For anybody who doesn't appreciate the hire, they haven't [seen] his teams play. He's a great coach. I've seen his teams play a lot, and several of my friends are former Washington State players and alums and they're heartsick over losing him." Walker

Coach Tony Bennett celebrates leading Virginia to the 2014 ACC Tournament title.

had been the general manager of the Seattle SuperSonics in the 1990s and played for both Seattle and Portland in the 1970s and '80s after graduating from Virginia.

Bennett had previously turned down offers from Marquette, a school from his native Wisconsin; LSU, the team located in his wife's hometown; and Indiana, the flagship school of what is arguably the sport's cultural hub. At his introductory press conference on April 1, Bennett said, "When my wife and I were flying over here, we started talking. We started talking about how the press conference is kind of like your wedding day. It's a celebration. There's a lot of promise. There's a lot of excitement. But what really matters, quite honestly, is the marriage, and that's the daily investment. That's the promise over time and that commitment, and I think that's what it takes to build a program, and I am so excited to do that here."

After some growing pains his first two seasons, the marriage between Bennett and Virginia has continued to blossom, in no small part as a result of Bennett's daily investment in a program that he has made his own. He's brought the Cavaliers into an era of unprecedented success with a multitude of NCAA Tournament berths and conference titles. In the process of elevating the program to nearly the upper echelon of the sport, he's done it while staying true to his "Five Pillars" of humility, passion, servanthood, thankfulness, and unity, as well as his devout Christian faith.

By Bennett's third season, the Cavaliers were back in the NCAA Tournament for the first time in five years. By Bennett's fifth season, the Cavaliers had won the ACC Tournament title and achieved a 30-win season for the first time since Virginia's 1982 Sweet 16 run. By Bennett's seventh season, the Wahoos were back in the Elite Eight.

The Miracle in Landover

The Virginia men's basketball team had traveled to Tobacco Road in search of a conference championship 22 times, and each time the Cavaliers had come up short. The only member of the league in its inaugural season to have never reached the championship game, Virginia was in its second season with Terry Holland as head coach in 1976. A streaky regular season—the Cavaliers only once went five games above .500—saw them enter the ACC Tournament as the No. 6 seed out of seven teams after going 4–8 in the conference and 15–11 overall.

The tournament was held outside the Tar Heel State for the first time that year, moving to the Capital Centre in the Washington, D.C., suburb of Landover, Maryland. To even get to the semifinals, the Wahoos would have to beat North Carolina State, a team that had beaten Virginia twice already in the season. The Wolfpack had won three of the last six ACC titles, but the No. 17 team in the country was no match for the likes of Wally Walker, Billy Langloh, and Marc Iavaroni, as Virginia outscored N.C. State by 16 in the first half and went on to win 75–63. Walker led all scorers with 25 points, going 10-of-15 from the field.

Walker's seventh straight 20-point outing made him one of two Cavaliers, along with Langloh, to score in double figures in the 73–65 semifinal win against second-seeded Maryland. Just eight miles from the Terrapins' College Park campus, Walker and Langloh combined for 47 points on 18-of-32 from the floor and 11-of-13 from the free throw line, along with 11 of the team's 30 rebounds. Bobby Stokes made two clutch free throws with around two minutes to play to put the Cavaliers up by five and make it a three-possession game. (This was before the NCAA instituted the three-point line.) He made three more free throws to ice the win and send UVA on to a Saturday night showdown against No. 1 seed and No. 4 North Carolina. The team that had never won twice in a single conference tournament—and that few expected to win a single game this time around—had shocked two teams in as many nights.

Walker was named second-team All-ACC at the end of the regular season, which many Virginia fans saw as a slight to what the senior, and eventual Academic All-American, accomplished his final season—22 points per game on 54.8 percent shooting. Holland, Walker, and the rest of the Cavaliers would see to it that the ultimate ACC team honor would belong to all of them for the first time.

After leading the Tar Heels 35–30 at the intermission, Virginia started the second half on the wrong end of a 12–2 run. It would be tied at 60 with four minutes left, and after an extended scoring drought from both teams, Langloh went to the line with less than a minute to go. Langloh sank both, and an ensuing layup from Otis Fulton, following a travel call on UNC, pushed UVA to the brink of a title.

With 10 seconds left, UNC lost the ball out of bounds. Langloh made one of two free throws to make it 65–60, and the celebration began. A late basket from North Carolina was followed by two last free throws from Langloh, and the game ended as the biggest upset in the history of the conference. The Virginia bench erupted as the sizeable Cavaliers portion of the crowd stormed the court in wild celebration of the monumental accomplishment.

It was the first time that a team had won the ACC championship by beating the top three seeds in the tournament, and Virginia had to do it against teams they'd gone a combined 0–6 against in the regular season. Walker went 7-of-9 in the final game, while shooting a perfect 7-of-7 from the line for 21 points and grabbing seven rebounds. His effort was redeemed in the end with the

Everett Case Award for the tournament's Most Outstanding Player. "Wonderful Wally's" No. 41 would be retired, and he would eventually be a world champion with the 1977 Portland Trail Blazers and 1979 Seattle SuperSonics.

10 Chris Long

When your father is in the Pro Football Hall of Fame and you're playing the same sport, at the same position, you're bound to be compared to him again and again ad nauseam. For defensive end Chris Long, son of the legendary Howie Long, flying under the radar was not much of an option growing up as he tried to make a name for himself as a high school student—and again at Virginia, working his way into the NFL.

Coming out of St. Anne's-Belfield School in Charlottesville, Long, unsurprisingly, was a standout multi-sport athlete, playing basketball, lacrosse, baseball, and, of course, football. A *SuperPrep* All-American, a PrepStar All-American, and the 2003 Gatorade Player of the Year in Virginia, Long was a four-star recruit who didn't drum up a lot of offers during his recruitment period. That's because, as a Class of 2004 recruit, Long gave a verbal commitment to the Cavaliers on November 3, 2002, becoming the earliest commitment in Virginia football history, according to *TheSabre.com*.

In his debut season in 2004, Long provided depth on the defensive line but wasn't able to make a big splash his first year, succumbing to illness and missing five games in the middle of the season. By his sophomore year, Long started every single game for the Cavaliers. His junior season saw more of the same. After that junior campaign, Long had already posted eight sacks and 24 tackles for loss out of 108 total tackles. He was named a second-team All-ACC his junior year.

By the time Long's senior season came around, there was no doubt that he had earned his scholarship based on his own ability and not based on his last name. Long became Virginia's third unanimous All-American in school history after recording 79 tackles, 19 of which were for losses, and 14 sacks. Long deflected nine passes, forced two fumbles, made one interception, and scored one touchdown his senior year. For his efforts Long, the ACC Defensive

Hall of Famer Howie Long (left) talks with Virginia head coach Al Groh while his son, All-American defensive end Chris Long, gets ready for spring practice. (USA TODAY Sports Images)

Player of the Year, was awarded the 2007 Ted Hendricks Award recognizing the nation's top defensive end.

With a resume like that, it's hard for a fan to pick a favorite play, but ask enough people, and one answer rises to the top. In Virginia's 2007 Maryland game at College Park with the Hoos down 17–10, the 284-pound Long drilled Maryland quarterback Chris Turner in the end zone for a safety late in the third quarter. Virginia's Mikell Simpson would score the game-winning touchdown with just 16 seconds remaining in the game to give Virginia a 18–17 win against the Terrapins.

Long was selected in the first round of the 2007 NFL Draft as the overall No. 2 pick to the St. Louis Rams. By comparison, his father was drafted in the 1981 NFL Draft in the second round as the 48th pick. "I'm not going to move out of my dad's shadow," Long said in an ESPN feature. "That's tough because he was a heck of a player, but I'm just going to try to make my own name and do a little something of my own."

Even amidst a successful NFL career, Long has not been shy about his Wahoo roots. In 2012 the then-five-year NFL veteran made a $300,000 contribution to the George Welsh Indoor Practice Facility for the football program. "I am so proud to be a part of a brotherhood like the Virginia football program," Long said. "Some of my greatest memories were experienced at UVA, working with my teammates to set a standard of excellence on the field that my university could be proud of. Virginia football players of the future deserve this same opportunity, and the construction of this facility goes a long way toward ensuring that reality."

Long's charitable nature and desire for social good didn't stop there. In 2015 Chris Long and Rams teammate William Hayes went undercover in the homeless community in St. Louis to walk 24 hours in their shoes. The two tried to panhandle for funds and slept in an empty box truck at night. The documentary aired on ESPN's *SportsCenter* to raise awareness for homelessness in

America. In 2012 Long had committed to donating $1,000 to the St. Patrick Center, a St. Louis resource center for the homeless, for each sack recorded. He has raised over $150,000.

For Virginia fans, who have followed him during his college career and beyond, none of this comes as a surprise, as the down to earth star athlete had won over the hearts of Cavaliers everywhere with not just his on-field performances, but also his off-the-field class. On November 24, 2007, the university retired Long's No. 91 jersey, making him the first player in Virginia history to have his jersey retired while still an active NFL player. The New England Patriots signed Long in 2016.

11 1989 ACC Championship

By fall of 1989, Virginia had been in the Atlantic Coast Conference for 35 football seasons, during which time the conference had as many as eight and as few as seven teams. By the start of the 1989 season, each of the charter institutions, including South Carolina, who left the ACC following the 1971 season, had won at least a share of the conference championship. Virginia and Georgia Tech, the Yellow Jackets didn't join the conference until 1979, were the last two teams remaining without any hardware.

Virginia had finished both the 1987 and 1988 seasons with a 5–2 conference record—good enough for a second-place finish in the ACC. With the return of honorable mention All-American Roy Brown at left guard; quarterback Shawn Moore, who had just come off throwing for over 2,100 yards the year prior; and the team's leading rusher in tailback Marcus Wilson, Virginia seemed poised for a strong season.

The Cavaliers opened that year against the defending national champion and No. 2 team in the country, Notre Dame, in East Rutherford, New Jersey, for the Kick-Off Classic. After a 36–13 shellacking by the Fighting Irish, nothing about this season opener had the Cavaliers faithful believing that the season would end with a championship ring in hand. "Never a prayer: Irish destroy Cavaliers in Classic," read the headline in *The Cavalier Daily* the next morning. Notre Dame had scored on each of their five possessions and jumped out to an insurmountable 33–0 lead over Virginia. "We got the hell kicked out of us," Virginia head coach George Welsh said after the game. "It was one of those games where you burn the films." Wilson carried the ball 15 times for 80 yards in the defeat. "I didn't see it as demoralizing," he said. "I saw it as embarrassing."

Virginia, though, was able to right the ship the following week when they traveled to No. 12 Penn State, defeating the Nittany Lions 14–6 in front of a crowd of 85,956, the second largest in Beaver Stadium at the time, to avenge a 42–14 loss to Penn State the year before. Each of Virginia's two touchdowns had come on a Moore-to-Moore pass, a 24-yarder and 15-yarder, respectively, from quarterback Shawn Moore to wide receiver Herman Moore, setting the stage for one of the strongest quarterback-to-receiver connections in all of Virginia football history.

The upset victory over Penn State, described by *The Cavalier Daily* as what may have been "the biggest win in Welsh's seven-year tenure," sparked life into the Cavaliers, who would go on to win the next three games, posting wins against Georgia Tech, Duke, and William & Mary to start the season with a 4–1 record. Other coaches, fans, and media began to take notice of the Virginia Cavaliers. "We had a chance to win, but obviously we didn't have much of a chance. Virginia's just way too good for us," Duke head coach Steve Spurrier said following their 49–28 loss to the

Cavaliers. Duke would go on to finish their season with an 8–4, 6–1 ACC record, tying Virginia for the conference title.

By the time Virginia traveled to South Carolina to face the No. 15 Clemson Tigers, the Hoos were beat up and bruised and in no shape to take on the three-time reigning ACC champions. Virginia had never beaten Clemson in 28 tries, and this year would be no different. The Cavaliers were without Shawn Moore (shoulder), tailback and prized recruit Terry Kirby (ribs), and defensive end Don Reynolds (ankle). Wilson had but one carry due to a hip injury.

Virginia put up a strong fight even with the limited roster. Backup quarterback Matt Blundin opened the second half with a 75-yard touchdown pass to Herman Moore, the longest pass of the season for UVA, to tie the game at 17 points apiece.

Two costly interceptions, however, would give the Tigers what they needed to blow the game open, ultimately winning 34–20. It was the Tigers' 29th consecutive win again the Cavaliers—then the longest active winning streak against any other Division I-A school by a team. Perhaps the silver lining to the loss at Clemson would be that the Cavaliers would return to Charlottesville the following week to defeat North Carolina 50–17 to give Coach Welsh his 100th career win in front of a home crowd.

Win after win just kept rolling in for the Cavaliers. The following week Virginia dispatched Wake Forest 47–28. It was the first time since 1968 that the Wahoos would score at least 45 points, 17 of which came from kicker Jake McInerney, who posted a school record with four field goals and five extra points. "You've got to be ahead by 26 to win. It's too easy to come back in college football," Welsh said following the game.

Virginia would escape the following week with a one-point victory against Louisville on a game-winning field goal from McInerney, who connected on his 10th, 11th, and 12th straight field goals to shatter the school record of 10 consecutive field goals.

The win was a big one for Virginia, and Welsh knew this. "Now we've got a chance for a great year," he said following the game, "a chance for one of the best seasons at Virginia in a long, long time."

A win against No. 18 North Carolina State the following week not only gave Virginia a sweep of the Carolina schools that season, but it also made George Welsh the winningest coach in Cavaliers history, breaking Art Guepe's school record. Virginia would dispatch Virginia Tech the week after as Wilson became just the fifth UVA player to rush for at least 1,000 yards in a season.

The regular season finale at College Park was a big one, as excitement for Virginia fans reached an all-time high. Virginia could reach a New Year's Day bowl, the Citrus Bowl. Virginia could achieve a 10-win season for the program's first time, breaking the nine-win record set in 1895, a record that hadn't been matched until this 1989 season. Finally, Virginia could win at least a share of the ACC championship.

Though Maryland was only 3–6–1 (2–4 ACC) that season heading into the game, the history between the two teams was enough for even just a casual observer to know how daunting of a task this high-pressure game would be. Virginia's record against Maryland was a mere 16–35–2, and even worse, Virginia hadn't won at Maryland's Byrd Stadium since 1971. Virginia's win against Maryland the prior season was the Cavaliers' first against Maryland in 16 years.

Behind the precision and athleticism of Shawn Moore, who rushed for two touchdowns and passed for three more, Virginia executed a near-flawless game, winning 48–21 to finish the regular season 10–2 (6–1). Virginia tied Duke for first place in the conference. Without any official tiebreaker policy in place, the ACC named both teams as co-champions. Duke claimed that they were more deserving of the championship crown because they had actually beaten the previous conference champions, Clemson, to get where they were. Virginia claimed that the Cavaliers were more deserving, as they had taken the head-to-head game against Duke.

The Citrus Bowl exercised its option to select the ACC champion for its New Year's Day bowl game in Orlando. Because the Cavaliers had beaten Duke and because the Cavaliers were ranked higher in the polls (No. 16 heading into the Maryland game), the Citrus Bowl opted to send Virginia to Disney World, while Duke was left with the consolation All-American Bowl in Birmingham, Alabama. The No. 15 Cavaliers would ultimately lose to No. 11 Illinois 31–21 and finish 18th in the AP poll.

Virginia's 1990 season is perhaps the program's most heralded season—in large part because the Cavaliers reached a No. 1 ranking for the first time in school history. But in many ways, the 1989 team achieved as much, if not more, than its 1990 brethren. And although the 1990 team might be more widely recognized for its accomplishments, the 1989 team has something the 1990 team never will: a championship ring.

12 2015–16 Basketball Season

When the Virginia Cavaliers' 2014–15 basketball season came to a premature end at the hands of Michigan State for the second year in a row, questions about the following season lingered. How would Virginia look without its All-American, Justin Anderson, who declared early for the 2015 NBA Draft, in which he was selected in the first round as the 21st pick by the Dallas Mavericks? Would the Cavaliers be able to replace the Lefty Driesell National Defensive Player of the Year in Darion Atkins, who was graduating? How would Virginia respond to a challenging schedule that included preseason out-of-conference Top 15 teams such as Villanova and California?

Though Virginia would lose the do-it-all Anderson and the defensive giant Atkins, the Hoos' leading scorer (14 points per game) and second team All-American Malcolm Brogdon would be returning and be supported by fellow seniors Anthony Gill, who had also been named to the All-ACC Defensive Team alongside Atkins, and Mike Tobey, who was the ACC Sixth Man of the Year.

An 86–48 win against Morgan State to open the season for Virginia was a sign that the Hoos were ready to pick up where they had left off, but then Virginia stumbled to a 73–68 loss against a George Washington team that was knocking on the door of the Top 25 rankings and would eventually win the NIT.

Virginia closed out the month of November scoring an average of 81 points—a far cry from the 65.4 points per game that the team had averaged in the season prior. The too-familiar storyline of Virginia dominating on defense but struggling on offense seemed to be losing steam, and fans began to wonder if head coach Tony Bennett had figured out the perfect balance between his renowned pack line defense with the firepower necessary to go further in the tournament.

Virginia's win streak included a 70–54 win at Madison Square Garden in the Jimmy V Classic against No. 14 West Virginia and a 86–75 thriller against No. 12 Villanova in Charlottesville in back-to-back games. It was followed up with a 63–62 overtime winner against California, a talented, freshmen-laden team ranked in the preseason at No. 14.

Ranked No. 4 with a record of 12–1, (1–0 ACC), the Cavaliers found themselves on the losing side of a 70–68 nail biter in Blacksburg against Virginia Tech. Junior guard London Perrantes' six three-pointers in the second half were not enough to come back from a 26–21 halftime deficit as Virginia gave up 26 points on 16 turnovers to the Hokies. It was a disappointing night for Virginia, but the rivalry game between the two schools had often been tight, and most Virginia fans chalked the loss up to a fluke.

The fluke, however, didn't stop in Blacksburg. The Hoos dropped two of their next three—on the road at Georgia Tech and again on the road at Florida State—and all of a sudden, Virginia had a losing ACC record after five games for the first time since Bennett's second year at Virginia in the 2010–11 season. "Virginia fans can officially start to panic," wrote Whitey Reid of *The Daily Progress* following Virginia's loss to Florida State. "There's been a disconnect with this team."

Virginia won the next two games against Clemson and Syracuse, both in Charlottesville, to bounce back to a winning conference record at 4–3. But there was no doubt that the Cavaliers in Charlottesville were as good as any team in the country. It was the road version that gave rise to questions, as all four of Virginia's losses at that point were on the road.

Virginia's next game was a trip to Winston-Salem to face a struggling Wake Forest squad. On paper there was no reason that the Demon Deacons should have been able to keep up with the Hoos. But road game woes reared their ugly heads again, and Wake Forest looked to be in the driver's seat as the Deacs came flying out of the gates and twice led by as many as 14 points, including with under eight minutes left on the clock. Virginia struggled offensively, shooting only 1-of-13 from beyond the arc in the first 39 minutes of the game despite being the ACC's leading three-point shooting team.

With a 10-point deficit and 90 seconds to play, it was statistically impossible for Virginia to come back, according to data analytics. What the numbers didn't take into account, however, was that the Virginia nets would catch fire. Virginia hit a perfect 4-for-4 on three-pointers in the final minute of the game and completed the miraculous 72–71 comeback victory with a buzzer-beating, three-point bank shot from Darius Thompson. "A miracle shot, a once-in-a-lifetime shot," Thompson said. "But it was our fault for putting ourselves in that situation to begin with."

The miracle shot was just what Virginia needed, and the Hoos finished the season with an 11–2 record. The Cavaliers' only two losses during the stretch were at Duke—on a controversial buzzer-beater by Grayson Allen in which many thought a travel should have been called before the shot—and at Miami. For the second year in a row, Virginia hosted ESPN's *College GameDay*, though this time the Hoos were on the right side of the win column against North Carolina.

Seeded second in the ACC Tournament, Virginia dispatched Georgia Tech and Miami to reach the finals against North Carolina. Though the teams were tied at 28 at the half, and Virginia led 44–40 with under 10 minutes remaining, the Cavaliers lost steam as shooters went cold, missing their next 12 shots and allowing North Carolina to use a 15–2 run that would give the Tar Heels the lead for good and the ACC championship.

Still, Virginia received a No. 1 seed in the NCAA Tournament for the second time in three years. For the third straight year, though, the NCAA Selection Committee slotted Virginia and Michigan State in the same region. Seeded No. 2, the Spartans seemed on a collision course to meet UVA again in the Elite Eight. But the Cavaliers would never get the opportunity to finally shake off the Spartan curse, as Michigan State lost in the first round to No. 15 seed Middle Tennessee State. With the loss of the other major powerhouse in the region, Virginia looked destined for a trip to the Final Four.

The Cavaliers looked dominant in the first weekend, defeating Hampton and Butler by a combined 44 points to advance to the Sweet 16. Newfound aggression from Tobey gave the entire team the lift it needed to set itself up for a long tournament run. Virginia continued to roll through its opponents, taking down No. 4 seed Iowa State in the Sweet 16 to set up an Elite Eight matchup with

ACC foe Syracuse, the No. 10 seed in the region. Syracuse was the lowest-seeded team to make the Elite Eight.

Virginia looked poised to cruise through another game, using a 19–2 run in the first half to take control of the game. Up by as many as 16 in the second half, the game seemed to be Virginia's to lose until Syracuse employed an uncharacteristic full-court press to slowly climb back into the game. It wasn't the press that stopped Virginia. The Cavaliers had faced a number of strong full-court press teams all season, including West Virginia, whom many referred to that season as "Press Virginia." But for the first time all season, Virginia allowed its opponent to dictate the pace of the game. Though Virginia was able to break the press without much difficulty—the Cavaliers were only once unable to get the ball over midcourt—they tried to take advantage of the resulting 2-on-1 opportunities. That's usually a sound strategy for teams that are able to pass the ball up the court to break the press, but Virginia's shooters had simply grown cold in the second half, and Virginia came up empty on most of the opportunities.

Perrantes was only able to score three points in the second half—compared to his 15 in the first. ACC Player of the Year Brogdon was limited to 12 points all game. Despite shooting 48 percent in the first half, including 45.5 percent from the three, Virginia was contained to 35.7 percent shooting in the second half and just 30 percent from the three.

On the other side of the ball, Syracuse went from shooting just 11.1 percent from beyond the arc (1-of-9) in the first half to 55.6 percent (5-of-9) in the second half. The Orange also made 16 of their 18 second-half free throws. That helped them outscore Virginia 47–27 after halftime and ultimately led to Syracuse's 68–62 victory and a berth in the Final Four.

Under head coach Tony Bennett, Virginia had never lost a game when heading into the locker room with a double-digit lead at the half. It was an impressive 68–0 record. After losing its

14-point halftime lead, that statistic dropped to 68–1 in what will certainly be a stinging memory in Cavaliers fans' minds for years to come.

Virginia finished the 2015–16 season at 29–8—just one win shy of reaching the 30-win mark for the third consecutive season. Though there's heartache that will stay with Virginia fans for some time, that's not to take away from the season's other accomplishments. A perfect 15–0 record at John Paul Jones Arena, Virginia was undefeated at home for the first time since 1981–82. The Elite Eight trip was the first for the Hoos since head coach Jeff Jones took the program there in 1995. Virginia also had a consensus first-team All-American in Brogdon, the program's first since Ralph Sampson.

Following the season-ending loss, Bennett told his team, "Weeping may endure for the night, but joy comes in the morning." The senior class of Brogdon, Gill, Tobey, Evan Nolte, and Caid Kirven, according to Bennett, made incredible strides toward establishing a national powerhouse program, and with a leading recruiting class coming in the for the following season, hope remains high for the Hoos faithful.

13 "Bullet" Bill Dudley

You're too small to play football.

The No. 1 pick in the NFL draft heard that again and again throughout grade school, but that wasn't enough to stop "Bullet" Bill Dudley, perhaps one of the most versatile players to ever play for Virginia. At a mere 5'9" and 110 pounds in high school, no one would have challenged that statement.

A late bloomer when he started as a first-year player at Virginia on scholarship in 1938, Dudley had managed to put on at least some weight, getting up to 5'10", 150 and beginning his career at Virginia as a punter and halfback. Dudley, a scholar of the game who was willing to put in more work than anyone else, was fifth on the depth chart at halfback, but a series of serendipitous (for him) injuries gave him a little playing time throughout his sophomore season, his first year lettering at Virginia.

That little playing time was all he needed to establish himself as a legitimate football player who could contribute mightily to a team that would get its first winning season in seven years that season. His junior season saw him as the starting halfback for every game, putting up impressive total offense numbers.

It was during Dudley's senior year in 1941, however, that he established himself not just as a well-rounded and effective player at Virginia, but also as one of the best college football players in the nation. Virginia finished the season 8–1—the Cavaliers' best season by far since a couple six and seven-win blips in the 1920s. Most notably, Virginia notched its first win against neighboring North Carolina, a team that had beaten the Cavaliers in each of the previous eight seasons, five of which were complete shutouts. In that game Dudley, just 19 at the time, was responsible for all three of Virginia's touchdowns (two rushing and one passing) en route to the 28–7 Cavaliers victory. His 325 all-purpose yards that game still ranks No. 2 in Virginia's annals.

Dudley would finish the 1941 season leading the nation in scoring (134 points), touchdowns (18), and all-purpose yards (1,675). His all-purpose yardage that season still ranks No. 6 in Virginia's history. Dudley was responsible for 206 of Virginia's 279 total points that season while playing as a rusher, passer, punter, place kicker, and punt returner.

Voted a consensus All-American (Virginia's first one), Dudley finished fifth in the voting for the Heisman Trophy that year. He was awarded the Maxwell Trophy as the nation's best player. In 1942 Dudley was selected as the first overall pick in the NFL draft by the Pittsburgh Steelers. He played his rookie season with the Steelers, earning Rookie of the Year honors after leading the league in rushing with 696 yards, as well as All-Pro honors. Dudley went on to serve in the Army Air Corps but returned to the Steelers for the 1945 and 1946 seasons. In his final season with the Steelers, Dudley earned the league's Most Valuable Player award, leading the NFL in rushing, punt returns, interceptions, and lateral passes attempted. He was the first person in the NFL to ever lead in four statistical categories. Also having spent time with the Detroit Lions and Washington Redskins, Dudley finished his NFL career with three Pro Bowl selections and six All-NFL first or second team selections.

In 1956 Dudley was elected to the College Football Hall of Fame. In 1966 he was elected to the Pro Football Hall of Fame. He was also the first player in any sport to have his number (35) retired at Virginia. His career after his playing days was wildly successful as well. He founded the NFL Alumni Association, for which he later served as president. From 1966 to 1974, he served in the Virginia House of Delegates. He also served on Virginia's Board of Visitors. At the age of 88, Dudley passed away in 2010 in Lynchburg, Virginia.

14 The Barbers of C'ville

There was no doubt that both Tiki and Ronde Barber, each a multi-sport athlete in high school at Roanoke, Virginia, were athletically talented. Both of the twins were selected as part of the

All-American team by the recruiting service, *SuperPrep* magazine, and were ranked in the top five among Virginia recruits during the fall 1992 season. Ronde had also won the high school boys' national championship as a hurdler (twice), while Tiki finished as high as second nationally in the long jump. Both were also members of the honor society, and Tiki graduated as valedictorian of his class.

When it came time to select their college, the twins knew two things: that they would only go to a school that gave offers to both of them and that they didn't want to go to hometown team Virginia Tech, the alma mater of both of their divorced parents. Though largely out of the picture during their childhood, their father, J.B., had played running back for the Hokies in the early 1970s, and the twins were born in Blacksburg. Their recruitment came down to five schools—Clemson, Michigan, Penn State, UCLA, and Virginia.

Penn State and UCLA quickly dropped off the radar. The twins first visited Virginia in early December 1992, as Virginia assistant coach Danny Wilmer was the first coach to recruit the brothers. Virginia seemingly had everything for the players—a football program that they could each contribute to almost immediately, a top-notch education as the NFL wasn't yet on the map for the brothers, and a close—but not too close—location to visit their mother.

In January the Barbers made an official visit to Clemson, though by then both players had made up their minds on Virginia. Following the visit to Clemson, Ronde said, "Clemson didn't show us what we wanted to see. I didn't feel we were as important to Clemson as we were to Virginia."

When they returned from their Clemson trip, they canceled their visit to Michigan and made a verbal commitment the following day to Virginia. "Our mom advised us to take a couple trips so we could make a comparison," Tiki said, "but our decision was sort of made as soon as we got back from Virginia."

Tiki played his freshman year at tailback, but he did not make much of a splash, carrying the ball just 16 times for 41 yards. He received more playing time his sophomore season both as tailback and as a kick returner, excelling particularly as a returner and earning All-ACC honorable mention honors for his efforts.

Ronde, on the other hand, took a redshirt his freshman year and immediately broke out as a star cornerback his sophomore season. Wreaking havoc on opposing teams' passing game, Ronde made eight interceptions during his breakout season, good for the second most in the nation. That year he was a first-team All-ACC selection and was named to the AP All-American third team. He was also named the ACC Rookie of the Year.

By their junior seasons in 1995, both Tiki and Ronde were ready to take the stage and lead Virginia. The season opened with a bang—a trip to Michigan in the Pigskin Classic to kick off the college football season on national television. No. 17 Virginia jumped out to an early 17–0 lead against No. 14 Michigan with both brothers contributing mightily to the effort. Ronde registered an interception, while Tiki, on third down from the Cavaliers' own 19-yard line, rushed 81 yards for a touchdown. The touchdown, was not without cost, though, as Tiki took a shoulder-separating hit from Michigan linebacker Jarrett Irons, forcing him to watch the reminder of the game from the sidelines. The fourth quarter saw the Wolverines score 18 unanswered points, winning on the last play of the game.

Loss notwithstanding, Tiki and Ronde continued to have standout junior seasons. Against second ranked Florida State, Tiki rushed for 193 yards and, together with his receiving and returning yards, logged 301 all-purpose yards en route to a 33–28 victory against the Seminoles, Florida State's first ever loss since joining the conference four seasons prior. Both the twins would earn first-team conference honors that season. Tiki entered Virginia's record book for rushing yards as a junior with 1,397 and most all-purpose yards as a junior with 1,906. Both are still records. Tiki and Ronde were named third-team All-Americans that year.

Both players continued their senior seasons with strong performances. Tiki was named the ACC Player of the Year. Ronde was named a second-team All-American by *Football News* and a third-team All-American by *The Sporting News*, while Tiki was named third-team All-American by *The Sporting News*.

On draft day in 1997, Tiki and Ronde spent the day golfing. It wasn't until the 17th hole that Tiki received a call from the New York Giants letting him know that he would be drafted in the second round as the 36th overall pick. Shortly thereafter, early in the third round, Ronde received a similar call from the Tampa Bay Buccaneers, letting him know that he'd be going as the 66th overall pick.

With one brother heading north and the other heading south, it would be the first time that the twins would be separated for any extended period of time since birth. According to an article on Mosaec.com that same evening over a celebratory dinner with their mother, Tiki said to her, "Mom, I want you to quit your job tomorrow. Ronde and I will take care of you."

15 1982 ACC Championship Game vs. North Carolina

Coming off a Final Four appearance and finishing third in the NCAA Tournament the previous year, the 1981–82 Virginia Cavaliers had high expectations. Ranked No. 7 in the preseason, the highest preseason ranking in the program's history, the Cavaliers tore through the regular season with a 27–2, 12–2 ACC record. Virginia's first loss was at the hands of No. 1 North Carolina 65–60, a loss later avenged when the No. 3 Wahoos convincingly upset the Tar Heels 74–58. Virginia's other ACC loss came to Maryland 47–46 in overtime, though it had defeated Maryland earlier in the season 45–40, also in overtime.

Though both teams had 12–2 records, North Carolina earned the No. 1 seed in the 1982 ACC Tournament, while Virginia received the No. 2 seed. The Tar Heels routed No. 8 seed Georgia Tech 55–39 and dispatched No. 4 seed N.C. State 58–46 to reach the ACC championship. Virginia, meanwhile, escaped No. 7 seed Clemson 56–54 and edged No. 3 seed Wake Forest 51–49.

North Carolina's roster was stacked with players who would soon become household names: Michael Jordan, Buzz Peterson, Sam Perkins, James Worthy, and Matt Doherty, for starters. The Tar Heels boasted six McDonald's All-Americans on the team and laid claim to four of the prior seven ACC titles, and North Carolina had just beaten Virginia in the 1981 Final Four semifinal the year before. Virginia wasn't without firepower of its own. The Cavaliers had legendary Ralph Sampson, the reigning two-time National Player of the Year, along with the likes of Othell Wilson and Jeff Jones. Virginia was also led by the reigning ACC Coach of the Year in Terry Holland.

It was the best matchup ACC—and college basketball—fans could hope for. Virginia was an offensive powerhouse; the team would finish the season leading the conference in points, average scoring margin, and rebounding average. North Carolina was known for their delay offense, a stalling tactic that would be known as the Four Corners.

The Tar Heels struck first, winning the opening tip and immediately scoring on their first possession. The Heels would jump out to an 8–0 lead and would continue to fire on all cylinders behind the herculean efforts of Carolina junior forward James Worthy, who scored 14 of his 16 points in the first seven and a half minutes of the game. All 16 of Worthy's points came in the first half, as he was a perfect 8-for-8 in field goals.

Despite the slow start, Virginia's baskets started dropping, and the Hoos closed out the first half trailing only 34–31. Virginia would open the second half strong to take a 35–34 lead within the first two minutes and would make six of their first eight field goal attempts in the second half. The lead, however, would not last long. North Carolina's Michael Jordan pounded away at the long-range jumper, including a 20-foot bucket that gave Carolina a 40–39 lead with 13:31 to play in the game. North Carolina would first go to the four-corner stall with 12:59 to play. "We tried the Four Corners to see if they would come out and chase us," North Carolina head coach Dean Smith said following the game. "When they did not attack, we went to our regular offense, setting a screen for Jordan. It worked, and we knew we would come back to it later."

With the Tar Heels up 44–41, Virginia's Jeff Jones would hit a 25-foot long bomb to cut the lead to just 44–43 with just more than seven minutes to go in the game. Smith called timeout to set up his Four Corners. "The four-corner stall was once called the four-corner offense, but no offense appeared to be intended today," *The New York Times* wrote. "James Worthy, Mike Jordan, Jimmy Black, Matt Doherty, and Sam Perkins played catch until Virginia committed its seventh foul of the half, which sent Doherty to the line with 28 seconds left [in the game]."

Doherty made the first but missed the second to give the Heels a 45–43 advantage. Pressured by Black, Virginia freshman Jim Miller had the ball go off his knee to give Carolina the ball back in a possession that likely sealed Virginia's fate. Doherty was fouled again, but this time made both buckets. Sampson made an uncontested dunk at the buzzer for the 47–45 final score. North Carolina would win its fifth ACC title in eight years.

The ACC Tournament, and especially the championship game, sent the nation into a heated debate on the rules of college basketball, the possibility of a shot clock, and the effect the North

Carolina brand of basketball was having on the country. "I don't care about the image of the sport," said Doherty, who would become head coach at North Carolina later in his career. "It was good for Carolina basketball because we won the game."

The day after, when asked whether he thought anything should be done about the delaying in college basketball, Smith responded, irritated: "Isn't it amazing? We saw a great basketball game until about 8:40 was left, and that's all you want to talk about. Are there any more questions except for those about the delay?" When asked about it, Holland chose the higher route. "I'm not getting involved in that controversy," he said. "North Carolina did what it thought it had to do to win."

But even North Carolina center Sam Perkins had reservations. "Slowdowns are hurting the game, at least according to the fans. More and more people are doing it, so I think they'll eventually introduce a device to stop it, a clock or something."

"We were just trying to win, and did," Smith said after the game. "They have a 7'4" guy you want to get out from under the basket, and he won't come out. If Sampson had come out, it might have been different. When I use the Four Corners and win, I'm a genius. When I use it and we lose, I'm all wrong."

The loss was deflating for Virginia, but the Cavaliers would still earn the top seed in the Mideast Regional. North Carolina was the top seed in the East Regional. Virginia would advance to the Sweet 16 before losing 68–66 to No. 17 UAB. North Carolina would go on to win the national championship. The ACC and a number of other conferences introduced a shot clock experimentally the following season. In 1985 the NCAA adopted a 45-second shot clock, which would be reduced to 35 seconds in 1993 and again to 30 in 2015.

16 Malcolm Brogdon

If you were to meet Malcolm Brogdon for the first time without knowing who he was, you'd probably guess that he was a senior business executive, a lobbyist, or perhaps a governor. The son of a lawyer and a university associate provost and a graduate of the Frank Batten School of Leadership and Public Policy at the University of Virginia, Brogdon isn't your typical college basketball player.

Regarded by recruiting services as a four-star recruit out of high school in Georgia, Brogdon received offers from Clemson, Harvard, Minnesota, Notre Dame, and Vanderbilt, among many others. After returning from his official visit to Virginia in August of 2010, the 6'5" guard committed to the university, citing an instant bond he felt with Virginia head coach Tony Bennett. As a member of a family that prioritizes academics above all else, he found pressure from his parents to delay the commitment until he had made official visits to two other schools in particular—academic powerhouses Vanderbilt and Harvard.

Still, Brogdon affirmed his commitment to Virginia. In his freshman season in 2011–12, Brogdon played in 28 games and started in one, missing the final four games, including the first round of the NCAA Tournament, with a left foot injury. The Cavaliers were routed by the Florida Gators in that first-round game 71–45.

Foot surgery that season left him out for the entirety of the 2012–13 season. Following the redshirt year, Brogdon came back during the 2013–14 season with a more refined game, playing in and starting all 37 games during Virginia's first Sweet 16 run since the 1994–95 season before losing to Michigan State. Leading the team with 12.7 points per game and an 87.5 free throw shooting percentage, Brogdon was named to the All-ACC first team by the ACC coaches. He was the only ACC player to score in double figures in all 18 ACC regular-season games, an impressive feat for a member of a team that played at the sixth slowest pace in the country with games averaging only a combined 60.9 possessions.

Brogdon's progression continued through his junior year when he led the team with 14 points per game, shooting 42.2 percent from the field, 34.4 percent from three, and 87.9 percent from the free throw line. For his efforts he was recognized by both the ACC coaches and media as an All-ACC first-team member and recognized by the national media on the second team All-American. He was named a finalist for multiple national player of the year awards. For the second year in a row, however, Virginia found themselves going home early from the NCAA Tournament, losing once again to Michigan State—this time in the second round.

When power forward Mike Scott declared for the NBA draft a year early in 2012, Virginia turned to junior guard Joe Harris to take command of a young team in need of leadership. When Harris graduated in 2014 and the Cleveland Cavaliers selected him in the draft, Virginia needed a new leader to rally behind, and Justin Anderson rose to the occasion with his passion and athleticism. When Anderson declared he would leave Virginia a year early to enter the 2015 NBA Draft and was selected in the first round by the Dallas Mavericks, Virginia again needed a new leader to emerge. A very different personality from Anderson, Malcolm Brogdon became that hero, leading the team with his calm demeanor.

So calming was Brogdon's attitude that his pregame ritual actually included a yawning session. "I've never met a player," said teammate Marial Shayok in a *Wall Street Journal* article, "who yawns on a consistent basis." It wasn't because he was bored of his competition in the NCAA. For Brogdon the involuntary yawning

The 2015–16 ACC Player of the Year, Malcolm Brogdon, dribbles the ball during a 2015 victory against Ohio State in which he had a game-high 22 points. (USA TODAY Sports Images)

could be a way to lower his brain's temperature and improve decision-making, according to the same article.

Whatever the reason, it appeared to be working. In Brogdon's senior season, he averaged a whopping 18.2 points per game while shooting 39.1 percent from the three-point line. Brogdon was named both the ACC Player of the Year and ACC Defensive Player of the Year, the first time in conference history that the same player received both honors. He was also the first player to ever receive back-to-back Defensive Player of the Year honors from the ACC coaches, having shared it with teammate Darion Atkins the year prior. Brogdon was the first ACC Player of the Year for the Cavaliers since Ralph Sampson in 1983.

His senior season had, by his standards, tipped off with a rocky start. During a 69–62 loss to Florida State, the third loss for the Cavaliers in four games, which gave a highly touted Virginia team a 2–3 conference record, Brogdon tried to take command of the game in a similar fashion to perhaps what he saw from Scott, Harris, and Anderson in years past. Brogdon attempted 17 field goals that night, trying to single-handedly carry the team's offense and be the spark the team so desperately needed. Only four of those shots went in, though, a percentage unacceptable to Coach Bennett.

In front of the entire team at a team meeting, Bennett specifically pointed to Brogdon's shot selection, using it as an example of what goes awry when an individual player does not follow the team mentality. "Coach Bennett definitely got on me hard," Brogdon said in an interview with *The Daily Press*. "He called me out in front of the team, and, really, I tried to be more within the offense from then on and get my shots out of the offense…It's part of being one of the best players on the team. Sometimes you're going to mess up. Sometimes you're going to need to be put back in check."

Following the criticism, Brogdon met with his teammates individually to solicit criticism and refine his game. Brogdon altered his game, recognizing that, while being a great shooter with good court vision, his strengths as a leader extend to being able to pull in his teammates to execute Bennett's game plan. Virginia went on to win the next seven games straight before falling to Duke in Durham on a controversial buzzer beater. By the end of the season, Brogdon was an unanimous consensus first-team All-American.

Virginia fans lovingly call him "The Governor." His brothers call him "Humble Moses," a play off his middle name. He's not like most star basketball players you'll meet. He knows that his future, while it may include some NBA playing time, holds a greater calling than the sport.

He says he wants to be a politician one day, while his mother, who believes he is too honest to be a politician, said he would more likely end up being a public policy lobbyist. Brogdon has also said that he would like to use his NBA money to one day create a non-governmental organization (NGO) to address poverty and hunger in developing nations. "People don't realize how motivated he is," Bennett said in a *USA TODAY* article. "His nickname is awesome because Moses was one of the humblest men. He was the prince of Egypt and had great courage going to Pharaoh. That's like Malcolm. He's very driven, very purposeful in what he does, but he has a humility and is unaffected by things that come his way. He has a plan and he's going to stay true to who he is."

17 Save UVA Sports

In 1998, as the university founded in 1819 began its preparations to enter into its third century, president John T. Casteen announced a "Virginia 2020" initiative to outline the university's agenda for the future, including acknowledging its successes to date, identifying areas for improvement, and proposing recommendations to move forward. In 1999 Casteen appointed the Virginia 2020 Strategic Planning Task Force for the Department of Athletics, a 17-member task force to critically assess the program's facilities, academics, Title IX and NCAA compliance, overall finances, and fund-raising. By April of 2001, the task force made a number of recommendations, but two of their findings in particular struck a chord with the university at large.

The first was that, in order to bring the university into full Title IX compliance, the athletics department would need to increase the number of female athletes from 47 percent to 54, which was reflective of the female student population at large. In order to do this, the task force recommended that the athletics department eliminate men's indoor track and add women's golf, which would bring the ratio up to 51 percent. The second finding was that at the time the university athletics department was operating at a deficit of approximately $200,000, a deficit that their most conservative financial forecasts projected would rise to $10.4 million annually by 2010 for a cumulative deficit of $47 million during that period.

To address the funding issue, the task force recommended classifying the university's 24 varsity programs into four tiers to be reviewed annually, each with disparate treatment: Tier One was football, men's basketball, and women's basketball. Each Tier One sport would receive full funding of grants-in-aid "to compete at the highest intercollegiate level." Tier Two included men's and women's lacrosse, men's and women's soccer, field hockey, rowing, and men's and women's swimming. Each Tier Two sport would receive full or substantial grants-in-aid and operating budgets to contend for a national championship.

Tier Three included women's golf (if added), softball, women's tennis, women's cross country, women's indoor and outdoor track and field, and volleyball. Each Tier Three sport would receive limited grants-in-aid or need-based aid and minimal staffs and operating budgets.

Tier Four included baseball, wrestling, men's golf, men's tennis, men's cross country, men's indoor track and field (if not dropped), and men's outdoor track and field. Each Tier Four sport would only receive need-based financial aid and would only receive a limited coaching staff. Tier Four sports would only be permitted to undertake regional travel, though they would continue to compete in the ACC.

Other recommendations were made, but the tiered structure garnered the most attention—and outrage—particularly from the student body. "To qualify for nationals in cross country and track," first-year student Walton Kingsberry, a member of the track and field and cross country teams, said in an interview with the *Cavalier*

ACC's Longest Winning Streak in Any Sport

It's incredible to think that as late as 2001 Virginia men's tennis was listed as a Tier Four sport with the threat of receiving only need-based financial aid, having only a limited coaching staff, and being permitted only regional travel. If these recommendations had been followed, not only would Virginia's trophy cases be a lot emptier—between 2001 and 2015, Virginia amassed six individual singles and doubles NCAA champions and two team national championships—but the ACC record books would be missing one of its most impressive stats.

On May 14, 2006, the Virginia men's tennis team under head coach Brian Boland defeated ACC opponent Wake Forest, a match that would spark a win streak that would span nearly an entire decade. During this time Virginia won 140 consecutive matches against ACC opponents, the longest such streak in the conference in any sport.

The streak was broken on February 15, 2016, when North Carolina defeated Virginia 4–2 in the finals of the Intercollegiate Association's National Team Indoors Championships at the Boar's Head Sports Club in Charlottesville. Virginia had previously won the title five times, in 2008, 2009, 2010, 2011, and 2013. It was North Carolina's first appearance in the championship match.

Daily in 2001, "you have to qualify through a regional meet, which is not in Virginia. Basically, it's taking us out of the national spotlight altogether. It's their way of killing the program off without pulling the rug out from under our feet."

Expectedly, the coaches of the Tier Four sports were vocal in their reactions to the task force's recommendations. Baseball coach Dennis Womack was among the most vocal of the group. "I don't think it's better to have this stated," Womack said in a *Cavalier Daily* article. "Nobody wants to be in Tier Four; you'd at least like to move up a tier or two. Five or six years down the road, we'll probably be the laughingstock of the ACC. It's a devastating blow in terms of competition, not only in the ACC, but also throughout the state of Virginia."

Similar sentiments were echoed by wrestling coach Larry Bernstein, men's golf coach Michael Moraghan, and track and field coach Randy Bungard. By early June, following continued vocal pressure from students, alumni, athletes, and others, and upon the recommendation of its Student Affairs and Athletics Committee and Finance Committee, the university's Board of Visitors commended the task force's efforts in identifying the athletics department's major issues but specifically rejected the proposals to tiering or eliminating any sports. Instead, the athletics department was tasked with working with the Board of Visitors to develop more creative methods of fund-raising to make up the deficit.

By the end of June, the university's athletics department announced that, thanks to anonymous donations of $2 million, the baseball program would be launching a $4 million upgrade to what would be named Davenport Field. Many suspected that the anonymous donor was famed legal thriller author John Grisham, whose son, Ty Grisham, was set to play for Virginia as outfielder. "We went from the outhouse to the penthouse," said Womack.

The baseball program, under head coach Brian O'Connor, hosted its first ever regional in 2004—just the fourth time the program had even reached the NCAA Tournament—and would go on to make the tournament every year thereafter, including a College World Series title in 2015. The men's tennis program since 2001 has also garnered multiple singles and doubles national championships, earning the reputation as one of the most dominant programs in the country, and in 2013 earned its first team national championship, following up with a second in 2015.

The wrestling program won an ACC Championship in 2010 finished 15th, a program best in the NCAA championships the same year. From 2008 to 2010, the men's golf program reached the NCAA championships for three consecutive years. They finished 11th in 2010, the program's best ever finish. Each of the men's cross country and track and field teams, though they have not yet found national team accolades since the task force's recommendations (the men's outdoor track and field had an individual 800m national champion in Robby Andrews), has continued to demonstrate improvement during that period.

18 Virginia Tech: A Rivalry Rooted in Controversy

The Virginia-Virginia Tech rivalry has its roots in the 19th century, but it wasn't always so heated. The two schools began playing each other in 1895, a contest that resulted in a 38–0 victory in favor of the Cavaliers. In the first eight meetings between the two teams from 1895 to 1904, Virginia Tech was shut out in seven of them, scoring only five points in the other. Virginia was 8–0 against the Hokies by a cumulative score of 170–5. The lopsided record did not sit well with a Virginia Tech player by the name of Hunter Carpenter.

Carpenter enrolled at Virginia in 1898, but he didn't begin playing for Tech until 1899, under the name Walter Brown because his father had forbidden him to play football. Eventually his father saw him in a game, and he was allowed to begin playing under his own name. As good as Carpenter was at halfback, there was one thing he was never able to accomplish during his four years of playing from 1899 to 1903: he was never able to beat Virginia.

Carpenter was so infatuated with beating the Commonwealth's flagship university that, after graduating from Virginia Tech in 1903 with an engineering degree, he entered law school at North Carolina, a school that had gone 6–3 in 1903, including a 16–0 win against Virginia. "I want to help Carolina beat the University of Virginia," he said.

He would again be unsuccessful. Virginia would win 12–11 on an extra-point attempt that bounced off another Virginia Tech transfer and over the crossbar. In his one record-setting season at North Carolina, Carpenter established himself as one of the greatest Tar Heels of all time.

What happened next, though, would ultimately be the start of a rivalry. With relaxed eligibility standards, Carpenter declined North Carolina's offer to be a team captain for the 1905 season. But still determined to beat Virginia, he decided to return to Virginia Tech for a *seventh* season at halfback—this time on a stacked team favored to win the game. Virginia protested the use of Carpenter in the game on multiple grounds. The Virginia Inter-Collegiate Athletic Association, of which Virginia Tech was a member, prohibited the use of postgraduate players. Unfortunately, Virginia had withdrawn from the VIAA earlier in the year, and therefore the rules were not applicable in the contest.

Virginia's efforts to protest Carpenter's eligibility didn't stop there. Professional players also were prohibited from playing.

The Virginia student newspaper claimed that they had proof that Carpenter was on an athletic scholarship—effectively getting paid to play for Virginia Tech during a time in which some conferences viewed athletic scholarships, as opposed to academic scholarships, to be a form of professionalism. The school demanded that Carpenter sign an affidavit against his professionalism, which he did, but that did little to comfort the Virginia administration or fanbase.

Virginia Tech dominated nearly every facet of the game behind Carpenter's outstanding play. With an 11–0 lead for Virginia Tech, Carpenter was ejected after throwing the ball directly at a Cavalier. Depending on who you ask, what prompted the outburst differs. Ask a Virginia fan, and they'll tell you that the Cavaliers' R.E. Barry made a hard tackle, leaving Carpenter banged up. Ask a Virginia Tech fan, and they'll say that for the third time Barry had clotheslined Carpenter, grabbing his neck and throwing a punch. Regardless of which story is to be believed, the passion that arose out of the incident sparked a rivalry that would last more than a century.

The controversy doesn't end there. Despite the ejection of Carpenter, Virginia Tech would go on to win 11–0, its first victory ever against the Cavaliers. After the game the story goes that Carpenter caught wind of the student paper's scholarship accusations, something his teammates worked to keep from him in the weeks leading up to the game. Carpenter threatened to sue the student paper for libel. Between the potential use of an illegal player, the threat of legal action, and the physical confrontations on the field, Virginia said that it would no longer play Virginia Tech, a promise held true until the two schools reignited the on-field rivalry in 1923. Virginia would lose that game 6–3.

19 The Shot

There have been many truly defining individual moments in the history of Virginia basketball—Barry Parkhill's jumper to beat No. 2 South Carolina, Ralph Sampson hitting a floater to beat Maryland in his final home game, Joe Harris' dagger three-pointer to seal the 2014 ACC Tournament against Duke. But for UVA fans, there is but one play worthy of the name "the Shot," and it belongs to Sean Singletary.

Going for their first win against Duke in five years, unranked Virginia (13–6) took on the No. 8 Blue Devils on February 1, 2007 in its first season at the sparkling new John Paul Jones Arena. Trailing by as much as 13 in the first half, Virginia clawed back to make it a seven-point deficit at halftime.

Coming out of the locker room, Virginia picked up right where it left off scoring-wise. UVA kept scoring but still trailed for the first 12 minutes and change of the second half. Duke's Jon Scheyer fouled J.R. Reynolds on a three as the Blue Devils led 49–46. Reynolds, who scored 20 of his 25 points in the second half, confidently stepped up and made all three foul shots to tie the game. Those shots, however, came in a three-plus-minute stretch where Virginia failed to make a field goal, and Duke would go back up 54–49 and then 59–51 with less than four minutes remaining.

Six straight Reynolds free throws gave Virginia a chance to tie, as the Cavaliers were down 61–59 with 44 seconds left in regulation. Singletary went for the drive from the right wing and pulled up from the elbow, knocking down a game-tying jumper with 26 seconds left. Josh McRoberts missed what would have been a game-winner for Duke with three seconds left in regulation, and the game went to overtime.

Virginia drew first blood in the overtime session, as Singletary hit a pair of early free throws. The two teams traded free throws throughout much of the overtime. A defensive rebound from Singletary with 31 seconds left gave UVA a chance to hold for the last shot, and Virginia coach Dave Leitao called for time with 17 seconds to go.

Singletary brought the ball up, and from the beginning, it appeared to be an isolation play for the point guard. He dribbled to the right and drove to the low block outside the paint, beating McRoberts in the process. Somehow, while beginning to lose his balance, he launched a teardrop as he fell backward to the hardwood. It was nothing but net with one second left, and the roof of the building nearly went off as the circus shot put the Cavaliers on the precipice of their first win against Duke under Leitao.

Greg Paulus had one final look from three at the buzzer that nearly went for Duke, but it bounced off the back of the iron. What Singletary did after the shot was almost as notable as the game-winner itself. He pointed and started at an ESPN camera that caught him in a group hug with Reynolds and Mamadi Diane, a cold-blooded look that earned the nickname "the Stare."

"I would come to shoot early before games, sometimes two or three hours, shoot until I almost passed out," Singletary told *The Daily Progress* in 2015. "Every time we played a game on ESPN, we'd get the same camera man, a tall, black guy. He told me, 'Anytime you make a three-pointer or something, look at me and do something.'"

20 George Welsh

George Welsh was a glutton for punishment. When he took over as the head football coach at Navy in 1973, he was taking on a program that had an embarrassing 12–41 record over the previous five years with no real sign that the program could be saved. In Welsh's nine seasons at the helm, Navy came away with five winning seasons, including a nine-win season that finished with a win in the Holiday Bowl. Welsh became Navy's all-time winningest coach at the time.

Just as he was proving that the military academy could enjoy sustained success, he left in 1982 to move to another flailing program: Virginia. Up until Welsh arrived, the Cavaliers were what athletic director Terry Holland would later describe as "cannon fodder," with an all-time 33–121–11 record in the Atlantic Coast Conference. Virginia had never been to a bowl game.

In a time when Virginia fans questioned whether the Cavaliers could ever be a national powerhouse given its rigorous academic requirements and high admissions standards, Welsh was unwilling to accept the premise. "Why can't Virginia be that?" Welsh asked. "If you accept limitations without trying to change them, you don't belong in football coaching. One of the things that attracted me to Virginia is that it is an outstanding institution. I like the idea that you can have high academic standards, a high graduation rate among athletes, and have a good football team that will be competitive each week. In recruiting I like to be able to sell a strong academic institution and attract athletes who are good students. There are plenty of those around."

It didn't take long for Welsh to turn the program around. After a losing campaign his first year, going 2–9 and 1–5 in conference,

Coach George Welsh sports his signature white bar hat during the 1990 Citrus Bowl, one of 12 bowls Virginia reached during his 19 years at the school. (*USA TODAY* Sports Images)

Welsh and the Cavaliers found their way into the winner's circle his second season, finishing 6–5 overall and 3–3 in the ACC. It was only the third time in 31 seasons that Virginia had finished with a winning overall record.

By Welsh's third season in 1984, Virginia put up an 8–2–2 record, finishing second in the conference with a 3–1–2 ACC record, and notched a win over Purdue in the Peach Bowl, Virginia's first ever bowl game. The Welsh era was officially underway. Except for a blemish in 1986, Virginia wouldn't experience another losing season under Welsh's tenure.

Welsh, who made the iconic white bar "UVA" hat famous, would throw it onto the sidelines whenever he got angry. He considered leaving Virginia following the successful 1984 season. Arizona State made an offer to Welsh that more than doubled his salary at Virginia and made promises of facilities and resources at his disposal far beyond what Virginia had offered at the time. Still, his work at Virginia wasn't done, and Virginia updated his contract to keep him in Charlottesville.

Virginia fans remember one time in particular when Welsh, who was generally reserved, just couldn't bite his tongue. Virginia's 1989 ACC championship was shared with Duke, then led by another legend, Steve Spurrier. In the game between them, the Cavaliers scored on seven straight possessions to run the score up to 49–28, the biggest offensive showing for the Hoos in decades. The following week Duke upset reigning ACC champions Clemson, who would rebound the following week with a win against Virginia, for the 29th time in a row. Duke's loss to Virginia would be its only ACC loss of the season. Virginia's loss to Clemson was also its only ACC loss. The Citrus Bowl, who invited the ACC champion, offered the bid to Virginia on account of the head-to-head result, though the conference had no formal tiebreaker in place. Spurrier disagreed. "I've always felt that to be the true champion you're supposed to beat the guy who was champion before," he said. "We're the ones who beat Clemson…Of course, as we all know, Virginia hasn't beaten Clemson in the history of the school, and I don't know if they ever will. If a guy wants to beat Mike Tyson, he's got to beat Mike Tyson. He can't beat 'Bonecrusher' Smith and be the champ."

This time Welsh didn't hold back. "One thing I could never understand about Steve Spurrier, and you can quote me, we scored touchdowns on seven straight possessions in that game," he said. "And…it could've been worse. And then he said, 'Well, we should have been champions, because we beat the kings.' They beat Clemson, and we didn't. I'll tell you what. I might have been able to score 70 that night if I wanted to."

Virginia went 134–86–3 under George Welsh, who became the winningest coach in both Virginia and ACC history and earned 12 bowl bids for Virginia during his 19-season tenure. He earned ACC Football Coach of the Year honors five times; was named 1991 Bobby Dodd Coach of the Year Award winner, which is given to the Division I Football Bowl Subdivision head coach whose team excelled on the field, in the classroom, and in the community; and was named the national Coach of the Year by multiple groups in 1998. "I am now and will be forever a Wahoo," Welsh said when he retired at age 67. "It's time for this old salt to sail off into the sunset."

21 Joe Harris

When Virginia hired Tony Bennett to coach the basketball team in 2009, Bennett promised the fans and university community one thing. "I came here to build a great team, but more importantly,

I came here to build a program that lasts, and the way you go about that is you have great integrity and you have great passion," Bennett stated at his opening press conference.

Coming from Washington State University, Bennett inherited a program clamoring for sustained success. Bennett was able to retain two commitments of former Virginia coach Dave Leitao's final recruiting class, point guard Jontel Evans and forward Tristan Spurlock. However, his initial recruiting campaign began in earnest with a commitment from Joe Harris the summer after taking the helm in Charlottesville.

Harris, a talented wing from the picturesque lake town of Chelan, Washington, was heavily recruited by Bennett at Washington State. Despite the change in location, Bennett continued his pursuit of Harris and convinced the versatile player to follow him east.

Born September 7, 1991, in Chelan to parents Alice and Joe Harris Sr., Harris was destined to become a basketball player. Harris grew up surrounded by the game and clamored to assist his father, the basketball coach at Chelan High School, any time the opportunity presented itself. This included four-year-old Harris running the scoreboard and clock at practice for his dad. Throughout elementary and middle school, Harris served as the team's manager.

Though Harris played three years of football and two years of baseball in high school, he really shined in basketball. As a four-year starter for his dad, Harris earned both the Mr. Basketball in Washington state and the Gatorade Washington Boys Basketball Player of the Year titles his senior season in 2010. At Virginia in his first season, Harris joined a top 15 ranked recruiting class that included K.T. Harrell, Billy Baron, James Johnson, Will Regan, and Akil Mitchell. Of the six players, just Harris and Mitchell stayed all four years at Virginia, helping Coach Bennett build the foundation for the program going forward.

As a freshman Harris played in all 31 of Virginia's games, starting 25. The team went just 16–15 with a 7–9 record in the conference. Harris averaged 10.4 points and 4.4 rebounds per game and amassed 27 steals and 11 blocks. His 65 three-pointers made put him in second among freshmen in Virginia's record books for three-pointers made in their first season. Harris finished the season shooting 41.7 percent from three, the best mark for a freshman in the ACC since 2000.

Harris's second season featured a December road trip to the West Coast, which saw the Cavaliers play Oregon and Seattle University, giving some of his friends and family an opportunity to see him play. After the particularly raucous game at Seattle, Coach Bennett addressed the fans in the arena. "A lot of those were Chelan fans," Bennett stated. "Joe Harris had over 200 people here. That was nice for Joe, and he had a nice dunk. He is a young man that when he is around people they are drawn to him. It was nice to see the town embrace him and come here to support him."

Throughout his sophomore campaign, Harris played a major role for the Cavaliers. He saw action in all 32 games, starting all but one due to a broken hand he suffered against North Carolina in February. Transfers and multiple injuries left the Cavaliers depleted, but they were selected as the 10 seed in the West region in the NCAA Tournament. No. 7 seed Florida was too much for the Hoos, ending their season and leaving Harris wanting more.

In his junior season, Harris broke out, starting all 35 games for the Cavaliers, a school record at the time. Harris averaged a career-high 16.3 points, 4.0 rebounds, and 2.2 assists per game en route to a 23–12 record. His standout game came in a home victory against No. 3 Duke when he scored a career-high 36 points. Although Harris was always hesitant to talk about himself, preferring instead to praise the effort and hard work of his teammates, his performance impressed Duke head coach Mike Krzyzewski. "Harris was fantastic, which we knew he would be," Krzyzewski said after the game to reporters. "He's just one of the best players in the country. When you have a guy playing at that level…it brings everybody up. You know you're playing with a stud."

The Cavaliers faded down the stretch, dropping a couple conference games and missing the NCAA Tournament but garnering the top seed in the National Invitational Tournament. Harris earned All-ACC first team honors voted by both the ACC coaches and media.

Joe Harris had become a fan favorite for his on-court performance, hard work, and affable personality over the course of his first three years in a Virginia uniform. His final season cemented him as a Cavaliers legend. The Cavaliers entered the 2013–14 season ranked No. 24, their first time ranked in a preseason poll since 2001–02. Losses to No. 14 Virginia Commonwealth University, No. 8 Wisconsin, and Wisconsin-Green Bay had the Hoos on shaky ground as they entered their final non-conference game at the University of Tennessee in December of 2013. Tennessee pummeled the Cavaliers from the opening tip until the final whistle. The 35-point loss had Virginia and its fans reeling.

Virginia's offense looked flat. Its hallmark "pack line" defense did nothing to slow the Tennessee players. How would the Hoos fare in the challenging ACC? On New Year's Eve, the evening following the loss to Tennessee, fourth year Joe Harris drove to Coach Bennett's house in a story that would become the anecdote of the season. Bennett and the player who followed him cross-country three years previously spoke frankly about the state of the team and what needed to be fixed in order for them to achieve the goals set out at the beginning of the season.

When the Cavaliers hit the court next at Florida State, a new team emerged. The offense utilized a more rigid "blocker-mover" scheme, and players like Malcolm Brogdon, Anthony Gill, London Perrantes, Justin Anderson, Akil Mitchell, and Darion Atkins blossomed. Defensively, Virginia was near impenetrable. Virginia opened the ACC with three straight wins over Florida State, Wake Forest, and North Carolina State, outscoring the three opponents by an average of 22 points. A loss at Duke dropped Virginia to an overall record of 12–5, (3–1 ACC), but the Cavaliers would not lose again until March 9, 2014, after 13 straight wins.

Virginia clinched the ACC regular season title with a 75–56 win against No. 4 Syracuse, the first time it got any piece of the title since sharing it with North Carolina in 2007. The last outright title for the Cavaliers had come during the 1980–81 season with Ralph Sampson. Harris earned a spot on the All-ACC second team.

As the top seed in the ACC Tournament, Virginia dispatched Florida State and Pitt to set up a rematch with Duke, the only ACC team it had not defeated that season. After a back-and-forth affair, Virginia pulled away from the Blue Devils when Harris drilled a three pointer in transition to give the Hoos a seven-point lead with under two minutes left. When the clock finally read all zeroes, the scoreboard read 72–63 in favor of Virginia, and the confetti started to fall. It was the first ACC Tournament title for the Cavaliers in 38 years, and Harris' performance was instrumental in bringing it home for just the second time in Virginia's history as he earned the title of ACC Tournament Most Valuable Player and a spot on the All-ACC Tournament first team.

The late season push and domination of the ACC led the NCAA Selection Committee to select Virginia as their final No. 1 seed. The Cavaliers held off a pesky Coastal Carolina team 70–59 in the first game and then routed Memphis 78–60 in the Round of 32 to earn the chance to play in the Sweet 16 at Madison Square Garden in New York.

Virginia faced Michigan State in the Sweet 16 and, after a brutally tough fight, ended their season with a 61–59 loss. Harris had 17 points in the loss, and the Cavaliers had a 30–7 record for the year. Over the course of his impressive career, Joe Harris scored 1,698 points for the Cavaliers, which was good for 11th place in the

Virginia annals. He finished his four years ranked first at Virginia with most games played (135) and second overall in Virginia history with a 40.7 percent average on three-pointers, of which he made 263.

Along with Akil Mitchell, his lone senior classmate, Harris brought Virginia basketball into the national discussion. His leadership helped the Cavaliers not only win the ACC regular season and the ACC Tournament, but also return to the Sweet 16 for the first time since 1995. Harris was selected by the Cleveland Cavaliers in the second round with the 33rd overall pick of the 2014 NBA Draft.

22 Terry Holland

With 16 years as head coach and another seven as the athletic director, Terry Holland oversaw a basketball and athletics program that rose to new heights under his leadership at the University of Virginia. Holland began his coaching career at his alma mater, Davidson College, under the tutelage of then-head coach Lefty Driesell. When Driesell left five years later to take the head coaching position at Maryland, Holland was named the head coach at Davidson, where he was selected as the Southern Conference's Coach of the Year three times over the span of five years. Davidson finished atop the Southern Conference in each of the first four years of Holland's tenure at head coach.

When Virginia's Bill Gibson retired at the end of the 1973–74 season, Driesell recommended Holland to then-athletic director Gene Corrigan. Corrigan had narrowed the list to three: Holland, Tom Davis (who would go on to lead Boston College to a Big East regular season title in 1981 and later earn AP Coach of the Year with Iowa in 1987), and Larry Brown (who played on the 1964 U.S. Olympic team and would go on to coach multiple NBA teams and be inducted into the Basketball Hall of Fame and College Football Hall of Fame).

Davis and Brown, though, never stood a chance. Corrigan hired Holland on the spot before either of the other two could even interview. "That was one of the best hires I ever made in my life—anywhere, anytime," Corrigan said.

Since joining the ACC in 1953 until Holland was hired in 1974, Virginia had only recorded one season with a winning conference record, and that came in 1972. Many questioned whether Virginia's rigorous academic standards were too restrictive to allow the school to achieve excellence on the court. "When I came from Davidson to Virginia, as restrictive as the academic requirements were, they weren't as strict as Davidson's. I was in heaven," Holland recalled. "I looked at it as a great positive. I don't think it was restrictive at all. It was very fair. There were rarely situations where we were denied the admission of a kid who I felt could do the work here and should be here."

Two years after arriving in Charlottesville, Holland had taken a big first step at turning the program around. He captured the school's first ever ACC Tournament title, leading a team no one thought capable of achieving such success. Virginia had beaten three ranked teams in as many days to accomplish "the Miracle at Landover."

During his time as head at Virginia from 1974 to 1990, Holland led Virginia to its greatest heights, the peaks of which have still not been replicated to this day. In his 16 seasons, he had a 326–173 record, earning the honor of being Virginia's winningest coach. He took the team to nine NCAA appearances, including two Final Four appearances and an NIT championship. During his tenure he was twice named the ACC Coach of the Year.

He also had the pleasure of recruiting and coaching Virginia's greatest basketball player in program history, Ralph Sampson, who was named the three-time National Player of the Year. In 1990 Holland stepped down as Virginia's head basketball coach to become the athletic director of his alma mater, Davidson. "People still ask me why I got out when I did," Holland told *The Virginian-Pilot* in 2013. "I really miss coaching basketball at tournament time because basketball is such a great tournament game, but the rest of it I don't miss that much.

"As I said at the time or shortly afterward, coaches can leave their job in one of two ways. Either they die on the job or they get fired, and I didn't like either one."

He spent five years as the Davidson athletic director, during which time he moved the school back to the Southern Conference, nearly tripled annual fund-raising, and led the school to host the NCAA men's soccer championship for three straight years, selling out each year. In 1995 he returned to Virginia to take on the athletic director position, where he would remain until 2001. During this time, in addition to chairing the NCAA Basketball Committee in 1997, Holland's legacy surrounded two major areas of accomplishment: raising the profile of the university's non-revenue sports and expanding and upgrading the facilities on Grounds.

In 1998 to 1999, Virginia rose to its then highest ever finish in the Directors' Cup, a standings race that took into account the entire portfolio of a university's athletics teams. Points are awarded based on each team's performance in the postseason. In 1999 Virginia finished eighth overall among Division I programs.

Holland's legacy also expands to the vast improvements in the university's facilities under his leadership and direction. Following successful fund-raising—both on a public level and on a private, individual level—Holland was able to oversee an $86 million expansion of Scott Stadium and related creation of the Carl Smith Center, the construction of the Aquatics and Fitness Center, expansion and naming of the Sheridan Snyder Tennis Center, the University Hall Turf Field, and the Park, home of Virginia's softball team.

In 2001 Holland stepped down from the directorship and became instead special assistant to president John T. Casteen. In this position Holland's primary focus was to raise funds for what would become the John Paul Jones Arena, a project that had been loosely in the works since the 1980s, though Holland had set the wheels in motion while he was AD. In 2004, with the new arena project physically underway, Holland left Virginia for East Carolina University rather than retire. Holland was inducted into the Virginia Sports Hall of Fame in 2003.

23 Upset of the Century

Perhaps the greatest upset in all of college sports history happened in front of a tiny crowd in 1982 at a high school gymnasium. The Virginia Cavaliers were on top of the college basketball world. Ranked No. 1 in the country, the Wahoos also laid claim to the best college basketball player in the country in senior center Ralph Sampson, who had already won back-to-back National Player of the Year honors and was en route to a third straight.

Chaminade University of Honolulu was not a ranked team. They did not boast a National Player of the Year. They barely had a home gym. The top team in the country playing a NAIA squad that had just lost two days earlier to Wayland Baptist wasn't supposed to be a big story. Virginia, meanwhile, was two weeks removed from surviving the "Game of the Decade," a 68–63 victory against No. 3 Georgetown that featured the two best starting centers in the country in Ralph Sampson and Patrick Ewing.

Following the big win against Georgetown, Virginia went to Japan to play two games against Houston and Utah. Sampson contracted a virus while overseas and was limited in both games. On the Cavaliers' return trip to the United States, they stopped by Hawaii for a quick game against an easy squad before heading back to Virginia to play some in-state rivals and continue ACC play. They had already beaten Duke 104–91 earlier in the season.

Chaminade had a student enrollment count of about 800 at the time. Its locker room was shared with the local high school, and it borrowed the team's towels from a nearby hotel. Head coach Merv Lopes was a professional high school counselor and only a part-time basketball coach. In order to prepare for the big game, Chaminade rented space at the nearby Blaisdell Arena, where 3,383 spectators would gather to get a glimpse of Sampson and the No. 1 Cavaliers. "The strategy was for us to go out there and give the people who came to watch the No. 1 team in the country some good basketball," Lopes said after the game. There wasn't any real expectation of coming away with a victory.

Chaminade did much more than that. Going into halftime, the score was tied at 43 apiece, and even then there was no doubt that the mighty Cavaliers would come back and put this game away. Matched up against Sampson was 6'7" center Tony Randolph, who knew Sampson from their high school playing days. "We used to play street ball all the time," said Randolph, who had also previously dated Sampson's sister. "I think he didn't really take me seriously."

Randolph, though, held Sampson to just 12 points on the night despite Sampson pulling down 17 rebounds in 38 playing minutes. In just 27 minutes Randolph put up 19 points and five rebounds. Chaminade's quick pace of play continued to rattle Virginia in the second half, and the Hoos were not able to break away from the close contest. With the Silverswords up 74–72 and only 35 seconds to play, Virginia missed three consecutive shots before Othell Wilson was called for a palming violation on a spin move with just 10 seconds remaining. Chaminade would make three more free throws, and the final buzzer sounded.

They had done the impossible. The unknown Silverswords had knocked off the top team in the country 77–72. Headlines read, "Yes, Virginia, there is a Chaminade." School officials were planning to change the name to the "University of Honolulu," but following the immense publicity from the victory, they elected to keep it "Chaminade."

In 1984 Chaminade established the Maui Invitational, in which the school invited three Division I schools to play an in-season tournament in Maui. Virginia accepted the invitation to play in the inaugural year, but the Cavaliers lost to Providence in the tournament's opening round and did not face Chaminade that year. The tournament has expanded to eight teams in total and is largely viewed as one of the premier early-season tournaments in the country. Virginia has participated four times but has never won.

In 2013 Terry Holland wrote to the Naismith Memorial Basketball Hall of Fame in support of efforts to elect the 1982 Chaminade team to the Hall. "Chaminade's monumental upset of our No. 1 ranked University of Virginia team was most significant in that it was not a fluke," Holland wrote. "Chaminade was simply a good team standing toe to toe with one of college basketball's best teams. The Chaminade victory paved the way for the NCAA Men's Basketball Committee to strongly consider allowing relatively unknown teams to compete for at-large bids to the NCAA Tournament. These at-large selections spawned a true national tournament and some truly exciting upsets on college basketball's largest stage. Chaminade's victory was therefore a catalyst that forced the world to acknowledge that, 'Parity had arrived in college basketball.'"

24 Heath Miller

In 2004 tight end Heath Miller became the second unanimous first-team All-American in Virginia's history. That distinction came 19 years after Jim Dombrowski in 1985. In just three years at Virginia, Miller, or "Big Money," managed to rewrite just about every tight end record, not only for the Cavaliers, but also for the Atlantic Coast Conference.

Originally recruited as a quarterback out of southwest Virginia, Miller transitioned to tight end during his redshirt year at Virginia in 2001. He started every game in 2002 at tight end, and it didn't take long at all for Miller to establish himself as a force to be reckoned with in the conference. If there was a record to be broken, Miller was up for the task. As a freshman in 2002, he recorded nine touchdown receptions, setting an ACC record and leading the nation that season for tight ends. It was the third most touchdown receptions in the country by any freshman and a school freshman record. He scored in each of his first five games of his career, setting the school record for the most consecutive games with a touchdown by a tight end.

By Miller's junior year, he and quarterback Matt Schaub had developed a clear connection on the field. In addition to being named a unanimous All-American in 2004, Miller was the recipient of the prestigious Mackey Award as the nation's top tight end, the first player in ACC history to win it. He set both Virginia and ACC records for most tight end receptions (144), yards (1,703), and touchdowns (20). He finished second overall in school history in receptions, seventh in yards, and tied for fourth in touchdown receptions. An outstanding blocker as well, he could do everything.

Miller became so dominant in his position that some commentators began calling Virginia "Tight End U," noting the history of NFL draft picks coming from this position out of Virginia, including Billy Baber (Round Five, 2001), Chris Luzar (Round Four, 2002), Tom Santi (Round Six, 2008), and John Phillips (Round Six, 2009).

For Virginia fans, Miller may forever stand out as the greatest tight end the university has ever seen. In part this is because of the dazzling one-handed catches prevalent throughout his collegiate career. However, the Virginia fanbase has always been obsessed not just with winning on the field, but also having a team full of stand-up individuals who can represent the university well off the field. For the fans part of Miller's appeal was that he was never one for showboating.

Virginia football coach Al Groh spoke highly of Miller's nose-to-the-grindstone mentality. He later recalled, "All Heath Miller wants to know is, 'Did we win, did I do enough and who do we play next?'"

For someone who set school and conference records his freshman year and continued this success all the way to national accolades, it would have been easy for Miller to be as loud as he was skilled, but his humility and team mentality cemented his position as a Virginia fan favorite during his time in Charlottesville and beyond.

Heath Miller left Virginia following his junior season to enter the NFL draft early, becoming only the fifth player in school history to declare early. Miller was drafted in the first round by the Pittsburgh Steelers as the 30th overall pick, where he helped the Steelers win multiple Super Bowl championships and has been selected to multiple Pro Bowls. In 2012 Miller was named the Pittsburgh Steelers' team MVP.

25 The "Amazin' Cavaliers"

Toward the end of the 1960s, Virginia basketball looked to be in danger of falling into a permanent state of basketball irrelevancy. Even on the best of nights, University Hall was half empty, and those who showed up were vocal in their desire for a new basketball coach as players and fans had lost faith in the leadership of then-head coach Bill Gibson.

By the start of the 1969 season, the Cavaliers had amassed a losing record in each of the preceding 15 seasons. The top four scorers and top three rebounders of the 1968 team that only finished 10–15 on the season had left, leaving a young, raw team that left little room for high expectations on the year. The ACC media picked Virginia to finish last in the conference.

Gibson pressed the administration to increase his authorized scholarships from five to seven to be more in line with—and competitive against—the other ACC schools, but the request was rejected. At the start of the 1969–70 season, Gibson was quoted as saying, "We're still playing catch-up basketball at Virginia, but we're getting there."

What the Virginia faithful saw throughout the 1969–70 season gave them hope for the program's future. Though the team again finished with a 10–15 record and seventh in the conference—just slightly above what the ACC media had predicted—there were flashes of brilliance, particularly near the end of the season, that gave Virginia fans a reason to stick around for next year. Virginia won six of its final 11 games, including a regular season home finale in which the Cavaliers shocked Duke 61–57 for the second year in a row at U-Hall. In the first round of the ACC Tournament behind Tim Rash's 25 points and Chip Case's and Bill Gerry's 21 points each, the

Hoos upset No. 2 seed North Carolina 95–93 for their first tournament game victory in 11 years. Virginia would lose by a single point to eventual ACC champions North Carolina State 67–66.

The wins against the Carolina powerhouses to close out the 1969–70 season, coupled with the return of four starters plus sophomore guard Barry Parkhill, who averaged 27 points per game for the freshman team, meant that for the first time in almost a full generation there was reason to get excited about the start of the next basketball season.

The 1970–71 team, consisting of forward Bill Gerry, guard Tim Rash, center Scott McCandlish, forward Frank DeWitt, guard Chip Miller, forward Jim Hobgood, and Parkhill, opened the season as advertised. The Cavaliers came out hot, winning 11 of their first 13 matches that season and earning the name, the "Amazin' Cavaliers," a moniker that would stick with them for years to come. Most impressive during their 13-game opening stretch was the buzzer-beating 50–49 victory against South Carolina, ranked No. 1 or No. 2 at the time, depending on the poll. Following that week the Cavaliers were ranked No. 19 in the AP poll, their first time ever cracking the top 20.

Though Virginia fizzled out to close the season, winning only four of their final 13 games, no one questions the significance of the 1970–71 season, which reenergized a lackluster fanbase and set the scene for seasons to come. The Amazin' Cavaliers brought U-Hall attendance records to new heights. Whereas there was only an average of 4,000 fans per game during the 1969–70 season, the Amazin' Cavaliers saw an average of 7,500 per game, numbers never before seen at U-Hall, which had just opened in 1965.

Virginia's success would continue in the coming seasons. The following year the Amazin' Cavaliers finished with a record of 21–7, (8–4 ACC), including a climb to the No. 6 spot in the AP poll after winning 18 of its first 19 games to open the season with its only loss coming to No. 3 North Carolina. It was Virginia's first season with a winning ACC record since joining the conference in its inaugural season. Though the final years of Gibson's coaching career at Virginia saw a dip in performance, by 1976 the Cavaliers would capture their first ever ACC Tournament title.

26 Wonderful Wally Walker

Following the Amazin' Cavaliers' performance in the 1970–71 season, Virginia and its fans thought the program had turned a significant corner and was ready to contend for an ACC title. Bill Gibson coached the 1971–72 team to a 21–7 season, going 8–4 in the ACC, earning a berth to the National Invitational Tournament, and earning ACC Coach of the Year honors with the help of ACC Player of the Year Barry Parkhill. Everything looked good for the Cavaliers.

The 1972–73 season had only two starters returning in guard Barry Parkhill and forward Jim Hobgood, who averaged 12.2 points per game the year prior as the team's second-leading scorer behind Parkhill's 21.6. But they also had an incoming freshman from Penn Manor High in Pennsylvania. Considered one of the top five high school players in the nation, Wally Walker had come off his final year with an average of 31.7 points and 21 rebounds per game and was a consensus prep All-American across the board.

From the second Walker came to the Grounds of Virginia, he had made an impact, earning a starting position on the young team. Though the team wasn't able to replicate its success the previous year, finishing just 13–12 overall and 4–8 in the conference, Walker made a statement during the Hoos' 84–78 win against No. 3 North Carolina at Chapel Hill. There, Walker connected on 12 of his 13 shots and pulled down 10 rebounds to cement his role as a player who would remain a force to be reckoned with for years to come. He finished his freshman season as the team's second-leading scorer with 13.7 points per game behind only Parkhill.

As his playing time and the team's reliance on him increased, so too did his point totals during his sophomore and junior campaigns, as he averaged 17.5 and 16.5 points per game. Legendary Virginia head coach Terry Holland took over for the 1974–75 season, Walker's junior year, and Virginia was ready to take on the conference.

It was during Walker's fourth and final season with the Cavaliers that the moniker "Wonderful Wally" was born and deservedly so. With the Cavaliers having finished the regular season only 4–8 in the conference, losing twice each to North Carolina (ranked No. 6 and No. 3, respectively), Maryland (No. 5 and No. 10), and N.C. State (No. 13 and No. 8), the Virginia fanbase's expectations heading into the ACC Tournament weren't high.

Luckily for Virginia, Holland wasn't ready to go down without a fight.

Unranked and No. 6 seed Virginia did what many described as the impossible that year, defeating three nationally ranked teams in as many days, starting with a 75–63 win against 17th-ranked N.C. State. The following night Virginia upset ninth-ranked Maryland 73–65 before taking down Dean Smith's fourth-ranked North Carolina Tar Heels 67–62 to claim the ACC Tournament title.

Walker, who had been left off the All-ACC team announced just prior to the ACC Tournament's start, averaged 24.3 points per game over the course of the tournament, shooting 28-for-41, earning himself the tournament's Most Valuable Player award, the first for any Virginia player. "When I cut the nets down," Holland said following the win, "I gave one to Wally and said, 'This one's for you.'"

Virginia was one of only three non-North Carolina schools to capture the ACC title, joining Maryland and South Carolina. According to Holland, the tournament title didn't "tell the whole story where Wally's concerned. It doesn't tell what he means to [Virginia] and what he's done for us all year in terms of leadership and inspiration. We played three days of perfect basketball."

What made it just a little bit sweeter for Virginia fans was that by capturing the ACC crown and earning a berth in the NCAA Tournament the Cavaliers had effectively kept Maryland out of the NCAA Tournament altogether. The NCAA had informed Maryland that if North Carolina captured the title, Maryland would be invited as well. With the Virginia upset, the NCAA instead invited North Carolina, leaving Maryland without any postseason play that year.

Walker finished his senior season averaging 22.1 points per game and 6.8 rebounds per game. His career average at Virginia was 17.8 points and 6.4 rebounds per game. Walker was drafted in the fifth round of the 1976 NBA Draft by the Portland Trail Blazers. He spent eight years in the league with Portland, the Seattle SuperSonics, and Houston Rockets, earning championship rings during his time at Portland and Seattle. After his NBA career, Walker spent a short time playing in Italy before enrolling at Stanford for his MBA.

Eventually, Walker would find himself back in the NBA in 1994 as the president and general manager of the SuperSonics. He stepped down from his role as president and CEO in 2006, just two years prior to the SuperSonics' move to Oklahoma City. His No. 41 jersey is one of just seven retired numbers at Virginia.

27 Frank Murray

Imagine someone who's never played the game of football becoming one of the hottest head coaches in the country. It's just about every fan's dream, but for Frank Murray, this was his reality. A graduate of Tufts University, and later Harvard and the University of Chicago for graduate work, Murray had always been a student of the game. Instead of following a career in journalism, Murray began coaching at high schools and smaller colleges before getting hired by Marquette in 1922 to lead the Golden Avalanches, as they were known at the time.

Undefeated his first two seasons at Marquette, finishing 8–0–1 his first year, outscoring its opponents 213–3 and 8–0–0 his second year with six shutouts, Murray finished his first two seasons with an impressive aggregate score of 374 points for Marquette and only 15 for its opponents. From 1922 to 1936 at Marquette, Murray would amass a 90–32–6 record, including a trip to the 1937 inaugural Cotton Bowl Classic, and only two losing seasons. He left Marquette to become head coach at Virginia in 1937.

Though he joined Virginia with high expectations of him from athletics director Norton Pritchett, who took over at Virginia with dreams of making Virginia an athletic powerhouse, Murray's first year at Virginia was not nearly as successful as his first at Marquette, or even his last at Marquette when he finished 7–2. Murray's 1937 Virginia squad finished 2–7, getting outscored by its opponents 52–169.

It wouldn't take too long, though, before Murray would assemble his team in Charlottesville. In the years leading up to Murray's hire at Virginia, Pritchett and company had been busy advocating to the university's Board of Visitors to begin offering athletic

Virginia Boxing

Long before collegiate football became the multi-billion dollar industry it is today, it was college boxing that reigned supreme in the eyes of the fans. Virginia fielded an official varsity boxing team as early as 1927, and it didn't take long for the Cavaliers to rise to the top of the sport.

With the newly built Memorial Gym as the venue, as many as 5,000 fans would gather into the packed gymnasium to watch what most considered to be *the* major college sport in Charlottesville. With tobacco smoke rising in the air and the balconies filled to the brim, fight nights under the bright lights at Memorial Gym were the social centerpiece for Virginia.

The product in the ring wasn't too bad either. From 1932 to 1937, Virginia went undefeated, winning consecutive Southern Conference championships. In 1938 Virginia became the NCAA national champions in the sport, sharing the title unofficially. The championship is deemed "unofficial" only because team points were not then officially awarded, though the NCAA continues to recognize Virginia's title.

By 1955 Virginia eliminated boxing as a varsity sport, largely as a result of growing concerns over student-athlete safety. By 1960, following a boxer's collapse with a brain hemorrhage that led to his death, the NCAA also refused to sanction the sport.

scholarships to bring stronger talent on board for the Cavaliers. When Pritchett hired Murray, the wheels were already in motion as Virginia was leaving the Southern Conference to remain independent, and Murray was the first head coach to offer an athletic scholarship, which went to Lee McLaughlin. McLaughlin earned his scholarship, ultimately becoming captain of the 1940 team before getting drafted by the Green Bay Packers.

By 1941 the right pieces had fallen into place for a successful season. "Bullet" Bill Dudley, an undersized but versatile player to whom Murray had offered a scholarship when Dudley was only 16 years old and 150 pounds, had grown into one of the most prolific scorers in college football. With Dudley captaining the 1941 squad,

Murray led Virginia to an 8–1 record, with the team's only loss coming to Yale 21–19, a team Virginia had just beaten the year prior for the first time in school history 19–14.

After Dudley graduated, Murray wouldn't be able to replicate the success he had in the 1941 season. Virginia fell into three straight losing seasons before finishing 7–2 in 1945, Murray's last year with the Cavaliers. He left Virginia to return to Marquette for four more years, resulting in four losing seasons for a struggling Marquette program. He finished at Virginia with an overall 41–34–5 record. His nine years at the helm of Virginia football remains the second-longest tenure of any Virginia coach behind legendary George Welsh and tied with Al Groh. Murray was succeeded by his star Marquette player Art Guepe, who had been an assistant coach under Murray at Virginia for five seasons. Murray finished his coaching record with a strong 145–89–11 record. Though he passed away in 1951, he was inducted to the College Football Hall of Fame in 1983.

28 Gonzaga Slays Another Giant

Charlottesville was abuzz with excitement throughout the 2000–01 men's basketball season. Third-year head coach Pete Gillen was about to take the Virginia Cavaliers dancing for the first time under his tenure and for the first time since 1997—when the No. 9 seed Hoos ran into an early exit against No. 8 seed Iowa.

The 2001 season was also the first 20-win season for Virginia since the 1994–95 Elite Eight team. Virginia was ranked seventh in the country heading into the regular season finale against No. 16 Maryland, a team it had beaten earlier in the season at home. The

Cavaliers had won four straight games heading into the Maryland contest, including wins over No. 2 North Carolina and No. 3 Duke, to reach the 20-win mark.

Unfortunately for Virginia fans, the Hoos would lose to Maryland in a blowout 102–67 and then bow out of the first round of the ACC Tournament in a 74–69 loss to Georgia Tech.

"We wanted to become one of the elite teams in the ACC, but we lost in the first round [of the ACC Tournament]," said senior point guard and team captain Donald Hand following the loss to Georgia Tech. "Man, we didn't prove nothing."

Following the losses Virginia would go on to receive a No. 5 seed in the NCAA Tournament and be paired against No. 12 seed Gonzaga (24–6, 13–1 West Coast Conference), who at this point had developed the giant-slayer reputation. In 1999 the 10th-seeded Bulldogs had taken down No. 7 seed Minnesota, No. 2 seed Stanford, and No. 6 seed Florida before finally losing to No. 1 and eventual national champion Connecticut in the Elite 8. In 2000, again as a 10th seed, Gonzaga defeated No. 7 seed Louisville and No. 2 seed St. John's to reach the Sweet 16.

Virginia fell behind early in the game behind the hot shooting of Gonzaga point guard Dan Dickau, who earned 21 points in the first half, including going 6-of-9 on three-pointers.

Midway through the second half, it looked as though Gonzaga would all but run away with the game up by 13 points with 12 minutes to play. But the Hoos finally heated up beyond the arc behind the three-point shooting of Hand, Keith Friel, and Roger Mason Jr. It was Mason who made back-to-back threes to give Virginia its first lead of the night 85–84 with only 1:28 remaining in the game, and suddenly, all the momentum had swung Virginia's way, and it looked like the Cavaliers might actually escape to the second round of the NCAA Tournament.

With only 21.4 seconds to go and the same one-point lead, Virginia freshman J.C. Mathis was fouled for a one-and-one to give the Hoos an opportunity to create some separation. Mathis, a 49 percent free throw shooter, missed the front end, giving Gonzaga at least one more chance to regain the lead in a game the Bulldogs had mostly dominated. Gonzaga senior forward Casey Calvary rebounded the ball. There was no doubt that Dickau would be the one to take the shot for the Bulldogs' final possession, especially with the Cavaliers cautious not to foul.

Dickau was indeed the one to drive to the basket. Virginia forward Adam Hall managed to get his hands up for the block, but the ball flew three feet out, right into the hands of a waiting Calvary, who hit the put-back to give the Bulldogs the go-ahead basket with just nine seconds to go.

It would be Mason, who had 30 points already that game, to drive and take the final shot for the Cavaliers, but he fought traffic all the way to the basket. A floater of a ball would go off the backboard and miss the rim entirely, and the final buzzer would sound with players scrambling for a loose ball. "It wasn't an upset in my mind," said Gonzaga head coach Mark Few. "It was a feather in our cap because we beat a great team. But I think we've proven we have a very good basketball program."

Gonzaga had done it again. The No. 12 seed Bulldogs had defeated No. 5 seed Virginia of the Goliath Atlantic Coast Conference and would advance to the second round of the NCAA Tournament. "They're much better than a 12 seed," Gillen said after the game. "Most people picked us to lose, and I guess the experts were real smart."

That would be the last time a Gillen-led Virginia team would reach the NCAA Tournament, leaving a sour taste in fans' mouths for years. The Cavaliers would not get to dance again until the 2006–07 season under head coach Dave Leitao.

1990 Football Season

Virginia had just come off the program's best football season. The 1989 squad had finished 10–3 with its only losses coming to No. 2 Notre Dame, No. 15 Clemson, and No. 11 Illinois in the Florida Citrus Bowl. It was the first—and still to this date only—time the Cavaliers had reached the 10-win mark and finished 6–1 in the ACC, earning ACC co-champion honors. The team was ranked 18th in the final AP poll.

The 1990 season opened on the road at Kansas with the Cavaliers ranked No. 15. It was the first time the Hoos had been ranked in the preseason. In the first ever meeting between the two teams, Virginia handily took care of business with a 59–10 victory despite the heat down on the turf, which registered a scalding 130 degrees.

Virginia, up to No. 14 in the rankings, returned home to play host to No. 9 Clemson. To say that this game was highly anticipated would be an understatement. In what would become known as only "the Streak," Virginia had never been able to defeat Clemson in the 29 previous times that the two teams had met. Clemson head coach Frank Howard once said, "Virginia? That's the white meat of our schedule."

It was the game everyone from Virginia was talking about. Could this finally be the year—behind the likes of Shawn Moore, Herman Moore, Terry Kirby, and Chris Slade—that the Hoos finally took down the Tigers?

In front of 46,800 fans in a stadium that only sat 42,000, the Cavaliers put together four quarters of nearly perfect football for the spectators to enjoy. Virginia started the second half down only 7–6 and didn't look back. The Virginia defense held Clemson scoreless for the entirety of the second half, while touchdowns from Kirby and the Moore-to-Moore connection made it a 20–7 victory for the Cavaliers.

Virginia had finally shaken off the Streak, and its storybook season was well underway.

Virginia demolished its next three teams—Navy, Duke, and William & Mary—to skyrocket to a No. 2 national ranking, the program's highest ever ranking at the time. Over the course of the three games, Virginia won by a margin of 178–49.

The No. 2 team would keep on rolling, shutting down North Carolina State 31–0. Later that day top-ranked Michigan would lose by a mere point to rival Michigan State, and Virginia players and fans knew what the headlines would read the next day. Virginia earned the program's first ever No. 1 ranking in the country.

After a slow start to the game, the top-ranked Cavaliers regrouped and dispatched Wake Forest on the road 49–14. A perfect 7–0 on the season and outscoring their opponents 337–80, the Cavaliers were in the best shape they've ever been in. After a bye week, Virginia would be looking to face No. 16 Georgia Tech, also unbeaten at 6–0–1. Georgia Tech's lone blemish was a 13-all tie to North Carolina.

Virginia had a commanding 28–14 lead at the half. Known for its dominant offense, Virginia was expected to keep hammering the Yellow Jackets in the second half, but Georgia Tech had something else in mind. The Georgia Tech offense took over in the second half, beating a Virginia defense that some had suspected to be weaker than the record would otherwise suggest. Mounting a remarkable comeback, the Yellow Jackets hit a 37-yard field goal with only seven seconds remaining to give them the 41–38 victory. "I don't know what it was. They seemed to do everything right," free safety Keith McMeans said following the game. "I can't explain it. Everything they did, they were able to move the ball on us."

With that Virginia saw its national championship dreams slip away. The Cavaliers would drop to No. 11 in the rankings the following week, when they had a bounce-back win against North Carolina 24–10.

The rest of the season, though, would fizzle away, as Virginia dropped back-to-back games against Maryland and Virginia Tech. The Hoos accepted an invitation to the Sugar Bowl.

Former Heisman Trophy candidate Shawn Moore struggled all game long, having injured his right thumb on Senior Day, which had caused him to miss the previous game against Virginia Tech. Unable to complete a single pass in the second half, Moore and the unranked Cavaliers lost to No. 10 Tennessee 23–22 despite leading 16–3 heading into the fourth quarter.

Virginia finished the 1990 season ranked No. 23 in the final AP poll, and the Cavaliers had four players selected in the 1991 NFL Draft. Wide receiver Herman Moore was picked 10th overall by the Detroit Lions. Defensive back Tony Covington was drafted in the fourth round to the Tampa Bay Buccaneers, tight end Bruce McGonnigal was picked in the ninth round by the Pittsburgh Steelers, and quarterback Shawn Moore went in the 11th round to the Denver Broncos. "I don't know how much we needed to prove," coach George Welsh said after the Sugar Bowl. "But we showed that we can play at this level."

30 Bryant Stith

Before playing a single minute as a Cavalier, Bryant Stith spoke to *The Cavalier Daily*. "I don't go up to people and say, 'I'm Bryant Stith the basketball player,' I just introduce myself," he said. "I really fit well into the crowd here; I've met a lot of people and made a whole lot of friends. [But] I want to be Bryant Stith the person, not Bryant Stith the athlete."

From then on, the Virginia basketball legend would require no introduction. Valedictorian of his high school class, having only received one B in high school, Stith was a four-year starting forward/guard for Virginia from 1989 to 1992, during which time the Cavaliers had four 20-win seasons. As a freshman Stith averaged 15.5 points per game and was named the ACC Rookie of the Year. He continued this success throughout his four years and by his senior year he was averaging 20.7 points per game.

During that time Stith and the Cavaliers made three NCAA appearances—an Elite Eight showing, a second-round exit, and a first-round exit—and won the NIT in 1992 behind Stith's impressive play. Stith was named the NIT Most Valuable Player. Despite not scoring a bucket in the first 18 and a half minutes of the championship game, Stith finished with a team-high 24 points in the 81–76 overtime win against Notre Dame.

Stith was a three-time honorable mention All-American and first-team All-ACC honoree, scoring double digits in all 33 games his senior season. Stith's career at Virginia was one for the record books. He put up a total of 2,516 points during his four-year career, which surpassed Jeff Lamp's previous career points record of 2,317, and Stith's record still stands today. He also still leads Virginia with most number of games started (128), which is tied with Ralph Sampson and Joe Harris.

Stith finished second in career rebounding (859) behind only the great Sampson. He still remains fifth on that list today. In 1992 he was named a Wooden Award finalist. He did all of this with humility. "Some athletes are flamboyant, but I don't believe in that," Stith said early in his career. "I don't go around acting like I've got the world by its tail. I just want to be myself."

Teammate Cory Alexander fondly recalls his playing days with Stith. "What people don't understand about Bryant Stith is, as great of a basketball player as he is, he's a better person. It was to a point where I would almost look at him and say, 'Look, I just have to touch you because you're not real. You don't make mistakes, you don't do anything wrong.' Being able to be around Bryant made me a better person."

Stith was drafted in the first round of the 1992 NBA Draft as the 13th pick overall by the Denver Nuggets, where he spent the first eight years of his career before he played a year for both the Boston Celtics and Cleveland Cavaliers before retiring from the NBA in 2002. Despite being plagued by injuries throughout parts of his professional career, Stith averaged 10.1 points, 3.4 rebounds, and two assists per game.

Following his retirement, Stith took some time away from the game that had brought him up but also worn him down over the years. "Working was not in my plans, I could tell you that," he said years later at the age of 41. "I wanted to rehabilitate my body. It had broken down from the rigors of my NBA career, so I just wanted to go to physical therapy and make sure I'd be in good shape for the next 30 to 40 years. When I was playing basketball, I never wanted to be a coach. I had some good coaches but also some not-so-good coaches, especially toward the end of my NBA career. That basically turned me away from the game."

Yet, Stith wouldn't be able to stay away for too long. After retiring from the NBA in 2002, he became the head coach of the Brunswick High School boys' basketball team, his alma mater in Lawrenceville, Virginia, in 2006. He immediately led the Bulldogs to seven straight state championship games, winning the title in each of the final three visits.

In 2013 Stith was hired as an assistant coach at Old Dominion under head coach Jeff Jones, who was Stith's head coach the year

Virginia won the NIT. His son, B.J. Stith, played at Virginia for one year before transferring to Old Dominion.

31 South's Oldest Rivalry

Ask the question, "Who is Virginia's greatest rival?" and you might get a few different responses. A current student or recent graduate might say Virginia Tech. Someone from the "DMV" (D.C.-Maryland-Virginia) area might say Maryland. A graduate from long ago will resoundingly say North Carolina.

The Virginia-North Carolina game is known as the "South's Oldest Rivalry," and shouldn't be confused with the *Deep* South's "Oldest Rivalry." The Hoos and the Heels date back 1892, a 30–18 Virginia victory in Charlottesville. In the inaugural season of the rivalry, the two football teams actually played twice with the second contest taking place Thanksgiving weekend, a 26–0 loss to North Carolina.

Virginia dominated the series until 1916, when both schools suspended football competition for two years during World War I. Following the 1916 season, Virginia had a commanding 17–5–1 lead in the series. The two teams resumed the rivalry in 1919 and have played every year since. Perhaps the two-year hiatus was good for North Carolina because the Tar Heels dominated the series for the better part of the 20th century, including a stretch from 1927 to 1949 when the Tar Heels won 20 of 23 meetings. North Carolina's command of the series was also during a time when the Cavaliers had just two winning seasons from 1953 to 1982, a stretch that included a 28-game losing streak, the second worst in college football history. Only one football series has been played more frequently than the South's Oldest Rivalry, and that is the game for Paul Bunyan's Axe between Minnesota and Wisconsin. The Deep South's Oldest Rivalry between Georgia and Auburn has been played 119 times—compared to North Carolina and Virginia's 120, as of the 2015 season.

Following the 2015 season, North Carolina held a 62–54–4 advantage in the series, winning the six most recent matchups as head coach Mike London was unable to find a win against the Tar Heels during his tenure. Nonetheless, among the 16 most recent meetings from 2000 to 2015, the series was at a dead even tie with each team winning eight times.

The reasons for the rivalry seem apparent on its face. Both schools are among the academic elite public institutions in the nation, and both schools share a similar cultural background as well. Being the flagship universities of border states, recruiting was always a heated battle between the two schools. The recruiting rivalry reached its climax in the battle for Ronald Curry, an All-American in both football and basketball.

Curry was both the top quarterback prospect in football and the McDonald's All-American Game MVP in basketball in 1998. Originally committed to Virginia football, he flipped his commitment to North Carolina after the Tar Heels basketball staff recruited him heavily even after the verbal commitment to Virginia. To this day Cavalier fans refer to him as "Benedict Ronald."

Multiple Virginia rally songs focus on the North Carolina rivalry. One song from 1897, which would have been sung throughout the game so long as the Hoos were up, ended with the lyrics, "The South is our land, and we're setting the pace / Good-bye, Carolina, Good-bye! / You cannot play ball, and you're out of the race, / Good-bye, Carolina, Good-bye!" Another, called "Oh, Carolina," from the Virginia Glee Club, goes:

See the boys from Carolina,
My, they look so mighty fine!
Brand new sweaters, pretty letters,
Fragrant with the smell of pine.

See the Tar Heels, how they're running
Turpentine from every pore.
They can manufacture rosin,
But they'll never, never score.

See them try our ends and tackles,
But alas! It is in vain,
For each time they hear their doom in
"Carolina ten to gain."

The rivalry had attracted the attention and attendance of not only both states' governors, but also those such as president Calvin Coolidge in 1928. Virginia's first university president, Edwin Alderman, was actually a North Carolina alumnus and former university president from 1896 to 1900. He arrived at Virginia to take the helm in 1904 and, after 20 years in Charlottesville, led a Virginia pep rally in 1924 with the words, "We praise Carolina for their constancy...in being good losers."

The passion was so strong among Virginia students and fans that it didn't matter if Virginia was playing the Tar Heels in football or even if Virginia was playing North Carolina at the time or not. Fans would delight in chanting "Carolina Sucks" regardless of sport or opponent.

32 Moore to Moore Connection

From 1988 to 1990, there was one name that Virginia fans heard more than any other. No matter if it was a running play or a passing play, it seemed that every offensive play involved this one name: Moore. And if it seemed like there were multiple of them on the field, it's because there were.

From the moment the two began playing together in 1988, Shawn Moore and Herman Moore (no relation), almost immediately began to make their way into the Virginia, ACC, and NCAA record books. Shawn Moore started as quarterback for the Cavaliers in 1988 as a redshirt sophomore. Herman Moore came in as a freshman wide receiver that same year. When the two connected, they proved to be one of the most potent quarterback-receiver duos in college football.

The two connected for a total of 27 passing touchdowns over their three-year careers together. During their careers the two led Virginia to two New Year's Day Bowls—the 1990 Florida Citrus Bowl and the 1991 USF&G Sugar Bowl—and in 1989 they captured the school's first ACC championship (which was shared with Duke). "We had this chemistry where if I saw him in man coverage, it was known I'm going to him," Shawn recalled. "If he is in single coverage, I'm throwing to him. I don't care what we had called. It didn't matter."

This perhaps came to the chagrin of quarterbacks coach Gary Tranquill. "But when Herman came and said, 'Look, I'm going to be open on this play,'" Shawn said. "He wasn't even in the progression, so if I went out of progression and threw it to him, I knew it would have to be a big play, because I knew I was going to get cussed out by Tranquill on the sideline. But I had confidence in him."

With the Moore to Moore connection firmly established, Virginia's offense was virtually unstoppable. At one point there was a stretch of 23 touchdown drives that averaged less than three minutes each. Shawn Moore still holds the Virginia record for career total yardage at 7,897, leading the ACC his senior season with 2,568 yards. He also set the record at the time for most career touchdown passes at 55. The previous record was a mere 33. Shawn's record would stand until Matt Schaub threw for 56 from 2000 to 2003.

Herman Moore still holds the Virginia records for most receiving yards in a single season, an ACC-leading 1,190 yards on just 54 plays (an average of 22 yards per catch), as well as most touchdown catches in a season at 13. He set an NCAA record by catching touchdown passes in nine consecutive games.

Both Shawn and Herman were named to All-American teams from various publications.

Shawn Moore finished fourth in Heisman Trophy voting that season, while Herman Moore finished sixth. Brigham Young's Ty Detmer was awarded the 1990 trophy.

Herman was selected in the first round (10th overall to the Detroit Lions), where he spent 11 seasons from 1991 to 2001, earning him four Pro Bowl appearances from 1994 to 1997 and three first-team All-Pro teams from 1995 to 1997. He finished his career after one season with the New York Giants in 2002. Shawn was drafted in the 11th round by the Denver Broncos but only spent four seasons in the NFL, playing in three games.

The Moore to Moore connection broke over 30 combined Virginia, ACC, and NCAA records during their time at Virginia.

33 Barry Parkhill

Although William Strickling and Buzzy Wilkinson were the first two All-Americans for the Virginia basketball program, it was a man from Pennsylvania who was the shining star of the University Hall era of UVA hoops paving the way for Ralph Sampson's arrival. His name was Barry Parkhill.

Arriving on Grounds in 1969 during an era in which freshmen were not allowed to compete on varsity teams, Parkhill made the most of his time as a Cavalier. In his second year (first on the varsity team), Parkhill joined the Wahoos to great fanfare as they looked to attain a winning campaign for the first time since 1953–54. After Virginia's best start in 30 years with six straight wins to open the campaign, Parkhill sank a baseline jumper with four seconds left that gave UVA a 50–49 win against No. 2 South Carolina on January 11, 1971. The win lifted Virginia into the Associated Press top 20 poll for the first time ever. A February win against North Carolina State ensured the first winning season at Virginia in 17 years. The team faltered down the stretch before advancing to the semifinals of the ACC Tournament as the No. 5 seed. The success of that season saw attendance at the relatively new University Hall skyrocket from an average of 4,000 to 7,500. Some of that can be attributed to Parkhill's average of 15.9 points per game.

The 1971–72 season was a breakthrough year for the Cavaliers. After a 3–0 start in the ACC, Virginia saw Parkhill set a record that might never be broken. Against Division III Baldwin Wallace at University Hall on December 11, 1971, Parkhill scored 51 points, setting the single-game scoring record at UVA. Wilkinson had already held the nine highest scoring games in university history but had never broken 50. After that game Virginia went on a tear,

Barry Parkhill, the ACC's Player of the Year in 1971–72, drives to the hole against Maryland. (*USA TODAY* Sports Images)

winning its next eight straight for a 12–0 start and rising to an all-time high of No. 8 in the national polls. Parkhill and the "Amazin' Cavaliers" would eventually reach No. 6 in the rankings with a record of 18–1. They dropped to No. 20 after losing four of their last six regular-season games, and any dreams of a first ever NCAA Tournament berth were eliminated with a semifinal loss in the ACC Tournament to rival Maryland.

However, Parkhill's average of 21 points, four assists, and four rebounds per game garnered the program just their second postseason invitation in history with their first trip to the NIT since 1941. A 72–71 loss to Lafayette at Madison Square Garden in New York meant the end to one of the greatest seasons that Virginia fans had experienced in their lifetime, but what a season it was. In addition to the 21–7 final record and a best ever third-place finish in the league standings, Parkhill was named the conference's Player of the Year and the Athlete of the Year. He was named a first-team All-American by the U.S. Basketball Writers Association and placed on the second team by two other outlets.

The 1972–73 season would not be as successful, with a fifth-place finish in the ACC and a first-round exit in the ACC Tournament. But Parkhill averaged 16.8 points per game and a career-high five assists, and Virginia achieved a third straight winning season for the first time since 1945 with a 13–12 record. The coaches named Parkhill a third-team All-American, and his No. 40 joined Wilkinson's as one of two to be retired at UVA.

After Parkhill's graduation as the school's third-leading scorer of all time, he played in the American Basketball Association before beginning a 25-year coaching career in the college ranks. He coached at UVA as a graduate assistant in 1977–78 before moving to William & Mary, where he spent five years as an assistant and four years as a head coach. He's been an administrator at Virginia since 1992, including as associate director of athletics for development. In the early 2000s, he was the chief fund-raiser for the building of the sparkling new John Paul Jones Arena on Grounds, and the practice court at the facility bears his name.

34 Joining the Atlantic Coast Conference

From 1937 to 1953, Virginia operated as an independent institution unaffiliated with any conference. The university had left the Southern Conference for a number of reasons, including the Southern Conference's prohibition on offering athletic scholarships, Virginia alumni's distain toward conference rival North Carolina, and the conference's prohibition on postseason play, though the state of Virginia football at the time was not one to be terribly concerned about postseason bowl invitations.

In 1953 seven other schools—Clemson, Duke, Maryland, North Carolina, North Carolina State, South Carolina, and Wake Forest—also left the Southern Conference for similar reasons. At the time of the split, the Southern Conference had 17 members of varying degrees of football pedigree, and one of the reasons the seven schools wanted to separate from the remaining 10 was to create a more level playing field in terms of competition, which included banning freshman eligibility and creating a round-robin schedule to better determine the true conference champion.

The new conference called the Atlantic Coast Conference was fully operational by the time football season came around for the 1953 season. The bulk of the ACC wanted Virginia to be its eighth member, but a standoff of pride, among other reasons, would prevent this from happening in time for the start of the football season. Virginia, independent at the time, would not beg to be let into the new conference. Meanwhile, the ACC institutions reportedly wanted Virginia to ask for the invitation and would not issue a formal one without the appropriate dance.

Duke was another reason for the ACC's delay in extending an invitation to Virginia. At the time a national powerhouse in football, Duke had rivalries with Tennessee, Navy, and Georgia Tech. To add Virginia as a conference member would have meant seven conference games in the round-robin format, plus Duke's out of conference three rivalry games, leaving no room for new rivals or other strategic games in a world of college football where schools were only beginning to move toward 10-game seasons.

But it wasn't only the then-ACC schools that led to the delay. Virginia itself was internally conflicted on whether the institution would want to join the conference or not. On the one hand, Virginia director of athletics Gus Tebell, a former UVA football coach himself, pushed the Board of Visitors toward joining the ACC. Among other reasons, he cited the increased publicity by playing in what could become one of the top tier conferences, noting that Virginia was not being challenged enough, having gone 18–1 during the previous six seasons against the remaining Virginia schools.

Virginia president Colgate Darden Jr., however, opposed the potential move to the ACC. He argued that the remaining five schools in the state, plus neighboring George Washington, were all still in the Southern Conference, and that remaining as an independent allowed the university to schedule all six of them should they desire, which they did in 1952, winning all six contests.

With strong alumni opposition to joining the ACC, Darden was not silent as to his position against joining the conference. Darden's track record already made clear that football was not his priority at the university, having made little effort to retain head coach Art Guepe, one of Virginia's most successful coaches, and having openly rejected the notion of playing in the Orange Bowl, or any postseason bowl, if invited. In presenting to the Board of

Visitors his position, he expressed concerns that the ACC's academic and moral standards may not align with Virginia's, which could make it more difficult for Virginia to adequately compete.

In a four-hour debate on whether Virginia would join the new ACC, the Board of Visitors' minutes reveal, among other reasons, Maryland was a significant factor to consider. Virginia had refused to play Maryland in football, though the two teams met in almost every other sport because of the "football factory" practices that Maryland employed. In an interview with renowned Virginia football historian Kevin Edds, 104-year-old football alumnus John Rishner said, "Maryland was a powerhouse, but they had some of the dirtiest players I ever saw. They were terrible. I don't know how they got away with some of the stuff. We didn't like Maryland. We didn't like the way they played."

Ultimately, Virginia's Board of Visitors agreed with Tebell that the university could benefit from joining the ACC, and the board voted 6–4 to accept an invitation to the new conference were one offered. South Carolina's J.T. Penney received word of the vote and shortly after called Virginia to extend a formal invitation. Virginia joined the ACC on December 4, 1953. As the 1953 football season had already passed, Virginia did not participate that season in football, though it competed in the league's inaugural basketball season as a full conference member.

The first five years in the ACC were not kind to Virginia. The Cavaliers won only four conference wins during this five-year stretch. By its sixth year in 1959, Virginia finished with an overall 0–10 record and then repeated the winless feat in 1960. It wasn't until 1968 that Virginia had its first winning conference record of 3–2.

35 Buzzy Wilkinson

Virginia basketball only had one winning season in the 1950s, and it never had a winning ACC record (though the conference hadn't formed until 1953). Still, any conversation about Virginia basketball legends must include the name Buzzy Wilkinson rising near the top. Indeed, any conversation about ACC players during the 1950s must acknowledge that Wilkinson may have been the single greatest ACC player of the decade. Named by his grandmother after a comic book character, Richard "Buzzy" Wilkinson lettered for the Cavaliers from 1953 to 1955, a three-year period during which Wilkinson broke nearly every scoring record at Virginia.

In Wilkinson's sophomore season, the 6'2" guard set the school record for most points in a season at 521. He broke this record the following year, putting up 814 points in 27 games and being one of the first three collegiate athletes to average more than 30 points. In his senior year, he broke the record once more with 898 points over 28 games, averaging 32.1 points and becoming the first to put up back-to-back 30-point scoring averages.

Wilkinson's senior and junior years still rank as No. 1 and No. 2 in most points per season—head and shoulders above No. 3 Bryant Stith, who put up 684 points in the 1991–92 campaign. The kicker? In Wilkinson's day there was no such thing as a three-point field goal.

Wilkinson finished his career with 2,233 points, a record that would stand atop Virginia's annals for more than two decades until Jeff Lamp eclipsed him with 2,317 points. Stith currently holds the record, just above Lamp and Wilkinson, at 2,516 points.

Over the course of his career, Wilkinson averaged 28.6 points per game, which continues to stand today as both a Virginia and ACC record. His 32.1 points per game his senior season also remain both UVA and ACC records. The numbers can be overwhelming, but the bottom line is that no Virginia player has been as prolific, yet efficient, of a scorer as Wilkinson in his three years at Virginia. It's not even close. His 28.6 points per game over his career is a full nine points per game higher than the next person on the list, teammate Bob McCarty, who played from 1954 to 1956 at Virginia. During the overlapping years, Wilkinson and McCarty were known as the "West Virginia Rifles" and combined to average about 52 points per game.

There are 10 Virginia players to have ever scored a 40-point game. Wilkinson is the only one to have done it more than once. In fact, he did it 10 times over two years. He had a single-game high of 48 points in 1954, a record that has only been bested by Barry Parkhill in 1971 with 51 points.

Wilkinson was drafted by the Boston Celtics, but a car accident caused him to sustain career-ending injuries before he even got on the court as a professional player. Wilkinson would return to Virginia as an assistant coach and obtained his law degree from Virginia in 1962 after serving in the military. He was inducted into the Virginia Sports Hall of Fame in 1975. Wilkinson's No. 14 jersey was retired in 1955, the first basketball player at Virginia to have his number retired and only the second Virginia athlete overall. Wilkinson passed away on January 15, 2016, at the age of 83.

36 Frank Quayle

At 5'10" and 200 pounds, running back Frank Quayle was as compact as he was fast, and believe me when I say that he was both. Quayle, who played for Virginia from 1966 to 1968, still holds the No. 1 spot in Virginia's records for all-purpose yards with 4,981 yards coming off rushing, receiving, punt returns, and kickoff returns.

When you think about Virginia's rich history of backs that includes Tiki Barber, Thomas Jones, Terry Kirby, and so on, that becomes just that much more impressive. If he got a single block, he'd be off to the races. If the defenses left any gap, he'd find the end zone. He didn't waste too much time running east-west. His only objective was to run forward, run fast, and not get knocked over.

During his three seasons at Virginia, Quayle set more than 20 ACC offensive records, including the career rushing leader at the time. He earned first-team All-ACC honors in 1967 and 1968, as well as ACC Football Player of the Year honors his senior season in 1968. A standout two-sport athlete, Quayle also earned honorable mention All-American honors in lacrosse in 1967. In his senior season, he was the first Cavalier to receive the Anthony J. McKevlin Award, given to the ACC Athlete of the Year.

Had Quayle done his research when looking at programs coming out of high school, it's not entirely clear that the New Jersey native would have picked Virginia. He began to take notice of Virginia, who was then actively recruiting him, as the Cavaliers climbed to No. 20 in the rankings and quarterback Bob Davis looked to be a legitimate All-American candidate. These things boded well for a running back looking to make an impact on an already successful team despite Virginia's previously woeful years. "I didn't know Virginia's football history," Quayle was quoted in

The Daily Progress. "I had no idea about its sorry past. It was an eye opener to learn when I got here."

Leading up to Quayle's recruitment, Virginia had been a lower-tier ACC school, having gone 14 years without a single winning season. Quayle, meanwhile, had offers from Boston College, Duke, Northwestern, and Notre Dame, among others. Virginia had the academics coupled with a football program and established lacrosse program, and that was good enough for Quayle.

In Virginia's final game of the 1968 season, also Quayle's final game of his career at Virginia, he had the opportunity to seize three records, which he kept a close eye on throughout the game. He could become the ACC's single-season rushing leader, the ACC's career rushing leader, and earn Virginia's single-season rushing record then held by John Papit and established in 1949.

Quayle amassed 216 yards on 29 carries that game, and with the win clinched, he knew that he had taken both of the ACC records. When given the option to return in the game to run out the clock in the final few plays, Quayle declined. He knew he had rushed for 1,213 yards that year and that Papit's record sat at 1,214. "For some reason I just didn't want the school record," Quayle said. "It seemed like too much."

Virginia would finish with a 7–3 record that season, the first winning season in 16 years. The Cavaliers wouldn't get back to a winning season for another 10 years.

Quayle was drafted in the fifth round of the 1969 NFL Draft by the Denver Broncos but only played one season in the NFL. Eventually, Quayle returned to Charlottesville in 1973 with a career in real estate, where he was one of just three brokers recognized by *USA TODAY* as one of the top real estate brokers in the United States. He joined the Virginia Sports Network as a broadcaster in 1983 and announced 346 of the 348 games over the course of the next 29 years before his retirement following the 2011 Chick-fil-A Bowl.

In 2012 Quayle was honored with the Order of the Crossed Sabres Award given to those who served Virginia football either on or off the field. He is only the 12th recipient of the award, which was inscribed, "In grateful recognition of your exemplary service, self-less commitment, and extraordinary impact on Cavalier Football."

37 The Persian Prince

Among every football player to have ever donned the blue and orange in Charlottesville, few have or will have had as remarkable a life as Jamshid "Jim" Bakhtiar, also known as the Persian Prince. Born in Tehran, Iran, Bakhtiar followed in his father's footsteps by leaving the country to come to the United States to pursue an American education. At the age of 11 in 1945, he disembarked from an American ship with 2,000 U.S. soldiers headed to a major naval base in Norfolk, shortly after which he and his mother, an Idaho native, moved to Washington, D.C. to begin their new lives.

In a new country with a new language, Bakhtiar discovered American football by following some kids to the local Boys Club, where he quickly learned that he was fast and could play a number of different positions. By the age of 16, his mother had returned to Iran, leaving him alone in D.C., supporting himself by working at a gas station.

After spending a year at prep school, Bakhtiar was recruited to Virginia, where he became a star fullback and linebacker from 1955 to 1957. During each of his three varsity seasons at Virginia, he led the team in rushing and scoring, the only player in school history to do so. He had also finished in the top 10 in the country in rushing for all three years. Following his three years, Bakhtiar set records in the young Atlantic Coast Conference in rushing (2,434 yards), rushing attempts (555), and 100-yard games (nine), records that stood for more than a decade. He earned All-American honors from the Football Writers Association of America following his senior season.

Bakhtiar's story, though, doesn't end with a record-setting, nationally acclaimed football career. Following his playing days at Virginia, he spent one year playing in the Canadian Football League, where he earned All-Canada honors. After the CFL he returned to Virginia, using his CFL earnings to attend UVA's medical school to study psychiatry, graduating in 1963.

After practicing in California for 11 years, Bakhtiar again followed in his father's footsteps, returning to Iran in 1974 with his son, Jim Jr., with the goal of integrating "modern psychology and modern psychiatry with some of the Islamic traditional elements in that part of the world," he told the *Daily Press*.

In Iran, Bakhtiar accepted a teaching position at the University of Isfahan. He established the country's first modern psychiatric unit, teaching others to treat mental illness as a medical condition rather than a social stigma. Not long after Bakhtiar's return to Iran, the Iranian Revolution broke out, overthrowing the American-supported monarchy to establish an Islamic Republic. Concerned for the future well-being of Jim Jr., who, at the age of 14, was nearing draft age and potentially impressionable to Iran's political propaganda to join the war, Bakhtiar decided that he would escape the country, which at the time was unwilling to issue passports to doctors.

One night as he was planning his family's escape at about 2:00 AM, a unit of Iranian revolutionary guards stormed his house armed with fully automatics and took Bakhtiar to a temporary prison in downtown Tehran. He was held and interrogated for months. "It was scary," Bakhtiar later recalled to the *Daily Press*. "It wasn't like playing Virginia Tech."

When Bakhtiar was finally released, he made the decision—without consulting his family—that they would try to escape in the middle of the night. On the night of their escape, he simply told his wife and three children to get in the car and that they were going on vacation. With only what they were wearing, the five of them made their way north, where they exchanged their family car for horses, which they rode in the middle of the night, hiding in caves during the day.

Finally, the family made their way into Istanbul, Turkey, where they were free. Six weeks later, they obtained passports and were able to return to the United States. Jim Jr. described Bakhtiar's incredible story as being not as significant as others have made it out to be. "[We] didn't have any choices. It was what we had to do," he said. But there was still one major issue.

Because Bakhtiar had left all of his money, jewels, and family possessions behind in Iran, he arrived in the United States without anything. The Virginia football family, though, does not leave its own stranded, and without hesitation former teammates and coaches met him with open arms. Former assistant coach Harrison "Chief" Nesbit, who had originally recruited Bakhtiar, housed the family for a month before Bakhtiar's former teammate Frank Kessler loaned him a townhouse. "There's not many people you're just going to *give* a house to," Jim Jr. later recalled in an interview with ESPN, "and they did it with pleasure."

In 2006, nearly 50 years after they first recognized him as an All-American, the FWAA awarded him the All-America Alumni Award to recognize his achievements after life on the gridiron. "There's a whole life after football," Bakhtiar advises young players. "If you get locked in and think it's only football, I think you're shortchanging yourself."

Bakhtiar's No. 34 jersey was retired during halftime of the Virginia-Virginia Tech game on November 28, 2009.

38 Justin Anderson

Even before he stepped foot on the Grounds as a student at the University of Virginia, Justin Anderson made a splash for Virginia basketball fans. For the small forward out of Rockville, Maryland, athleticism was never a doubt. In a story he recounted to *Sports Illustrated* in 2015, Anderson describes his first dunk in an auxiliary gym at Washington & Lee University when he was in the fifth grade. By the time he was in the eighth grade, he already had a national recruiting ranking. As he was making his college recruiting trips, he was a consensus top-50 recruit.

Initially, Anderson committed to Maryland and longtime Terrapins legend Gary Williams. However, when Williams suddenly retired from the school, he was succeeded by Mark Turgeon, who decided not to keep assistant coach Rob Ehsan, Anderson's lead recruiter. Shortly following this decision, Anderson announced his de-commitment from Maryland, and his recruitment was open once again. By then he had risen to be a five-star recruit, and *Rivals.com* ranked him the No. 23 overall prospect in the class of 2012. He had also been named Gatorade's 2012 Boys Basketball Player of the Year. About a week after visiting coach Tony Bennett at Virginia, Anderson announced his decision to attend Virginia, much to the chagrin of rival Terrapins fans.

Behind fellow shooting guard Joe Harris on the depth chart, Anderson didn't find immediate success at Virginia and learned a valuable lesson along the way. "You can't just expect things to just be given to you," Anderson told *Sports Illustrated*. "When I was younger, I think everything was given to me because I was so athletic. People started to tell me how good I was, and I think I started to listen to it. I never worked hard. I maybe got some shots up, played a little pickup basketball. It's much more than that. You have to make sure you put your work in. You have to make sure you value the little things. There were a lot of life lessons."

In his freshman year, Anderson played in 35 games, starting 17 of them. He averaged 7.6 points and 3.3 rebounds, and while he had some flashes of brilliance—as you'd expect from someone with his innate athletic ability—he lacked the consistency Bennett needed in order for Anderson to earn a permanent position in the starting lineup. In the 2013 NIT, Anderson led Virginia, averaging 19 points per game during the three-game tournament run.

Anderson continued to show promise during his sophomore year, but with Harris, then the senior shooting guard, showing complete domination on both ends of the court on an already well-balanced Cavaliers team, getting into the starting rotation would still not be in the cards for Anderson. Though he started only five games, Anderson played 21.5 minutes per game, and while his stats line looked similar to his freshman campaign, it was the energy that Anderson brought onto the court that was among his greatest contributions to the team. For his contributions coming off the bench, Anderson was named the ACC's Sixth Man of the Year.

His junior season proved to be Anderson's breakout season. With Harris having been drafted by the Cleveland Cavaliers, everyone turned to Anderson to step up as the next leader of the team. In a heart-to-heart with Anderson, Bennett said to him, "Be sound and tough. You just do it the way you have to do it. You don't have to be Joe Harris, [just] because Joe Harris left. Understand how you help this team."

The summer leading up to Anderson's junior year, he attended a training facility in Illinois to continue working on his conditioning, footwork, explosiveness, and shooting. The work proved invaluable. With some tweaks to the mechanics of Anderson's shot, suddenly Anderson became not only an athletic freak of nature

Justin Anderson dunks over North Carolina's Brice Johnson during Virginia's 75–64 road victory in 2015.

when it came to defense, dunking, and alley-oops, but he had also become a mid and long-range shooting threat.

That junior season Anderson's three-point shooting percentage skyrocketed to 45 percent and up from a mere 29.4 percent the year prior. He became infuriatingly frustrating for opponents to defend because it didn't matter where on the court Anderson was. He was always a genuine threat to shoot with a legitimate jumper.

Ranked as high as No. 2 in the country and jumping out to a 19–0 start, the 2014–15 Virginia Cavaliers had a realistic shot of going deep into the NCAA Tournament, but a fractured finger on February 7 in a win against Louisville and a surprise appendectomy in early March left Anderson out of commission for eight games late in the season. Virginia, talented and team-oriented as it was, had difficulties recovering from the injury—in part trying to make up for the lost talent and in part trying to reintegrate Anderson back into the system post-injuries.

Virginia's NCAA Tournament run was cut short by Michigan State for the second straight year. It's impossible to speculate how the Cavaliers would have fared if Anderson was healthy through the final stretch, and after a season with results that finally rivaled those of the Ralph Sampson era, Virginia fans couldn't help but feel a little disappointed in the abrupt end to the record-setting season.

Anderson was named to the All-ACC second team and the National Basketball Coaches Association's All-American third team following his junior season. He entered the NBA draft that year with still one year of eligibility remaining at Virginia. Anderson was drafted in the first round by the Dallas Mavericks with the 21st overall pick, becoming the first Virginia player taken in the first round since the San Antonio Spurs selected Cory Alexander in 1995. Anderson joined Mavericks head coach Rick Carlisle, who was on Virginia's 1984 Final Four team. On draft day Carlisle called Anderson with just one word: "Wahoowa."

39 Art Guepe

In seven seasons from 1946 to 1952 and amidst a challenging time for college football nationwide, head coach Art Guepe's Virginia teams never had a losing season. Amassing a 47–17–2 record during his career as head coach at Virginia, Guepe's .727 winning percentage remains the highest in school history for any individual who coached more than two seasons at Virginia. Originally a quarterback out of Marquette from 1934 to 1936, Guepe had led the team to a 7–1 record in 1935 and a 7–2 record in 1936, including a trip to the first Cotton Bowl Classic in 1937. There, Guepe scored the only touchdown of the game for Marquette, returning a 60-yard punt for the Cotton Bowl's first ever touchdown in a game Marquette lost 16–6 to Texas Christian.

Guepe's head coach at Marquette, Frank Murray, would leave the school to become Virginia's head coach in 1937. After coaching Marquette's freshmen for a season in 1937, Guepe followed Murray as an assistant coach at Virginia from 1938 to 1942 before serving in the Navy during World War II.

Following the war Guepe became Murray's successor as Virginia's head football coach in 1946. His first season at Virginia was his worst, finishing with a 4–4–1 record that included a shutout 40–0 loss to perennial national powerhouse Penn. Following that season, though, Guepe found success on the football field, including winning the first six straight games in the 1947 season that gave Virginia its first top 10 ranking in the Associated Press poll. Just two years later in 1949, Virginia defeated No. 20 Penn for the first time in 14 tries, giving them a No. 9 ranking in the AP poll. Virginia finished the 1949 season with a 7–2 record and the 1950 season with an 8–2 record.

The Gooch Report

The fall of 1951 was one of the most perplexing years in the history of Virginia football, and it would set the stage for three decades of futility to come. A faculty committee headed up by Robert Gooch, a political science professor, called for not only faculty control of athletics, but also an end to athletic scholarships. The move would have effectively turned Virginia into a "college division" athletic program—or a Division II or III-level school in modern sports terms.

The weekend after the report came out, UVA lost to underdog Washington & Lee. "I do not want to suffer Saturday after Saturday with a losing team. I just saw de-emphasized football, and I didn't like it," one student told *The Cavalier Daily* at the time.

The committee convened in the spring after the NCAA repealed the Sanity Code, which imposed severe restrictions on financial aid or any admissions preference for student-athletes. Instituted in 1948, it stated that colleges could grant scholarships and give jobs to players based only on financial need rather than athletic or academic potential.

At the end of the last season, Virginia's 8–1 effort would be rewarded with an offer to go to the Orange Bowl against future ACC counterpart Georgia Tech. Virginia president Colgate Darden, a known opponent of postseason bowl games, had a different mind-set.

Despite this success the 1951 season was met with controversy as professor and former Virginia quarterback Robert Gooch and the three-man Gooch Committee released the 43-page report now referred to as the Gooch Report, which recommended faculty control of extracurricular activities, including football, as well as opposing athletic scholarships based on athletic ability rather than need and academic merit.

This seeming de-emphasis of athletics at the university created great controversy and cast a shadow over the 1951 team, who, prior to the report's release, was 2–0 on the season, beating George Washington and Virginia Tech by a combined 53–0. In the week immediately following the Gooch Report's release, the team would

Although Darden wasn't particularly opposed to the football program in general, he was suspicious of big-time football and knew that it would be up to the Board of Visitors to decide whether UVA would go to Miami. They wouldn't be meeting until December, and the idea was nixed.

Virginia would join the Atlantic Coast Conference two years later for a number of reasons. Although it was an athletically focused conference, institutions like UVA, Duke, and North Carolina added academic credibility to the new league. UVA's first year in the ACC would also be their first year without Guepe, arguably the best coach they'd ever had. After going 8–2 in 1952, Guepe had become disillusioned with the state of affairs at Virginia and left for Vanderbilt. Although the Gooch Report was effectively dead a year after it was published, Guepe determined that it was in his best interest to leave an environment where football was not a priority. After Guepe left, Virginia would have just two winning seasons between 1953 and 1982. That stretch featured a 28-game losing streak between 1958 and 1960.

One interesting point about Gooch is that not only was he a football player at UVA, but he was also a star. As a senior quarterback in 1914, he was part of the team that split the South Atlantic Intercollegiate Athletic Association title with Washington & Lee and was named to the All-Southern team.

lose 42–14 to Washington & Lee. Undeterred, Guepe led the team to six straight victories to finish the season 8–1. The Orange Bowl offered Virginia a spot in the New Year's Day bowl game to face Georgia Tech, an invitation that was met with great excitement from the Virginia players. Guepe was quoted as saying, "I don't want to be a bowl maniac, but these kids did a tremendous job this season, and they deserve a good trip if they want it." It was the school's first ever invitation to a postseason bowl game.

However, Virginia president Colgate Darden, a known opponent of postseason competition and bowl games, declined the invitation—in particular because of the faculty's opposition toward subsidized football and the national attitude trending away from big-time football. Still, Virginia would finish ranked No. 13 that season in the final AP poll. Following this season the Board of Visitors approved Darden's recommendation of a $100 salary raise for Guepe.

A year later, following an 8–2 season in 1952 with losses coming to national powers Duke and South Carolina, Guepe went to interview at Vanderbilt for the head coaching position. Prior to the interview, Guepe requested a five-year contract at an annual salary of $10,000. Upon his return from Nashville and prior to hearing back on whether his requested contract would be accepted, Guepe announced that he would be leaving Virginia for Vanderbilt with a $12,000 annual salary. "While I regretted to see Mr. Guepe go," Darden said, "I do not think he could have refused the offer made him at Vanderbilt, nor do I think we could have equaled it without giving to football here an emphasis in comparison with other activities, which would have been injurious in the long run."

When he retired from Vanderbilt in 1962 to become the commissioner of the Ohio Valley Conference, Guepe left with a strong statement to Vanderbilt that was equally applicable to Virginia: "There is no way you can be Harvard Monday through Friday and try to be Alabama on Saturday."

It was Guepe's opinion that in order to find success and become competitive on the gridiron, Vanderbilt—and certainly Virginia as well—would need to relax its academic and admissions standards for its football players. Art Guepe passed away on November 3, 2001, at the age of 86 and is buried in Nashville, Tennessee.

40 Hooville: Charlottesville's Tent City

In the college basketball world, there's only one tent city that garners national attention, and that's the one in Durham. But Duke fans aren't the only ones to celebrate in this time-honored tradition of sleeping outdoors in February on concrete. At least for a period of time in Virginia basketball history, beginning in the mid-1970s and going well into the Pete Gillen head-coaching era, Charlottesville also played home to a tent city known as "Hooville."

Before the days of points accumulation and online student ticketing systems at Virginia came the days of old-school, first-come, first-served waiting lines. During the peaks of Virginia basketball under Ralph Sampson and throughout the turn of the century, Virginia basketball fans, growing ever hungry for a top-notch program to go deep into the NCAA Tournament, began to line up earlier and earlier in hopes of getting floor or lower-bowl seats at University Hall, a cozy 8,457-seat arena. Hours turned into days and days turned into weeks, and before you knew it, for big games at U-Hall, it was like there was an entire city right there on the concourse between U-Hall and Onesty Hall.

For outsiders and professionals well beyond their college years, the tradition seemed to be a silly one. Hoards of students spent days and nights in the bitter winter cold—not in hopes of getting a ticket, which could readily be done for most games—but in hopes of getting seats closer to the floor of a fairly small arena. From a logical perspective, it made little sense.

However, students who camped out for days or weeks remember these times fondly. For them it wasn't just an opportunity to skip classes and it wasn't just the chance of getting courtside seats. It was a time to bond with their fellow basketball fanatics: groups of first-year hall and suitemates, fraternity brothers and sorority sisters, student organizations, or just a hodgepodge group that found each other one way or another. Everyone on the concourse was there for the same, united reason: to cheer on the Wahoos to victory.

As groups grew larger and crowds rowdier, a new student-run organization was formed: the 'Hoo Crew. The 'Hoo Crew with the tagline "Keepin' You in Line" was created not only to ensure a fair camping out process, but also to address the university administration's concerns that students were skipping classes to camp out for basketball games. They did so, for example, by limiting the number of students in each group and only requiring that one person from a group be present at any given time, thereby allowing students to coordinate camping schedules around their class schedules.

On weekends the concourse was the place to be. Groups brought out generators in order to blast music throughout the tent city. Every group brought their own collection of snacks, beverages, and entertainment, and for a few months out of every year, U-Hall, and not Rugby Road, became the center of the social scene for the Wahoo faithful.

At its peak, tents flooded the U-Hall concourse and stretched almost entirely around Onesty Hall to Emmet Street with upwards of more than 200 tents for some of the biggest games, such as the 2002 contest featuring No. 8 Virginia and No. 3 Maryland. Those who were there remember Hooville fondly as the biggest party of the year, though the Cavaliers would ultimately fall 91–87 to the Terrapins that game.

Former Virginia basketball head coach Pete Gillen, who led the Cavaliers from 1998 to 2005, knew and understood what the campouts meant to the student body. Despite only one NCAA Tournament appearance during his seven seasons at Virginia, Gillen holds a soft spot in the hearts of many Virginia basketball fans who were students at the time. In the week and days leading up to a big game, Gillen would often come out to greet the dedicated students camping out in the bitter January and February cold. And knowing the plight of the modern-day college student, he did not come empty-handed, frequently handing out Krispy Kreme doughnuts or pizza for the fans. It wasn't just Gillen who displayed his appreciation for the fanbase. Alumni recount stories of student athletes like Travis Watson ('03) coming out and spending time with the fans, including playing video games inside of one of the tents that had a generator.

In each of the final three seasons under Gillen, the Cavaliers finished with six or fewer conference wins. Subsequently, student interest began to dwindle, and the population in tent city followed. Shortly after, Virginia implemented an online ticketing system that eliminated the need for camping out early for best seats. Instead, students were awarded loyalty points based on the basketball games they attended, as well as their attendance at other Cavaliers sporting events. The students with the highest number of points not only increased their chances of getting tickets, but they also improved their group entrance time.

Today the 'Hoo Crew name has been repurposed to refer to the official student fan group at the university, which received the 2014 Naismith Student Section of the Year Award.

41 2014 ACC Regular Season Title

After a blowout loss to Tennessee in December of 2013, Virginia soon-to-be-legend Joe Harris drove his red pickup truck to head coach Tony Bennett's house on New Year's Eve to talk about how the 9–4 Cavaliers could turn their season around during conference play before it was too late. Harris and Akil Mitchell were seniors, the only remaining two of Bennett's first recruiting class that was nicknamed the "Six Shooters." Whatever words were exchanged that night sent the Cavaliers into a winning frenzy that turned the season around, losing only twice more in the regular season and holding a total of 12 opponents to 50 points or fewer in the regular season.

Two months later in his final game at John Paul Jones Arena, Harris nailed a dagger three from right in front of the Virginia bench to all but secure the program's first outright ACC regular season championship in more than three decades.

For almost all of the 2014 ACC season, newcomer Syracuse had been in first place, ranked No. 1 or No. 2, and undefeated. Its perfect run ended with an overtime loss at home to Boston College on February 19, but after starting the season at 25–0 overall and 12–0 in conference play, many thought that the Orange would run the table through the regular season and the ACC Tournament in Greensboro, North Carolina.

About 500 miles to the south, however, Virginia was going on a remarkable run of its own. After Harris' famous visit to Bennett's house, one nail-biting loss at Duke was the only blemish on their league record, and the Cavaliers were off to one of their best ever ACC starts. The matchup that had been talked about for weeks reached hype of nearly unprecedented levels after a UVA win against Miami on Wednesday of that week and a Syracuse win against Maryland that Monday. With Syracuse at 13–2 in the conference and UVA at 14–1 heading into the Saturday afternoon showdown, the game was a de facto championship game for the regular season crown, something that the Hoos had shared four times without claiming outright since 1981.

Fourth-ranked Syracuse started well, but momentum went back to the No. 12 Cavaliers with a London-Perrantes-to-Mitchell alley-oop from half court early in the first half that pushed the Virginia crowd to its breaking point. The two teams traded buckets, including a stretch where they combined for four straight three-pointers, for much of the second half. After Syracuse's Tyler Ennis picked up his fourth foul, coach Jim Boeheim took him out of the game with the Orange trailing 46–42 and 9:11 remaining on the clock. Perrantes "Call-cool" responded with a long three from the tip of the sabre at midcourt, a play that would spark a run that would eventually secure the regular season title. A three from Justin Anderson helped strengthen the Cavaliers' grip on the crown with 7:36 left.

Harris' three with 4:45 remaining put UVA up 60–47, and it was all over from there. Harris left the floor of John Paul Jones for the final time with 39 seconds left, hugging every coach, player, and support staff member on the bench to a long, loud ovation. Thomas Rogers, a senior walk-on-turned-scholarship-player from a town 60 miles to the southeast of Charlottesville called Farmville, provided potentially the most memorable moment of the day just seconds later. Rogers drained a three-pointer from the right wing, and the players on the bench celebrated more than they had for any basket all day or all of them put together.

The Hoos had finished the game on a 29–14 run to secure the regular season title. In front of a home crowd that had been starved of championships for decades, Tony Bennett led the team in cutting down the nets of JPJ for the very first time.

42 1984 Peach Bowl

Following a 55–0 blowout by Clemson at home to open up the 1984 season, it looked to be more of the same for a Virginia team that had only three winning seasons in the previous 31 years. However, behind sophomore quarterback Don Majkowski, who had replaced sophomore Kevin Ferguson as the starter midway through the season, running backs Barry Word and Howard "Beaver" Petty, and potent defense, head coach George Welsh led the Cavaliers to nine straight unbeaten games before finally falling to Maryland to finish with a 7–2–2 regular season record and a second-place finish in the ACC.

With just two games remaining in the season, Welsh recalled a conversation with athletics director Dick Schultz, who informed him that a Peach Bowl bid was likely. Welsh thought they could do better than the Peach Bowl, a bowl that at the time was a lower tier bowl with smaller payouts (ranked 11th of the then-18 bowls) and certainly less fanfare. But after an injury to Virginia's star defensive back, Lester Lyles, Welsh went back to Schultz, suggesting that they instead should go ahead and accept the invitation, which they did. This worked out well for Virginia, considering it tied North Carolina that weekend and lost to Maryland the following weekend.

Virginia drew Purdue, a team that had gone 7–4, (6–3 Big Ten) in the regular season to finish tied with Indiana for second in the conference. Though the Boilermarkers had not been to a bowl game since 1980, this was their program's fifth bowl game, having won all four of their previous trips. The Peach Bowl was Virginia's first ever bowl game.

Virginia ran into problems from the very beginning. In fact, several of Virginia's players, including at least seven or eight starters, had gotten stuck in an elevator at the team hotel and missed the team bus. This group, including defensive tackle Tom Kilgannon, barely made it in time—just five minutes before the opening kickoff. Purdue quarterback Jim Everett had his way with Virginia in the first half, showing why the Los Angeles Rams would go on to select him as the overall No. 3 pick in the 1986 NFL Draft and why he would go on to a successful NFL career that included a Pro Bowl selection in 1990. Everett threw for 158 yards in the first half, including three touchdowns, each for double-digit yardage.

Heading into the locker room at halftime, Virginia trailed 24–14. The Cavaliers' two touchdowns had come from an 11-yard scamper by Petty and a three-yard pass from Majkowski to Geno Zimmerlink. Running backs Petty and Word recalled having an inspiring halftime in the locker room. Running backs coach Ken Mack challenged Petty and Word to "suck it up at halftime and to take over the game," Word said after the game. "[Mack] told us we were great backs, and we could change the game ourselves. He had never told us we were great backs before, so it really meant something to us."

That's exactly what happened. Virginia rushed for nearly 200 yards in the second half to take control of the game. The defense, equally inspired, shut down the Boilermakers offense for the entire half. Purdue was limited to just four possessions in the entire second half, which resulted in a punt, a missed field goal, a fumble, and an interception.

Virginia scored a touchdown on a one-yard Majkowski dive early in the third quarter and tied the game up early in the second quarter with a 19-yard field goal. Tied at 24 all, Virginia drove down to the Purdue 1-yard line with 7:17 remaining in the game. Having watched Virginia take risks all season long to gain the upper hand, spectators were expecting Welsh to go for the touchdown to give the Cavaliers a seven-point lead. "When you get a chance to go ahead," Welsh said after the game, "you've got to go ahead and make them beat you. There are some arguments both ways…I was concerned. But I think when you've got a chance to go ahead, most of the time I'll do that."

Welsh called on kicker Kenny Stadlin, who had already hit two field goals and three extra points that evening, to come in for the chip shot. The successful 22-yard field goal gave Virginia a 27–24 lead. Virginia's defense would hold with Ray Daly intercepting Everett at the Virginia 15-yard line and 4:56 to play, ultimately sealing the deal for Virginia.

Virginia's first ever bowl game was a success, as the Cavaliers handed Purdue its first ever bowl game loss. The Cavaliers finished with an 8–2–2 record, its most wins since 1952. Welsh was offered a head coaching position at Arizona State, a position that offered greater national attention, had better facilities, provided a bigger salary, and had a strong pipeline of recruits coming in. Welsh declined the offer, citing that his children had just moved to Charlottesville and didn't want to move again so soon. The university extended Welsh's contract and eventually upgraded its facilities, including the McCue Center and an expanded Scott Stadium. Welsh would go on to be the most successful coach at Virginia.

43 The Corrigan Report

Fewer individuals have had as great an impact on Virginia, the Atlantic Coast Conference, and the entire NCAA as Gene Corrigan, the university's athletic director from 1971 to 1980. No stranger to the university, Corrigan had served as the head coach of men's lacrosse from 1958 to 1967 and the head coach of men's soccer from 1958 to 1965. He also served as an assistant basketball coach from 1958 to 1960. Yes, for those of you who are counting along at home, it means that for an extended period of time he was coaching three sports concurrently.

During his tenure as each team's respective head coach, Corrigan accumulated winning records in both lacrosse (52–49) and soccer (39–35–7), but it was in his capacity as the university's athletic director where he made his biggest impact.

In 1969 Corrigan was named the athletic director at Washington & Lee University, where he had previously coached both lacrosse and soccer. Virginia hired Corrigan back in 1971 to serve as AD, where he would find himself fighting an uphill battle to establish athletics as a priority for the university. Having previously coached a number of sports at Virginia, Corrigan was no stranger to the university's attitude toward athletics. The school prided itself on being an academic institution first and foremost, and previous university presidents and administration had taken the approach that a school could not excel at both academics and athletics without some level of compromise.

For the University of Virginia, this meant that academics would get the spotlight. The school would keep the athletics budget relatively small compared to the rest of the conference, and this made it difficult for Corrigan to recruit the talent he needed—both in terms of players and coaching staff—in order to succeed and bring Virginia to the next level. Frustrated with the state of affairs, in 1979 Corrigan drafted what would become one of the most important documents affecting the university's approach to athletics, a report that would later become known simply as the "Corrigan Report."

The report outlined the university's deficiencies as they related to athletics and proposed a plan that would allow the school to amplify its athletics profile within the ACC without compromising its rich tradition of academics. Corrigan later recounted in an interview with *The Daily Progress*'s Jerry Ratcliffe that, as he filed the report with then-university president Frank Hereford, he said, "Please read this over the weekend…you might want to fire me on Monday."

Among other things the report recommended that the university provide greater support in the way of housing, meals, and scheduling; reserve a number of spots in each incoming class for student-athletes of non-revenue sports; defer the foreign language requirement for certain student-athletes; and relax the admissions standards for the Commerce School and School of Education. The report also asked Hereford to be certain whether Corrigan was "the right person to be in charge of [the athletics] program." And if he wasn't the right person, Corrigan would leave.

President Hereford did read the report as requested, and when he summoned Corrigan to his office, he had the university's vice presidents in attendance. Instead of terminating Corrigan as athletics director, Hereford directed the vice presidents to read and review the report and contribute to President Hereford's and AD Corrigan's plan to implement some of Corrigan's suggestions outlined therein. "We didn't change a lot," Corrigan said. "But what I saw was huge. It was the beginning to a road map for success."

With the support of Hereford and his staff, and a newfound university-wide focus to give athletics the resources it needed to succeed, Corrigan had some of the tools he needed to change the landscape at Virginia. During his time Corrigan would make several hires that would become household names among the Virginia faithful, including men's basketball coach Terry Holland, women's basketball coach Debbie Ryan, and men's soccer head coach Bruce Arena, each of whom would bring their respective sports to new heights.

Gene Corrigan would go on to be the athletic director at Notre Dame from 1981 to 1987 and then ACC commissioner from 1987 to 1997. In his final two and a half years as ACC commissioner, he also served as president of the NCAA. Corrigan would finally return to Charlottesville in 1997 for his retirement, though he has remained an active and knowledgeable advisor in the world of collegiate athletics.

44 Recruiting Ralph

Ralph Sampson, the 7'4" center out of Harrisonburg, Virginia, towered head and shoulders above his peers, both literally and figuratively. As a freshman at Harrisonburg High School, Sampson was already 6'7". In his junior and senior years of high school, he would lead the team to consecutive Virginia state titles. As a senior he averaged 30 points, 19 rebounds, and seven blocks. Sampson was unequivocally the most highly recruited player in 1979. In fact, he's arguably one of the top 10 most highly recruited players of all time. At the time there were two highly sought-after centers: Sampson and 7'1" Sam Bowie out of Pennsylvania. After those two there was a giant (pun intended) gap, and then there was the rest of the country. Sampson had more than 50 colleges and universities recruiting him by his senior year.

For Sampson's high school coach Roger Bergey, this was unfamiliar territory. Harrisonburg wasn't a basketball powerhouse and certainly had never experienced a recruiting season like the one Sampson brought upon them. After consulting with Sampson and his family, as well as with the NCAA, Bergey created a list of 14 rules that all colleges wishing to recruit Sampson needed to follow. Included on the list was that all contact must be made through the high school coach, and that Bergey wouldn't be taking calls after 11:00 PM (EST), to the chagrin of schools on the west coast.

As the recruiting period continued, Sampson was able to narrow down his list to four schools: Virginia, Virginia Tech, North Carolina, and Kentucky. Though four teams made the final cut, ultimately, the decision came down to Virginia and Kentucky. Kentucky had a lot going for it—namely, that it was a preeminent basketball program that boasted five national championships at the time, including one just the year prior. Kentucky's incoming class, it seemed, was going to be one of its most heralded recruiting classes, which included multiple *Parade* All-Americans at just about every position.

Virginia, on the other hand, was an upstart program. There was no rich history of national championships. While Kentucky was boasting its fifth national championship, Virginia was touting its first conference title from three years prior. But Virginia did have other things weighing in its favor. Perhaps most importantly, Charlottesville was close to Harrisonburg, which meant that he would be close to his family. It was also in the Atlantic Coast Conference, which most viewed as the strongest basketball league in the country.

Virginia head coach Terry Holland and assistant head coach Craig Littlepage, both of whom would later become athletics directors at Virginia, didn't engage in the same type of recruiting game as other schools. "Here at Virginia," Littlepage once said, "we feel as though the kids in our program are the most important. We, as coaches, try not to hotly pursue any young man at the expense of any of our present players. We don't want our kids believing that we don't care, that we're always trying to find replacements. We told Ralph right off that we were very interested in him. But once the season began, as with all of the other prospects, we just let him play. The senior year is a very important one for any young athlete, and especially for one as talented as Ralph."

In some respects this tactic of giving Sampson some space his senior year may have worked. Prior to Sampson's commitment, Littlepage explained Sampson "is a quiet, dedicated youngster, who doesn't seek all of the attention that many others do. In that respect our gameplan might prove successful in the long run. I sure hope so." Bergey would agree. "Just the other night," the high school coach said, "I saw him sitting on the bleachers before a game holding a little kid on his lap. Not many guys getting the kind of attention he gets would have time for kids like that." Said

Littlepage: "You're talking about the difference between greatness and goodness."

In a world before the Internet and national recruiting services, it wasn't common to know the daily goings-on for any given recruit. But with Sampson it was different. "Ralph Sampson. Ralph Sampson. Ralph Sampson. I've had it up to here with Ralph Sampson," wrote one *Cavalier Daily* columnist in April, 1979. "Rarely has a week gone by during the past four months without Sampson appearing in the newspapers. He seems to have become daily copy in local newspapers...It's enough to make a student sick."

Finally, Sampson called for a press conference on May 31, 1979, to announce his decision. The night before, he hadn't gone to bed until 2:00 AM and spent most of the night pacing, according to his mother, who didn't know where her son would be headed until moments before the press conference.

More than 100 media members showed up for the announcement, when Sampson admitted that in making the decision he had changed his mind at least 50 times. "It came down to Kentucky and Virginia," Sampson said during the conference. "So I think I'm going with Virginia next summer...next semester."

The announcement, though exciting for Virginia, didn't instill too much confidence in the Virginia coaches, as Sampson seemingly left the door open for second thoughts. Sampson admitted that he had not signed any scholarships and that he would leave it open for a couple days in case he changed his mind once more. "I haven't signed yet, but Virginia, I'll probably be going to Virginia. You know, Kentucky. I just didn't want to go there." When specifically asked about whether he was actually leaving the door open for a possible change, he responded, "It could happen. I'm not leaving it out."

Sampson did sign his letter of intent and scholarship package the following night, but 35 years later, when asked in an interview at what point he was fairly confident that Sampson would pick

Virginia, Holland revealed that even the paperwork didn't make him feel confident. "I was not sure until Ralph actually showed up on campus," Holland said. "Ralph's [May] pubic announcement was, 'I am going to Virginia…I think,' so we weren't taking anything for granted in this long-running recruiting battle."

The recruiting wouldn't stop even after Sampson actually started playing for the Cavaliers. "In the spring of every year," Holland continued, "NBA teams came to recruit Ralph with offers to make him the first pick in the draft while offering carloads of money. So we had to recruit him again each spring."

It worked out pretty well for Virginia. Sampson stayed with the Cavaliers all four years, fulfilling a promise to his mother to graduate in four years with his class from Virginia and bringing Virginia to heights it had never achieved, most of which have still not been replicated to this day.

45 Rick Carlisle

In deciding to transfer from Maine following the 1982 season, sophomore Rick Carlisle said that he wanted "to play at the greatest level of college basketball." For Carlisle this meant one of three schools: Providence, Syracuse, and Virginia. But he only flirted with Providence and Syracuse, then both in the Big East, for a short moment. "Once I got off the plane in Charlottesville and saw the city, the university, and met the people, it was pretty clear that was the place to go if I really wanted to test myself," Carlisle recalled to *The Daily Progress* in 2013.

It didn't hurt that Virginia had just reached the Final Four for the first time in program history. All signs pointed to Virginia being

Rick Carlisle, who would go on to become one of the NBA's best coaches, scrambles for a loose ball against Duke in 1983.

an upstart program. Forced to sit out his first year at Virginia, Carlisle watched Sampson and Jeff Jones take the Cavaliers on an incredible 27–1 start to the season, rising to the No. 1 spot in the national polls. That season would end with a record of 30–4, (12–2 ACC), including a memorable 47–45 loss to North Carolina in the ACC Tournament finals, in which the Tar Heels held the ball for over seven minutes because it employed their infamous Four Corners.

In his first year of eligibility at Virginia, Carlisle, who was named by *Playboy* as a top college player to watch, played alongside Sampson to lead the 1982–83 team to a record of 28–5, (12–2 ACC). The season itself was one of ups and downs as Cavaliers fans witnessed both the Game of the Decade, where Ralph Sampson and the No. 1 Cavaliers defeated Patrick Ewing and the No. 3 Georgetown Hoyas 68–63, as well as the Upset of the Century, where unranked Chaminade took down that same No. 1 Virginia team 72–77 just two weeks later. Carlisle averaged 10.9 points per game that season.

With Sampson out of the picture, the media didn't expect much out of Virginia's 1983–84 team, who would almost certainly need some time to rebuild after the country's three-time National Player of the Year had graduated. Whereas the 1982–83 team had a preseason No. 1 ranking for the first time in program history, this team was unranked altogether in the preseason despite finishing fourth in both polls the year prior.

Though Sampson and starting forward Craig Robinson, who combined for nearly 28 points per game for the Cavaliers, had both graduated, three of Virginia's starters were returning: junior guard Tim Mullen and senior guards Othell Wilson, a first team All-ACC selection, and Carlisle. The season started better than most were expecting, as Carlisle, along with Wilson, Kenton Edelin, and Ricky Stokes paced Virginia to 10 straight wins and a No. 20 ranking. That's not how the season would continue, though, as the Cavaliers lost seven of their next 10, and those were all conference games. Virginia struggled throughout the rest of the season, finishing the regular season 17–10, (6–8 ACC) and squarely on the bubble of the NCAA Tournament.

In a time when "seven and seven, you're going to heaven" meant a 7–7 ACC record would all but guarantee a team a spot in the NCAA Tournament, Virginia thought it needed a strong showing in the ACC Tournament in order to push themselves over the hump and squarely into the NCAA Tournament. But instead it lost to Wake Forest in its only ACC Tournament game 63–51.

With perhaps a little bit of luck, Virginia received an invitation from the NCAA as a No. 7 seed. In the opening round game against Iona, Virginia saw a big halftime lead dissipate, but the Cavaliers ultimately came away with the 58–57 victory. Virginia's second round game would be against No. 8 Arkansas, a game in which one reporter wrote that "it would take a near-miracle performance to beat the Razorbacks."

That miracle came in the form of Rick Carlisle, who hit a mid-range jumper in overtime to give Virginia the 53–51 victory. The Cavaliers would cruise past No. 18 Syracuse en route to edging out Indiana 50–48 to reach their second Final Four in just four years. Virginia would lose to second-seeded Houston by a mere two points (49–47). "That was a beautiful moment that I will always remember because we were a bubble team that got hot at the right time and played a lot of close games," Carlisle said. "It was a fantastic experience."

Carlisle finished his senior season at Virginia with 11.1 points per game as the Cavaliers' second leading scorer behind three-time first-team All-ACC selection Wilson. He would go on to be drafted in the third round by the Boston Celtics, where he played for just three seasons, including the Celtics' 1986 NBA championship season. In 1989 Carlisle became an assistant coach for the New Jersey Nets. After 11 seasons as an assistant coach with various teams and a stint as a radio analyst for the Seattle SuperSonics, Carlisle became the head coach of the Detroit Pistons for two seasons and the Indiana Pacers for four seasons. In 2008 he was hired as the head coach of the Dallas Mavericks, a team he guided to an NBA title in 2011.

46 Debbie Ryan

When Debbie Ryan resigned from her 34-year role as Virginia women's basketball head coach in 2011, the storyline wasn't all about the number of wins she had to her name, the number of coaches or WNBA stars she had produced during her tenure, or even individual or team accolades. Instead, writers, fans, alumni, and colleagues reflected fondly on what a good human being she was, what a good role model she served as for both players and fellow coaches, and what great accomplishments she had achieved off the court.

Ryan began as an assistant coach under Dan Bonner at Virginia, a program that was founded only two years prior. In 1977 after Bonner left the post, Ryan, then only 23 years old, was hired to take over. "I was totally oblivious to my age, to my inexperience," Ryan said years later. "I was a little too cocky. I really thought I knew quite a bit and I knew nothing. It was one of those things where I went like I was a bull in a china shop. I just thought I was going to change the world at a very young age. I was aggressive. I had a lot to learn and I did learn a lot."

Thirty-four years later it turns out Ryan did alright for herself and for Virginia women's basketball. Ryan's teams finished with an overall 739–324 record as one of only nine active Division

I women's basketball coaches at the time to have reached the 700-win milestone. She led the Cavaliers to 23 seasons of 20 wins or more and two seasons of 30 wins or more. Virginia made 12 Sweet 16 and seven Elite Eight appearances and reached three consecutive Final Fours from 1990 to 1992, including a trip to the national championship game in 1991, falling to Tennessee 70–67 in overtime. That year Ryan was named the Naismith College Coach of the Year, and Virginia's Dawn Staley was named the NCAA Tournament's Most Outstanding Player.

In 2008 Staley went on to become the head coach at South Carolina, where she went from a record of 10–18, (2–12 SEC) her

First Woman to Earn Varsity Letter

Twenty-one years before the university would have any official women's varsity teams, Mary Slaughter joined the Virginia men's tennis team in 1954. In doing so, she became the first woman to play a varsity sport at Virginia and to earn a varsity letter. She didn't just play the sport—she was good at it, winning the women's Eastern Intercollegiate Title.

Following her graduation, the United States Tennis Lawn Association crowned her the Virginia State Champion in women's tennis 1959, 1961, and 1963. She also won the 1965 Illinois State Tennis Championship in both singles and doubles. She earned her doctorate and taught at Illinois before finally returning to Virginia.

The university was no stranger to the Slaughter family. Her father, Edward, also known as "Butch," was hired in March 1931 as an assistant football coach at UVA, where he remained until 1940, when he joined Virginia's faculty in the physical education department while assuming the role as coach of Virginia's golf team at the same time. Under Butch Slaughter's guidance, Dixon Brooke won the NCAA Division I Men's Golf Championships that year. Butch coached the golf team until at least the 1958 season, a stretch that included his return as an assistant football coach from 1946 to 1948. From 1957 to 1973, he was the director of department of intramurals at Virginia, and to honor him in this role, the university named the Slaughter Recreational Center after him in 1982.

first season to five straight seasons of 20 or more wins, beginning just three years later, including a Final Four appearance in 2015. Staley, one of the most successful young coaches today, continues to hold the utmost respect for Ryan. "As I have grown older and now become a coach myself, I have an even deeper appreciation for Debbie," Staley said. "She is one of the most honest, dependable, and trustworthy people I know."

Others who have come out of Ryan's program include 2010 alumna and WNBA guard Monica Wright. "Coach Ryan, to me, is one of the greatest coaches I have ever played for," Wright said. "During my four years at Virginia, she not only taught me how to be a better basketball player and how to work hard, but she also taught me a lot about how to be a good person and to have integrity in everything that you do."

Integrity is a word that comes up over and over when Ryan's name is mentioned. Former Virginia player Jenny Boucek, who played for Ryan from 1992 to 1996, recalled a story of how Ryan was so strict in adherence to NCAA rules that if players happened to use a phone in the basketball offices, they had to pay for the call themselves. "At the time you're a kid and you think, *This is ridiculous*," she told ESPN. "But her integrity is unwavering. And now that's the thing I respect most about her. There were things I didn't understand then, but they were so important to my development."

Also tied to Debbie Ryan is Val Ackerman, who played under Ryan at Virginia until 1981. Ackerman went on to found the WNBA and serve as its first president. Even Connecticut's legendary coach Geno Auriemma has ties back to Ryan as an assistant coach under Ryan from 1981 to 1985. "Debbie has been one of the most influential people in my life," he said. "Without the opportunity that she gave me and the support I received at the University of Virginia, my life would be totally different than it is today. She will be missed by all her players, present, and former, but most importantly, the game will miss her."

She was named the ACC Coach of the Year seven times, and her teams won 11 ACC regular season championships and three ACC Tournament championships. Yet despite the accolades, Ryan will be remembered as a legend at Virginia not only for the success she found on the court and the new heights she achieved for a fledgling team, but for one of her greatest victories, on or off the court.

In 2000 Ryan was diagnosed with pancreatic cancer, which has single-digit survival rates. Only about four percent of those diagnosed with the disease go on to live longer than five years. Doctors removed the tumor, and after six weeks of radiation and chemotherapy, Ryan had beaten the odds. The following year Ryan went on to coach the U.S.A. women's basketball team to a gold medal at the Beijing World University Games. Ryan never missed a beat.

After stepping down from the head coaching position in 2011, Ryan, who has been cancer-free for more than 10 years, now works in development in the UVA Health Foundation, raising money for the cancer center. Few individuals have had as great an impact on any one area of the university as Debbie Ryan had on Virginia women's basketball and continues to have in the area of cancer research.

47 The Miracle Catch

When George Welsh agreed to become the head football coach of the Virginia Cavaliers in 1982, Virginia football was in shambles. The program had only two winning seasons to its name since 1953, and there were no signs of improvement in the years to come. Luckily for Virginia, Welsh was a really good football coach. It only took two seasons at the helm before Welsh put together a winning season, going 2–9, (1–5 ACC) the first year, and improving to 6–5,

(3–3 ACC) in 1983, which included a big 17–14 win against No. 19 North Carolina.

The 1984 season opened up with some question marks for Virginia, who had three legitimate contenders for the starting quarterback role: sophomore Kevin Ferguson, sophomore Don Majkowski, and redshirt freshman Scott Secules. The nod was given to Ferguson, but Welsh was not shy to admit that neither Majkowski nor Secules was far behind on the depth chart, though Majkowski was the more likely candidate to receive playing time should it come to that.

The season opened with a 55–0 shutout at the hands of football powerhouse No. 3 Clemson. Unshaken, the team bounced back with two consecutive and convincing wins: a 35–7 win against VMI at home and a 21–9 win against Welsh's former team, Navy, on the road.

When the Cavaliers had to travel to Lane Stadium to take on Virginia Tech the following week, they did so with a purpose: to avenge last year's 48–0 shutout loss to the Hokies at home. No one on the team had beaten Virginia Tech at the time, having lost to their in-state rivals in four straight attempts.

Error after error, mistake after mistake, the first three quarters of the game were unbearable to watch, as both teams committed penalties, dropped passes, and ran poor routes throughout the afternoon. To make a sloppy game worse, neither team was able to take full advantage of the other's mistakes. On Virginia Tech's first possession, the Hokies were able to drive to the Virginia 7-yard line but ran into trouble when an offensive lineman jumped offside on third down. The play would result in a pass out of the end zone, and the Hokies would be forced to settle for three. Virginia ran into similar troubles of its own. Despite forcing and recovering a fumble on the Virginia Tech 9-yard line, Virginia was forced to kick a field goal on fourth and 2 to tie the score at three apiece.

Virginia Tech regained the lead on another punt, and with just over four minutes to go in the first half, Welsh pulled Ferguson and replaced him with Majkowski. "Sometimes a quarterback change helps, sometimes it doesn't," Welsh said of the decision. "I didn't think we were going that well offensively...Majkowski has been practicing well and he deserved to come in."

Majkowski quickly earned his stripes on the field, taking 10 plays to complete a drive that ended in an 18-yard touchdown pass to Virginia freshman John Ford, who had already become the first Virginia freshman to ever catch a touchdown pass.

Virginia's David Bond would also make an interception with just 18 seconds remaining in the half, which set up kicker Kenny Stadin to attempt a 56-yard field goal. The kick went up, and it was good—just barely so, but it was enough to set the Virginia record for the longest field goal. Virginia would go into the locker room with a 13–6 lead. The lead wouldn't last for long, however—not with the way Virginia came out in the third quarter. "I was concerned in the third quarter," Welsh said after the game. "I could sense the momentum slipping away from us. The first three or four possessions we couldn't make a first down, and that's no good."

Though Virginia Tech was not able to capitalize on Virginia's mistakes, the Hokies would find their way into the end zone on an interception as Ferguson, who split playing time with Majkowski in the third quarter, tried to ditch the ball under pressure. Another Virginia interception would give Virginia Tech another field goal. The Hokies offense would finally earn its first touchdown in the fourth quarter to give Virginia Tech a 23–13 lead.

With a 10-point deficit into the fourth quarter, Virginia was on the verge of a fifth straight loss to Virginia Tech. Momentum was entirely on the Hokies' sideline, and it looked like the Virginia talent was just not there. Virginia drove to the Tech 34-yard line, but the drive began to stall, and the Hoos were facing fourth and inches. The fans were expecting a quarterback or halfback sneak.

Welsh, though, had something else in mind. "I was very excited about the call," Majkowski said after the game. "I knew it was a great call. It couldn't have come at a better time."

Instead of any sort of short yardage play, tailback Howard "Beaver" Petty faked the sneak, drawing the attention of the entire Hokies line. Majkowski aired the ball toward toward Ford. "I gave [Tech cornerback Leon Gordon] two steps to the outside and released inside," Ford recalled. "I didn't think I could get it at first. I took my eye off the ball for a few seconds to get my speed up. I happened to look up, and there it was. I got six fingertips on it. The route wasn't supposed to be that long, but when I saw the ball in the air, I said, 'I gotta go get it.'"

Completely outstretched, Ford was able to pull the ball in at the 1-yard line, setting up the touchdown for Petty on the next play. Virginia was suddenly down just four. The Virginia defense shut down the Hokies, and Majkowski devised a 59-yard drive that ended in a 14-yard touchdown pass to Ford, giving Virginia a 26–23 lead.

The Hokies got the ball back with just over five minutes remaining in the game. Their drive stalled, and a 52-yard field goal attempt went wide right. The Hokies would get the ball one last time with just 31 seconds left on the clock, but were unable to make anything of it.

Ford's "Miracle Catch" is often referred to among the Virginia faithful simply as, "the Catch." "UVA football was not very good until that season," Majkowski later recalled in an article in *The Daily Progress*. "That year was the start of turning the program around, and that was a pivotal game."

Virginia wouldn't lose another game that season until its regular season finale against Maryland, a 45–34 home loss. The 7–2–2 regular season record gave Virginia a bid to the Peach Bowl, the school's first ever postseason bowl game, where the Cavaliers defeated Purdue 27–24.

48 1995 Virginia Football Season

By the start of the 1995 season, Virginia had been to five bowl games in the six preceding years, going back to Virginia's first ACC co-championship. Accustomed to success under head coach George Welsh, Virginia players and fans alike were ready to take the program to the next level to gain national respect and prove that this wasn't just another phase in a football program that had largely struggled throughout modern history.

The Cavaliers had an opportunity right at the start of the 1995 season when the No. 17-ranked team traveled to No. 14 Michigan to play in the sixth annual Pigskin Classic. It was an opportunity to take on a perennial powerhouse on the road, in front of a national audience, and prove to the country that Virginia football was a force to be reckoned with.

For three quarters Virginia was doing exactly that. Senior captain and quarterback Mike Groh ran in a one-yard touchdown at the end of the first half to strike first for the Cavaliers. Virginia running back Tiki Barber followed that up in the third quarter with an 81-yard touchdown run. Add in a field goal, and Virginia was up 17–0 in the fourth quarter.

With more than 12 minutes remaining in the game, Michigan switched to its two-minute offense, and the entire momentum of the game changed instantly. A touchdown, a Virginia stop, and another touchdown (with a failed two-point conversion), and suddenly the game went from a statement win for Virginia to what the *Associated Press* would later describe as "the greatest comeback in Michigan history." "It's never over until it's over and it wasn't over," Welsh told the media afterward. "If we had gotten a first down, it would have been over."

Virginia wasn't able to get the final first down it needed in the following possession, though they managed to consume 5:07 off the clock. Michigan would recover the ball with just 2:35 to play and 80 yards to go. With four seconds remaining and 15 yards to go on fourth down, the freshman quarterback Scott Dreisbach lobbed one into the end zone. Wide receiver Mercury Hayes made the catch with just one foot in bounds. Michigan would escape 18–17 with no time left on the clock, and no extra point was needed.

Deflated as the Virginia locker room was after missing their opportunity for a big win, the Cavaliers still proved to the country that they were able to hang with the big dogs and were mere seconds away from defeating a powerhouse Big Ten school. The pollsters took note and, despite the loss, kept the Cavaliers at No. 17 for the following week against William & Mary.

Refocused, Virginia rattled off five straight wins, including a ranked opponent in North Carolina State. The No. 9 Cavaliers traveled to Chapel Hill to face a North Carolina team trying to win its third game in a row after losing its first two on the season. Despite having a fourth-quarter lead, Virginia once again succumbed to its opponent's comeback, falling 22–17 on the road. "When they needed a big play, like on third down, they were getting them," Virginia receiver Patrick Jeffers said after the game. "When we needed them, we just weren't able to hit them. It's a tough loss for us, but you've got to give them credit."

After a bounce back 44–30 victory against Duke in Charlottesville the following week, the No. 14 Cavaliers were off to Texas to face the No. 16 Longhorns. Neither team played particularly great in the gusting wind, and both teams were plagued by penalties, missed field goals, and turnovers, but in the back-and-forth game, Virginia pulled ahead 16–14 on a 56-yard field goal with just over three minutes to play. On the final play of the game, Texas kicker Phil Dawson nailed a 50-yard field goal into the wind just over the crossbar. Once again, Virginia would lose with no time left on the clock 17–16.

Virginia wouldn't be afforded too much time to think about the loss to the Longhorns. After an open week, Virginia was set to face the mighty Seminoles of Florida State, a team that had never lost a single ACC game since joining the conference in 1991, on a Thursday night in Charlottesville. "Florida State was so dominant during that era that the NCAA officially declared them a 'dynasty,'" sportswriter Jerry Ratcliffe told *Streaking the Lawn*, 20 years later. "No program since then has earned that sort of recognition by the NCAA."

Though Florida State struck first on a touchdown, Virginia wasn't too far behind in responding with a touchdown of its own. The teams exchanged another pair of touchdowns before the Cavaliers began to break away with a 35-yard field goal followed by a 72-yard pass from Groh to receiver Demetrius "Pete" Allen for a 24–14 lead. At the half Virginia led the Seminoles 27–21, and suddenly the players, the fans, and the entire nation began to believe this was possible. But against an offense that scored an average of 57 points per game, nothing was certain. Virginia maintained its lead throughout the second half. With a 33–28 lead on the Seminoles, the Virginia defense needed one more stop to seal the deal.

With four seconds left in the game, the Cavs were up by five, and Florida State was driving four yards away from the end zone. Seminoles tailback Warrick Dunn took the direct snap and plowed his way forward. For a brief moment, as Dunn's body made its way into the end zone, Cavalier fans thought, *Not again*, bracing themselves for another last-second defeat.

The officials ruled, however, that while Dunn made it into the end zone, the ball had not. Virginia's Adrian Burnim and Anthony Poindexter had successfully stopped the ball just inches short of the goal line.

Charlottesville was euphoric. Fans rushed the field. Goalposts were torn down. One made its way over to the Rugby Road and ended up on the Lawn the next morning. Virginia had given No. 2 Florida State not only its first loss of the season, but also its first ACC loss ever. Virginia had found its statement win.

The Cavaliers closed out their regular season with a win against Maryland on the road and a loss to Virginia Tech—by a mere touchdown. Each of Virginia's four losses during that 1995 season were by a touchdown or less. Capturing a share of the ACC championship, Virginia went on to defeat Georgia in its backyard to claim its second Peach Bowl title in Atlanta.

Ranked 16th in the final AP poll, the 1995 Virginia Cavaliers squad produced five All-Americans in punter Will Brice, safety Percy Ellsworth, running back Tiki Barber, cornerback Ronde Barber, and kicker Rafael Garcia. It produced 22 All-ACC honorees. It also produced what's arguably the single greatest moment in all of Virginia sports history.

49 Curtis Staples

You can't mention three-point shooting at Virginia without at least tipping your hat to Curtis Staples, who played for the Cavaliers from 1995 to 1998. In fact, you can't even really think about three-point shooting in college basketball without at some point referencing Staples. The 6'3" guard from Arizona finished his Virginia career as the NCAA's career leader in three-point field goals made with 413. The record would stand for eight years until 2006 when Duke's J.J. Redick broke the mark.

From the outside it looked like Staples had hit the ground running his freshman year on the team. Off the bench he provided Virginia an average of 11.9 points per game en route to an ACC regular season co-champion title and an Elite Eight appearance in the 1995 NCAA Tournament.

For Staples, though, it was a challenging season. After having dominated the competition in high school, Staples played for 11 scoreless minutes in his college debut. When he spoke to head coach Jeff Jones the following morning, he was told that Jones didn't feel he was ready, and that the confidence in Staples wasn't yet there. "That was probably the worst basketball experience of my life," Staples was quoted by the *Daily Press* in February of 1995. "I wasn't prepared for that. I had never in my life sat on the bench that long watching a game. It hurt me real bad. I was so mad, I was fed up, I didn't feel like I belonged."

Following the advice of those closest to him, Staples decided to stick it out at Virginia, a decision that paid off in dividends. Staples saw his playing time—and point totals—steadily increase. "By his third game," the *Daily Press* reported, "Staples scored 17 points in 24 minutes. By his 13th Virginia ran the final play of overtime to him."

Staples continued to climb the record books throughout his collegiate career. He led the conference in three-point field goals made per game during each of his four seasons at Virginia, setting the Virginia record in the category each season as well, records that still stand today.

During his final season in 1998, he earned third-team All-ACC honors, averaging 18.1 points per game. On November 12, 2006, Virginia retired Staples' No. 5 jersey.

When Redick broke Staples' NCAA and ACC three-point field goal records earlier that year at Cameron Indoor Stadium in Durham, North Carolina, Staples was on hand not just to witness the bucket, but afterward he also presented Redick with the game ball. "I held [the record] for about eight years," Staples later recalled. "I think I held onto it long enough…I think I've put my mark and my stamp on college basketball."

50 2015 College World Series

The 2015 Virginia baseball season started off with high expectations. The Cavaliers were coming off a heartbreaking College World Series Championship loss to Vanderbilt and returned quite a few key contributors from that team. Most notably, weekend starters Brandon Waddell and Nathan Kirby were returning to form one of the most formidable one-two pitching combos in the country. The college baseball media took notice, tabbing the Cavaliers a consensus top five team in their preseason rankings.

Some of the preseason excitement was tempered when two weeks before the season was set to start, it was announced that the team's leading offensive threat and All-American candidate Joe McCarthy had back surgery and would be out until April. Only four games into the season, it was then announced that John Laprise, the Hoos' returning leader in batting average, would be out for the season with a hip injury. Despite the losses Virginia would roll off 10 straight wins to start the season, but something didn't seem right for the team.

Perhaps Virginia hadn't tasted home cooking in a while. Due to massive amounts of snowfall in Charlottesville, the Cavaliers had to start their season on the road, canceling some mid-week games and having to scrounge at the last minute to find ballparks far enough south to host an impromptu weekend of college ball, such as a home series at a high school field in Charleston and another at a youth tournament facility in Myrtle Beach.

It wasn't until almost a full month after the start of the season that the Hoos had their home opener. Unfortunately, it wasn't much to write home about either as the 14–5 loss to in-state foe Old Dominion was the start of a stretch of six losses in eight games. The struggles were punctuated by some very uncharacteristic occurrences, the first being typically mild-mannered manager Brian O'Connor being ejected and subsequently suspended for four games after making contact with the home-plate umpire in a loss to Virginia Tech. The second was the Cavaliers pitching staff giving up 25 runs in just four games. For a program that prides itself on quality pitching, this was especially tough to swallow.

March and April were tough on the Hoos and, following a weekend series loss in Atlanta, Virginia stood 7–11 in the ACC at the conference season's midway point. In that span Virginia was swept at Virginia Tech, lost a home series against Florida State, was swept at home by Louisville, and lost mid-week games to the likes of Georgetown and VMI. Virginia was in a difficult position, being forced to go on a run if they had any hope of making the ACC Tournament, much less the NCAA Tournament.

Virginia found a glimmer of hope when McCarthy made his return to the lineup on April 15 in a 3–2 win against William & Mary. The following weekend the Hoos took a series from nationally ranked Miami, which was highlighted by Connor Jones' outing, the start of a streak where he was virtually unhittable as he grew into the team's ace. Although the Hoos started the ACC Tournament strong, defeating Georgia Tech 11–0 in only seven innings in a game that was ended by the ACC Tournament mercy rule, the week was one to forget as the Cavaliers dropped their remaining three games by a combined score of 27–9.

From there the Hoos set their eyes on the NCAA Tournament. When Selection Monday came, Virginia fans breathed a sigh of relief as the baseball team was selected as the No. 3 seed in the Lake Elsinore Regional. Virginia breezed through its first two regional games, defeating USC 6–1 and San Diego State 3–1. The Hoos would then face the Trojans once again with a trip to Super Regionals on the line. In a game that didn't end until 4:18 AM (EST), the Hoos pulled out a 14–10, 11-inning win. To add to the good fortune, the No. 1 seed, UCLA, lost to Maryland, setting up the most improbable of home Super Regionals for the Hoos.

In the first game of the series, the Hoos trailed 3–0 and hadn't registered anything until Kevin Doherty hit a bases-clearing double off the left-field wall that helped propel the Cavaliers to a 5–3 win. In the second game, Virginia didn't shy away from the dramatic. Trailing 4–2 heading into the bottom of the ninth and facing Maryland's shutdown closer, the Hoos would find triumph from an unlikely source. After Maryland walked in a run, freshman Ernie Clement stepped to the plate and delivered a walk-off, two-run single that would send the Cavaliers to their second straight College World Series.

After an opening game win against Arkansas 5–3, the Hoos faced offensive juggernaut and College World Series favorite Florida. Behind a stellar performance from Waddell, the Cavaliers defeated Florida by the score of 1–0. This was the same Florida team that had averaged nine runs per game in the NCAA Tournament. The win put Virginia in the driver's seat, but the Gators would not go away. In Virginia's first shot at a spot in the College World Series Finals, Kirby took to the mound in his first start since mid-April, but the Gators proved too much, winning 10–5. In the rubber match between Virginia and Florida, Waddell put up another good outing, but the real story was closer Josh Sborz, who came into the game in the sixth. Though he gave up an earned run early, he allowed only two Gators to reach base over the final three innings to preserve Virginia's 5–4 win.

The championship series featured a rematch of the 2014 Championship Series against the Vanderbilt Commodores. This time the roles were reversed as Vanderbilt was the juggernaut, having six players drafted in the MLB draft's first six rounds. Virginia dropped the first game 5–1, and heading into Game 2, Virginia's pitching availability was so bleak that they were forced to turn to center fielder Adam Haseley, who on the season had only pitched 23 innings. Haseley stepped up and then some, pitching five scoreless innings before turning the game over to Sborz. The Hoos won the game 3–0, setting up another winner-take-all final in Game 3.

Virginia turned to Waddell, who once again pitched a gem. The Cavs got a huge home run from Pavin Smith, and then in the bottom of the fourth, Virginia's Kenny Towns came up with a diving grab down the third-base line that made Hoo fans believe the win was possible. Then for a case of poetic justice, Kirby, after having the worst outing of his career the previous year, came in to shut the Commodores down in the game's final two innings.

Virginia prevailed 4–2, picking up their first College World Series title and the first by any ACC team since 1956. Virginia's improbable run to the College World Series title was a true underdog story. After nearly missing out on the ACC Tournament altogether and going just 1–3 in the tournament itself, Virginia became just the third regional No. 3 seed ever to win the title. Of the eight teams that made the 2015 College World Series, Virginia had the fewest regular season wins at just 33. Sborz was named the Most Outstanding Player of the series. "I'm just so proud of these guys," Virginia head coach Brian O'Connor said after the game. "They hung together all year and got to this postseason. It's just amazing what a group of guys that stay together and play for each other and pick each other up and don't give up can accomplish. We're very, very proud of this championship and feel very, very fortunate."

51 Virginia Leads the Sinful Seven

In the 1920s and 1930s, the college football landscape was surprisingly similar to today's landscape in which the issue of student-athlete compensation was at the heart of many debates surrounding collegiate athletics reform. By the 1930s money began to drive the growth and continued success of college athletics. Live television made it possible for schools to garner attention and attract top recruits outside of their regional recruiting base. Bowl games incentivized coaches and athletics programs to intensify their approaches in order to get coveted national attention and, of course, financial rewards. Air travel was becoming more accessible for coaches, which meant schools were recruiting well outside of their traditional bases. It was becoming expensive to run a college football program.

Responding to pleas to "return to sanity," the NCAA gave itself investigative and judicial powers in 1940 to look into alleged violations and issue interpretations, though it still lacked enforcement ability. In 1946 the NCAA drafted what it called "Principles for the Conduct of Intercollegiate Athletics" that would eventually be unanimously adopted as Article III for the NCAA Constitution in 1948. Included in these principles were:

- an adherence to a definition of amateurism, which prohibited "pay in any form" for participation in athletics,
- a charge to the institutions that the control and responsibility for the conduct of athletics ultimately lay in the institutions themselves,
- a requirement that student-athletes be admitted on the same basis as any other student and that they must maintain the same academic standards,

- a limitation that awarding financial aid to student-athletes, though permitted, must be done without consideration for athletics ability
- a prohibition on coaches or anyone representing an institution from recruiting a player with an offer of financial aid. Institutions were also prohibited from paying for travel expenses or "excessive entertainment" during campus visits.

These principles became known as the "Sanity Code," and it called for a three-person Constitutional Compliance Committee to make rulings on alleged violations. The sole penalty for violations of the Sanity Code was expulsion from the NCAA. In 1949 the Committee examined 20 violations. The University of Virginia was one of these schools being investigated.

Shortly after that announcement, president Colgate Darden Jr. declared that the school would withdraw from the NCAA if the Sanity Code were not amended. Specifically, the university opposed the NCAA's financial aid policy, arguing that athletes needed to get paid in order to allow them sufficient time to participate in athletics and maintain their academics. Participating in athletics and maintaining a job would mean, Darden argued, sacrificing an athlete's academic career, and Virginia's rigorous academic standards would independently be upheld for those on athletic scholarships. Virginia had been offering athletic scholarships since 1936, when it left the Southern Conference.

Still, in 1950, the NCAA announced that it would officially bring up seven institutions, including Virginia, for expulsion under the Sanity Code. These seven institutions openly admitted to the conduct but refused to enforce the Sanity Code. Led by the University of Virginia, this group, known as the "Sinful Seven," included Virginia Tech, Virginia Military Institute, the Citadel, Maryland, Villanova, and Boston College. Of the five southern schools and two Catholic schools, only Maryland was deemed a football power at the time. Of the seven, only Maryland, Virginia, and Villanova had winning records in 1949.

Of the seven, six of the schools, with Virginia leading the charge, mounted a defense. The Citadel offered to withdraw from the NCAA, refusing to lie to stay in the association.

The defense was centered around Virginia athletic director Norton Pritchett's argument that the Sinful Seven were doing what all other schools were—only that they admitted to their actions.

"If you feel that we are at variance with the general practice," Pritchett argued, "then I welcome you in turning thumbs down on us."

Following six hours of floor debate, the expulsion of the Sinful Seven was put to a vote. Though a majority of those voting were in favor of expulsion, that required a two-thirds majority, and the vote failed to pass by 25 votes.

The inability to expel seven open violators of the Sanity Code—seven schools who not only admitted to their violations but who would make no promises as to compliance to the principles—was a major blow to the NCAA. Without the ability to enforce, the code held little water. Ultimately, its single sanction was too harsh a penalty for member institutions to support against a fellow member institution. The 1951 convention repealed the code in favor of additional research and recommendations for regulatory authority with enforcement going forward. By 1954 the NCAA established a Committee on Infractions to review complaints and administer punishment proportional to the offense.

52 Tom Scott, Two-Sport All-American

Tom Scott played for Virginia football from 1950 to 1952. He also played lacrosse. He also played basketball. He also played baseball. With today's specialized focus on college athletics, Virginia likely will never see another four-sport athlete and certainly not one as talented as Scott. Under head football coach Art Guepe, Scott helped lead the Cavaliers to an overall 24–5 record, achieving eight wins each year and a No. 13 national ranking at the end of the 1951 season.

Scott didn't just play in four sports. He excelled in them. He was named a football All-American in 1952 by both the Associated Press and the Newspaper Enterprise Association. A member of Virginia's 1952 USILA National Champion lacrosse team, he was also named an All-American defenseman in 1953, becoming Virginia's first ever two-sport All-American.

Playing in the days of single-platoon football, Scott played as both an offensive and defensive end, though he most excelled on the defensive side of the ball. "I did play both ways, offense and defense," Scott said in an interview with the ACC Digital Network following his selection to the ACC Legends class of 2013. "And I did all the punting and all the kicking, but I liked playing defense the best. I guess I just liked to get after people and make the tackle. Tackling was something I always liked to do."

Having grown in up Baltimore, Scott played a lot of lacrosse growing up, but his heart was with football. "I started playing [lacrosse] as a very young boy and I also played baseball. When I got down to Virginia, I just kept playing them all. I played football and lacrosse at Virginia, and I also played on the basketball and baseball teams. I found that the studies came pretty easy to me and in my free time I just wanted to be playing a sport. I enjoyed it, and that was the way that I was brought up."

The Los Angeles Rams selected him in the fifth round of the 1953 NFL Draft, but his stay there didn't last long. "The Rams drafted me as their No. 2 choice," Scott recalled to *The Daily Progress's* Jerry Ratcliffe. "I went out there, and a guy comes up and taps me on the shoulder. I think it was [NFL commissioner] Pete Rozelle and said, 'Tom, we're going to loan you to the Eagles.'"

The "loan" worked out pretty well for Philadelphia, as Scott would earn the league's Rookie of the Year honors as a linebacker for the Eagles. According to Ratcliffe, Scott had performed so well that the Eagles disputed that there was ever a loan and refused to return Scott back to the Rams. Scott would stay with the Eagles for five more seasons and would be named to the Pro Bowl team twice in 1957 and 1958. From 1959 through 1964, Scott played for the New York Giants and reached the NFL Championship Game in each of the 1961, 1962, and 1963 seasons.

Following his NFL career, Scott worked in insurance in New York for more than 30 years. He also served as the director of the NFL Alumni Association from 1968 to 1971. He retired and returned to Charlottesville in 1995. Scott died on August 31, 2015.

He was inducted into the College Football Hall of Fame in 1969, and Virginia retired Scott's jersey in 2008. Gene Corrigan, former athletic director for both Virginia and Notre Dame, and a former ACC commissioner, helped compile the list of the top 10 athletes in Virginia history. "Well, No. 1 is very simple. It's Tom Scott," he said.

53 Anthony Poindexter

No Virginia alumnus knows the highs and lows of a football career better than Anthony Poindexter, who played safety for the Cavaliers from 1995 to 1998. If you ask a Virginia fan for Poindexter's most memorable moment, you'll get just one unified response: he stopped Florida State.

Only a redshirt freshman during that 1995 season, Poindexter, who played both inside linebacker and safety that year, and teammate Adrian Burnim stopped Florida State's Warrick Dunn just inches shy of the end zone in the final play of the game, cementing a 33–28 victory against Florida State for the Seminoles' first ACC loss since joining the conference four years prior.

Although that was certainly Poindexter's highest profile play, his career at Virginia was a living highlight reel. During his sophomore season, he recorded a school-record 98 tackles. Following a successful junior season campaign, he was named a first team All-American by *The Sporting News*. Following his junior season, many experts projected that Poindexter, if he decided to enter the 1998 NFL Draft that year, had a strong chance at being a first-round draft pick and certainly going no lower than the second round. Poindexter had two options that year—take the chance and enter the NFL draft a year early or stay for his senior season and try to improve his draft stock. He chose the latter.

Through the first six games of his senior season, Poindexter was a terror on the field as the Cavaliers went 5–1, shutting out two teams in the process, including a ranked Auburn team on the road. Against North Carolina State in the seventh game of the season, however, Poindexter's entire future changed in a heartbeat when he tore three of the four ligaments in his left knee. "A play lasts maybe eight seconds," Poindexter said years later. "In eight seconds I lost it all."

Poindexter was unable to recover fully from the injury and was forced to miss both the NFL Scouting Combine and Virginia's Pro Day. Instead of guaranteeing himself a first round, possibly top 10 NFL draft pick, Poindexter limped, both literally and figuratively, into the 1999 NFL Draft. The Baltimore Ravens took a chance on the injured Poindexter, drafting him in the seventh round. He was placed in the injured reserve list for his rookie season and played on and off the next two years for the Ravens, which included a Super Bowl championship in which he did not see any playing time. He was released in 2001 but picked up by the Cleveland Browns before being released again later that year. "What helped me get over it was, I knew I had done it a certain way every day," Poindexter recalled years later. "So my career was over, but it wasn't like I wished I could get this play back or I could get that play, or that practice, or that day back.

"That's the one thing: I didn't have any regrets. Obviously, I wanted to do some things for my folks that I was unable to do, but it wasn't like they had their hands out waiting for me to become the savior anyway. My dad was going to work regardless of what kind of money I made."

There was no shortage of awards and accolades in Poindexter's career while at Virginia. The school's only two-time, first-team All-American, Poindexter was also named the ACC's Defensive Player of the Year in 1998 and was the third Cavalier to be named a three-time, first-team All-ACC player. He was also the recipient of the Brian Piccolo Award honoring the ACC's most courageous football player. Poindexter's coach, legendary George Welsh, thinks back fondly of the star. "Anthony Poindexter was created to be a great football player," Welsh recalled. "He had size, speed, and great instincts, and no concern for his body—or anyone else's he hit. There is such a thing as no physical fear, and not many people have it. But he did."

Other prominent Virginia figures recognized greatness on the field, too. "I've often told people this," said 1992 All-American linebacker Chris Slade. "Out of all the great players who played before me and played after me at UVA, Anthony Poindexter is the one guy I wish I'd had the opportunity to play with."

Poindexter's story would serve as a cautionary tale to other college players deciding whether to go pro early or to stay in college an extra year. Many college players, including Virginia Tech quarterback Michael Vick, who went as the overall No. 1 NFL Draft pick in 2001, have cited Poindexter as a reason for leaving college while their stock was high.

Poindexter would return to Virginia in 2003 as a graduate assistant and over the span of 11 years would coach various positions for the Cavaliers, finishing in 2013 as the safeties coach. In 2014 Poindexter left Virginia to become defensive coordinator and safeties coach at Connecticut. In 2009 his jersey was retired. "Dex is UVA football," former Virginia linebacker Butch Jefferson said. "You say Anthony Poindexter, and people think UVA Football."

Experience the Basketball Venues

The Virginia basketball program has called four different sites home throughout its century plus of existence, and each has its own character, history, and names indelibly attached.

Fayerweather Hall is on Rugby Road across from Madison Bowl—or Mad Bowl—and hosted the Cavaliers in their first ever game against the Charlottesville YMCA on January 18,

1906—a 30–9 win for the university. It was the team's home court throughout much of the Henry Lannigan era, playing host to an undefeated 1914–15 campaign and the first great Virginia player, William Strickling. Currently, it houses the University's McIntire Department of Art.

In 1924 the Wahoos moved to Emmet Street's Memorial Gymnasium, popularly known as Mem Gym. It was built as a monument to the 2,700 UVA students and alumni killed in World War I. The early years of the building witnessed the coaching transition from Lannigan to Gus Tebell, who led the program until 1951. The late Buzzy Wilkinson was undoubtedly the most famous Cavalier to ever play at Mem Gym, holding many of school and conference scoring records even after he passed.

At the time the 2,500-person arena was the third largest gym on the East Coast. Without air conditioning and with the gymnasium frequently filled at or beyond capacity, Mem Gym made for one of the most menacing venues Virginia's ever had. "If it was a packed house," recalled Gene Flamm, who played for Virginia basketball from 1958 to 1963, "especially a game that was contested, with the screaming and the cheering and applauding, your ears would actually hurt."

Perhaps the most notable non-athletic event to occur at the school's various football and basketball facilities throughout the years occurred when president Franklin D. Roosevelt delivered the commencement address to the Class of 1940 in June of that year. While giving his speech, Roosevelt was alerted of a new alliance forged against France between Nazi Germany and Italy. "On this 10th day of June, 1900 and 40, the hand that held the dagger has struck it into the back of its neighbor. On this 10th day of June, 1900 and 40, in this university founded by the first great American teacher of democracy, we send forth our prayers and our hopes to those beyond the seas who are maintaining with magnificent valor their battle for freedom," the president said.

Mem Gym currently houses the Virginia wrestling and volleyball teams and is also a hub for intramural sports on Grounds.

University Hall, once called a "pregnant clam," had a 41-season run as the stomping grounds for many Virginia basketball legends, including Ralph Sampson, Terry Holland, Barry Parkhill, Jeff Lamp, Dawn Staley, Debbie Ryan, Wally Walker, Bryant Stith, Jeff Jones, Junior Burrough, Harold Deane, Travis Watson, and Donald Hand.

One of the toughest tickets in college basketball in the early 1980s, University Hall rocked for four decades, as the acoustics of the building (the noise traveled up along the curved ceiling and straight down to the floor) combined with a consistently raucous crowd helped make for an all-time record of 402–143 for UVA at "U-Hall." The last men's game there was on March 5, 2006, a 71–70 loss to rival Maryland. Sampson dunked twice for the ceremonial final baskets, and head coach Dave Leitao walked the ball out of the building and across Massie Road to the almost-completed new home of Cavalier basketball.

Virginia's mascot, Cavman, rappelled from the rafters of John Paul Jones Arena on the night of November 12, 2006 with (supposedly) that same ball in his hand. A sellout crowd was on hand to witness Virginia take on No. 10 Arizona in the first game at "JPJ" in an opening night that was opened by Michael Buffer delivering his signature "Let's get ready to rumble!" A comeback win rang in the shiny, spacious facility whose capacity, 14,593, was almost double University Hall's 8,457.

Through the 2015–16 season, the Hoos are a stout 160–37 at their current home, which features amenities for fans like wider concourses, a massive lobby, several merchandise locations, a plethora of concession stands, and the Virginia Basketball Hall of Fame. Today, Fayerweather Hall has been renovated and expanded and serves as home to the McIntire Department of Art at the university. University Hall occasionally hosts school events.

1989 Blowout of North Carolina

Coming off a disappointing 13–18 record the previous year for Virginia's only losing season of the decade, the 1988–89 basketball season was off to a strong start with a 5–1 record and the only loss coming at the hands of No. 18 Connecticut. The Cavaliers returned two starters from the previous year in guard Richard Morgan, who had averaged 10.1 points per game, and Bill Batts, who had averaged 7.9 points per game as the starting center, though Batts was a natural forward.

Coming back from exam break, however, Virginia looked to be playing uninspired basketball. The Hoos barely defeated Jacksonville 86–81 and would need an overtime period to overcome UC-Irvine 99–89. That's when things unraveled. Virginia would lose five straight games, including two conference games, in a tough stretch that included Seton Hall, Louisville, and No. 1 Duke. By the time Virginia played host to North Carolina in mid-January, the Cavaliers were 7–6 on the season and a shadow of their former selves.

For starters Batts, who was the only player who had started all 31 games the previous season, was placed on academic suspension, which meant that he would not be a student for an entire year and therefore would be off the team for the rest of the season. And the Cavaliers lacked their head coach, Terry Holland.

During the break Holland underwent intestinal surgery at the University Medical Center. During this time assistant coach Dave Odom stepped in for Holland, which proved to be a difficult task given that the Cavaliers were traveling to No. 13 Louisville, only to host top-ranked Duke three days later.

Holland was finally released from the hospital just prior to Virginia's game against No. 8 North Carolina, a team that had beaten Virginia in 13 of the previous 14 meetings. In what Odom described as "a truly heartfelt experience," Holland paid a visit to the locker room before the game and tried to provide inspiration to a Virginia team trying to find its way out of a five-game losing streak.

It worked.

Virginia came out of the gates running. While North Carolina was able to earn open looks and sink 53.1 percent of its shots the first half, Virginia wasn't too far behind, making 47.5 percent of its shots. "I was surprised they came out running," North Carolina head coach Dean Smith said. "That was a good move on their part. They were able to score quickly after we did."

Virginia led at the half 50–41 and didn't look back. When all was said and done, the Cavaliers had completely shut down the No. 8 Tar Heels 106–83. It was North Carolina's worst loss in 25 years since Duke beat Carolina 104–69. Much of it was due to Morgan's hit-it-from-anywhere night. After starting the game 0-of-7 from the field, the guard scored 39 points from all angles and distances, including hitting eight three-point buckets. "He showed what a fantastic player he is when he's making those rainbows and everything else," Smith said. "I don't think he had an open one all day."

Morgan wasn't the only one playing inspired basketball for Holland. Three other Cavaliers—Kenny Turner, Curtis Williams, and Anthony Oliver—all scored 12 points off the bench. The win ignited the Cavaliers, who would go on to win their next five games. Virginia finished the season with a record of 22–11, (9–5 ACC) and reached the Elite Eight of the NCAA Tournament, falling to No. 10 Michigan. Morgan would be named to the All-ACC first team, while forward Bryant Stith, who recorded seven points and six rebounds against North Carolina, would earn ACC Rookie of the Year honors.

56 Cory Alexander

The nation's top-ranked point guard in high school brought to the University of Virginia promise and hope, followed by excitement, and ultimately disappointment. No one was disappointed in his game, but instead a series of unfortunate ankle injuries prevented him from becoming the All-American that fans knew he could be.

A 6'1" point guard out of Waynesboro, Virginia, Cory Alexander was heralded as the No. 1 point guard coming out of high school in 1991 and the No. 9 player overall. Named a *Parade* first-team All-American and a McDonald's All-American, Alexander joined what would be a top five recruiting class in the country, alongside Yuri Barnes, Jason Williford, Junior Burrough, and Chris Alexander. It was perhaps head coach Jeff Jones' best incoming class at Virginia.

Alexander had an impact almost right from the beginning, earning a starting spot on a 1991–92 team that would go on to with the NIT championship. That year he averaged 11.2 points and 4.4 assists per game. The following year would be a breakout season for Alexander, who would average a whopping 18.8 points and 4.6 assists per game en route to a Sweet 16 appearance. It would also be his highlight season.

Unfortunately for Alexander and the Cavalier faithful, Alexander's junior season lasted approximately 11 minutes. In Virginia's season opener against Connecticut, the junior point guard fractured a bone in his right ankle, a season-ending injury. Without Alexander, Virginia would suffer a second-round exit from the NCAA Tournament in a 71–58 loss to Arizona.

Rested and ready to return the following year as a redshirt junior, Alexander picked up right where he had left off two years prior, averaging 16.7 points and 5.5 assists through the first 20 games of the season. On that 20th game, however, a 65–55 win against North Carolina State, Alexander again broke his right ankle in the first half. "Cory has a stress-type fracture in the inside bone of his right ankle, in the same general area of the injury he suffered in November of 1993," said Virginia team physician Dr. Frank McCue in *The Cavalier Daily*. "It's not displaced and it's a new fracture. It's not the same fracture as the one he suffered last season. He will not play again this season."

Even without Alexander, however, the 1994–95 Cavaliers would go on to win a piece of the ACC regular season title and reach the Elite Eight before falling to Arkansas.

Instead of staying for a fifth year and potentially risking further injury, Alexander declared as an early entrant to the 1995 NBA Draft, something he had informed the Virginia staff of as far back as October of that season. His three-season career at Virginia finished with 401 assists—good for sixth in Virginia's record book at the time. His tally still stands at ninth today.

Alexander was drafted in the first round of the 1995 NBA Draft, 29th overall by the San Antonio Spurs. In all he spent seven years in the league, playing for the Spurs, Denver Nuggets, Orlando Magic, and, after playing in the NBA Developmental League and in Italy, one more season with the Charlotte Bobcats. Following his NBA career, in which he averaged 5.5 points and 2.7 assists per game, Alexander now works as a college basketball announcer for ESPN.

57 The Greatest Comeback?

Many have called it the greatest comeback in Virginia football history. To make it sweeter, it happened at Lane Stadium in Blacksburg, Virginia.

Both Virginia and rival Virginia Tech were enjoying successful football seasons in 1998. Heading into the regular-season finale between the two teams, the Cavaliers, ranked 16th in the country, were 8–2 overall with losses coming to No. 25 Georgia Tech and No. 6 Florida State. Meanwhile, the No. 20 Hokies, who were also 8–2 overall, had losses to unranked Temple and Syracuse. The series between the two was close with the Hokies having a slight advantage at 39–35–5.

Having beaten the No. 19 Hokies in Charlottesville the year before as an unranked team, Virginia knew that Virginia Tech would be seeking revenge, and Virginia Tech indeed came charging out of the gates. A field goal within the first three minutes, a touchdown on a 51-yard run by running back Shyrone Stith, and a fumble recovery leading to another touchdown less than two minutes later, and suddenly the Hokies were up 17–0 on Virginia. Though Virginia running back Thomas Jones would find the end zone before the end of the first quarter, Virginia Tech would find another touchdown (with a failed two-point conversion) and two more field goals before the end of the half. Down 29–7 at the intermission, Virginia looked just about down and out. If a comeback were to happen, it would have to be a herculean effort.

But whatever the Virginia players and coaching staff did in the locker room at halftime should be replicated in every game. Both the Virginia offense and defense came out in the second half with a new-found passion that would lead to the perfect comeback execution.

In the opening possession of the second half, Virginia quarterback Aaron Brooks overcame a third-and-17 situation and converted on a fourth-down play to find the end zone on a 24-yard touchdown pass to redshirt sophomore receiver Kevin Coffey. After an exchange of fruitless possessions, Virginia sophomore linebacker Byron Thweatt caught an interception and returned it 53 yards to bring the Cavaliers within 29–21 with 2:33 to go in the third quarter.

A minor miracle was in the works.

The Hokies would find a 46-yard field goal early in the fourth quarter to go up 32–21. Virginia would respond with an 18-yard touchdown pass from Brooks to Jones followed by a successful two-point conversion. Virginia trailed just 32–29 and were within striking distance for the comeback victory with only 7:02 left in the game. As Virginia Tech methodically moved the ball down the field, the Hokies crossing the 50-yard line had Virginia fans feeling as though the nails were being hammered in. A touchdown would seal the deal.

The Cavaliers defense, though, held their ground, forcing a punt. With the ball downed at the 7-yard line by Shane Beamer, son of Virginia Tech head coach Frank Beamer, Virginia had the daunting task of moving 93 yards if they were to win the game right then and there.

But Aaron Brooks began to work his magic. After an incomplete pass, Brooks orchestrated a nine-yard completion to tight end Casey Crawford, followed by a three-yard toss to Jones for the first down. After a 23-yard pass from Brooks to Coffey, the Cavaliers were in business.

Brooks aired the football 22 yards to find the open arms of wide receiver Ahmad Hawkins at the 25-yard line. "When I caught the ball, my first thought was to get out of bounds," Hawkins said. "But when I turned around, I didn't see anybody. So I kept running."

He did just that. He kept running all the way into the end zone with 2:01 left on the clock. After the extra point, Virginia went up for the first time in the game 36–32 in what would become an insurmountable lead. "I was thinking field goal," Welsh told the media following the game. "Three points ties it. Ironically, we had just talked about overtime in the staff meeting. It's hard to get a touchdown. That's why I was thinking field-goal range. I was hoping to get on the 15-yard line, not the 25 or 30 where we seem to stall out so much."

In the final minute, middle linebacker Wali Rainer pulled down an interception to end Virginia Tech's final possession. "Anything is possible," he said. "But that's the danger of getting up 17–0 so early sometimes. It's dangerous for them. I think they got tired on defense."

58 "Benedict" Ronald Curry

Recruiting is the lifeblood of any major college athletics program. Imagine how different Virginia's basketball program would be if it hadn't been able to sign Ralph Sampson. And imagine where Virginia Tech football would be if the Hokies hadn't signed Michael Vick.

But recruiting can also leave scars, and UVA hasn't suffered a bigger recruiting injury than it did when it lost two-sport All-American Ronald Curry to North Carolina in 1998. Curry, a Hampton, Virginia native, was an all-world talent. He was a four-time all-state quarterback who set state records for passing yards and total yards. He led Hampton High School to three straight state football titles and was named the Gatorade National Player of the Year during his senior season.

In addition, Curry was a gifted point guard for the Crabbers' basketball team. He was named the McDonald's National Basketball Player of the Year as a senior. He led Hampton to a state basketball title as a junior. And he was the MVP of the McDonald's All-American game.

With Curry's abundant talent, Virginia fans were downright giddy when he committed to play quarterback for George Welsh at UVA. His announcement in early September 1997 made headlines throughout the state. "Most recruiting analysts rank the 6'3", 195-pound Curry as the nation's top quarterback prospect in football and among the best point guards in basketball," wrote *The Virginian-Pilot*.

Curry committed to UVA alongside Hampton teammates Bobby Blizzard and Darnell Hollier. His cousin, Almondo "Muffin" Curry, would eventually don the orange and blue and become a fan favorite while playing in the UVA secondary. Curry's high school football coach, Mike Smith, approved of his decision to head to Charlottesville. "I've known for a long time these three would go to Virginia," Smith told *The Virginian-Pilot*. "They're like family. That's why they're going together. I'm real proud they're staying in state."

But all the Virginia fan excitement about Curry would eventually turn sour. He started talking more about his desire to focus on basketball rather than football. And he announced in October '97 that he'd be taking an official visit to UNC. "I'm just keeping my options open," he told the *Daily Press*.

With its more ballyhooed tradition, North Carolina appealed to Curry from a basketball perspective. Although Smith told *The Fayetteville Observer* that "Ronald Curry will go to Virginia, and that's that," Curry's basketball coach, Walter Brower, encouraged him to keep an open mind. "I didn't like the way Ronald's recruitment was handled," Brower said. "I just felt he should take some visits and look around before making an announcement."

As the winter continued, the tide turned in North Carolina's favor. Curry didn't sign with Virginia on Signing Day in February, leaving the door open to switch allegiances. The hammer eventually fell on March 25. Just before the McDonald's All-American game, Curry announced that he had signed with UNC. If his change of heart wasn't bad enough, his remarks only added insult to injury for Cavaliers supporters. "Going to North Carolina, I'll just blend in," Curry told the *Daily Press*. "I won't be the superstar. Everybody's going to be watching, you know, 'Is Ronald Curry as good as the hype?' Hopefully, they'll win a national title [in basketball] this year, and I'll just go and blend in."

Since Curry's defection he's remained at the top of the hate list for many Virginia fans. Alongside him sits Boo Williams, the insurance salesman and Hampton AAU program director who many feel steered Curry towards UNC. One could argue that Curry's defection helped bring about the end of George Welsh's tenure at UVA and usher in the 15 years of dysfunction that followed. With Welsh putting all of his quarterback recruiting eggs in the Curry basket, the Hoos missed out on another local quarterback: Vick. As a result the program trajectories for the in-state rivals diverged overnight.

59 Sean Singletary

Philadelphia point guard Sean Singletary was certainly a highly regarded recruit when he committed to play for Virginia head coach Pete Gillen, though few UVA fans could imagine just how quickly he would become face of the program. He immediately brought energy and consistency to the point guard position for the team, and by the time Singletary left Charlottesville for the NBA he would become one of the most decorated players in team history and a leader of one of the best Virginia teams in a decade.

As a freshman he was the only Hoo to start every game of the 2004–05 season and was named to the ACC All-Freshman team. However, it was in his second season that Singletary, already a co-captain of the team, emerged as the team leader and one of the premier players in both the conference and country. As a sophomore Singletary became the first Virginia player to be named to the All-ACC first team since Bryant Stith in 1995, collecting numerous state and national media awards, and leading the Wahoos in assists, steals, and minutes. His 35-point performance on the road against Gonzaga established Singletary on the national scene, and though the team's overall season was relatively disappointing because of an opening round NIT loss at Stanford, Singletary's many accolades set an optimistic tone for his junior year.

The 2006–07 season opened with the inaugural game at the John Paul Jones Arena, in which Singletary and his 25 points led the Wahoos to an upset win against No. 10 Arizona. Along with his backcourt partner J.R. Reynolds, Sean led the Hoos to their best season since the mid-1990s, including a 16–1 home record, a share of the ACC regular season championship, and a No. 4 seed in the NCAA Tournament.

However, it was an overtime win against No. 8 Duke that will forever cement him the minds and hearts of UVA fans. During the primetime ESPN game, Singletary scored 17 points, tallied four assists, and played 43 minutes. Though seemingly a contradiction, he scored a bucket that was both a fadeaway and a one-handed teardrop. That game-winning, baseline shot, later known only as "the Shot," remains among the pinnacle of UVA video highlights, and the win established UVA as a title-contending-level team for the first time in more than a decade.

After flirting with declaring for the NBA draft before his fourth year, Singletary returned to Grounds for his final season, in which he would earn All-ACC first-team honors for the third straight year. Although the season was not nearly as successful for the Hoos as the previous one—the talented point guard alone wasn't quite enough to make a run to the NCAA Tournament—Singletary finished fifth in all-time scoring, third in three-point scoring, third in assists, and second in steals in Virginia program history.

Following hip surgery Singletary was drafted by the Sacramento Kings in the second round of the 2008 NBA Draft. After a couple of trades, he saw playing time with both the Phoenix Suns and the

Sean Singletary puts up "the Shot," a game-winning, fadeaway bucket to defeat Duke 68–66 in 2007. (USA TODAY Sports Images)

Charlotte Bobcats in the 2008–09 season. After being waived from a free-agent contract with the Philadelphia 76ers the following year, Singletary spent time playing professionally in Europe as well as the NBA Development League. Virginia retired his jersey prior to his final home contest of the 2007–08 season.

60 Go Streaking

At the heart of the University of Virginia lies a plot of grass that stretches 740 feet long and 192 feet wide. At one end is the historical Rotunda, while Old Cabell Hall stands tall at the other end. Lining either side along the way are 54 rooms used for student housing and 10 pavilions that are used both as faculty housing and classroom and meeting space. This area, known as the Lawn, forms the university's "Academical Village" and, together with Monticello and the other historical buildings at the University of Virginia, is designated as a UNESCO World Heritage Site.

By day students, faculty, and visitors walk down the Lawn with a certain air of reverence for the site that Thomas Jefferson selected to serve as the academic center of the flagship university. As day turns to night and as the nearby bars close up shop for the evening, many students choose to walk down the Lawn with an entirely different approach—specifically, quickly and without clothes, just as Mr. Jefferson himself would have wanted, probably.

Whether it's to celebrate a big Virginia victory or just because it's a Friday night, the student tradition of streaking the Lawn transcends generations at the university. It's not clear when the tradition first began, though there are reports of such festivities dating back as early as 1934 in the *College Topics*. "At the Lewis boarding house last Thursday night, some of the first-year men got terribly thirsty. So they all went down to the Corner in their pajamas. This was around 2:00 AM. Evidently they had been thirsty earlier in the night, but this is beside the point. When the over-jolly crowd got back to the Lewis, a couple of them forsook their pajamas and rushed pell-mell, Adam and Eve fashion up to their rooms. And to think that a nudist colony is in the making at Virginia. That's Jeffersonian Democracy for you."

The custom begins with the runner at the top of the Rotunda steps, streaking down the Lawn toward the Homer statue. Remember that there are five different levels to the Lawn, which means that there are four changes in elevation for which the runner will need to adjust speed. Upon reaching the Homer statue toward Old Cabell Hall, the runner is to climb the statue and give Homer a kiss—a quick peck on the Greek poet's posterior. The runner then turns and begins the journey back toward the Rotunda. Some versions of the tradition dictate that the runner—at the top of the Rotunda steps—must look through the keyhole into the Rotunda to bid the statue of Thomas Jefferson good night before putting his or her clothes back on.

Before a student earns his or her diploma at Final Exercises, the tradition is that the student must have streaked the Lawn at least once during his or her undergraduate career. Of course, the administration does not enforce this unwritten rule, and no one will know any better if you did or did not. But you'll know—as will Thomas Jefferson.

A piece of advice for anyone seeking to embark on this journey: sprinting down the Lawn toward the Homer statue may not always be the best approach. The entire round trip is just over a quarter of a mile with hills that could easily do damage if you're not paying attention—or a bit inebriated. In the spring, as the university prepares for Final Exercises, oftentimes portions of the Lawn are roped off, adding hurdles to the course. A quick jog down the Lawn allows a runner to sprint on the return trip, should they find law enforcement—or possibly worse, a mischievous Lawn resident with a spotlight—waiting for them at some point down this noble journey.

61 2011 Lacrosse National Championship

When the Virginia men's lacrosse team lost to Maryland 12–5 on April 2, 2011, coach Dom Starsia's squad was in a difficult position. The team had clear team chemistry issues and the team looked to be falling apart. While the earlier losses—a two-goal loss at Syracuse and a one-goal heartbreaker at Johns Hopkins—were closely contested, the loss to its ACC rival left a lot to be desired. The Johns Hopkins and Maryland setbacks were Virginia's first back-to-back losses since 2007 and the first back-to-back regular season losses since 2004. The coaches, players, and fans were not used to losses, let alone two in a row.

Virginia, who badly needed a victory to right the ship, got an overtime, game-winning goal from Steele Stanwick to take down North Carolina 11–10. Two straight losses to Duke in the regular season and ACC Tournament left the Cavaliers with an 8–5 record and in serious jeopardy of missing the postseason. Just one week after their last loss and one day before their Senior Day matchup with Penn, Coach Starsia released fourth-year midfielder Shamel Bratton from the team for violating team policies. Bratton's twin brother, Rhamel, was suspended at the same time. Shamel finished his career with 89 goals and 129 points, which put him in third and first place in the Virginia midfielder record books, respectively.

Coach Starsia had to make adjustments to his defense that was giving up more than 14 points per game and finagle his offensive scheme to get the team back on track before No. 13 Penn came to Charlottesville with the season on the line. Senior defender Bray Malphrus, one of Virginia's captains, moved to close defense from the long stick midfielder position. Although Virginia had historically played solely man-to-man defense, Coach Starsia introduced zone to the mix, so his young and inexperienced group could hopefully reduce the number of shots on top of the crease. Offensively, the Cavaliers reverted back to a more traditional UVA offense, consisting of ball movement and strong off-ball cutting instead of trying to initiate one on one to the goal. These combinations, coupled with an apparent improvement in team communication, led to a convincing 13–2 rout of Penn.

As a result, Virginia snuck into the NCAA Tournament as a No. 7 seed, meaning it would host the first round at Klöckner Stadium in front of a raucous home crowd. The Hoos drew the Bucknell Bison for their first game, and there was plenty of excitement when the teams finally took the field after over an hour lightning delay on May 15, 2011. Bucknell controlled the game, building to a 10–6 lead with just more than two minutes remaining in the third quarter. Though the Cavaliers would not go quietly, it seemed that every time the Cavaliers seemed poised to make a run, Bucknell responded. At one point Virginia successfully executed pulling the goalie to force a turnover and giving the attack another chance to get back in the game. Virginia eventually tied the game with under two minutes remaining, forcing the improbable overtime period. Matt White scored the game-winner in the extra frame, capping off an epic comeback. Junior attackman Chris Bocklet put away five goals on nine shots. Stanwick, a finalist for the Tewaaraton Trophy—the Heisman for lacrosse—scored three goals, had his second straight game with five assists, and had a hand in six of Virginia's final seven goals.

Next up, the Cavaliers headed to the NCAA Quarterfinals to take on second-seeded Cornell and Rob Pannell, whom many lacrosse pundits believed to be the best player in the country. Virginia got off to a slow start, finding themselves down 4–1 in the first quarter, but rattled off 10 straight goals to jump to a comfortable lead that did not get challenged again. The Cavaliers found an unlikely contributor in Nick O'Reilly, who had an assist and two goals, including a nifty behind-the-back score to tie the game at four. In addition to booking Virginia's ticket to the Final Four, the 13–9 victory meant that Coach Starsia had passed Jack Emmer to become the winningest coach in Division I lacrosse with 327 wins.

No. 6 Denver was Virginia's opponent in the semifinals, a team led by legendary coach Bill Tierney. The Cavaliers jumped to a 9–2 halftime lead after winning 8-of-13 faceoffs and controlling possession for most of the half. Coach Starsia got another balanced performance from his attack with three players, Bocklet, Stanwick, and Mark Cockerton, all scoring three goals apiece. Cockerton, who almost did not make the field after getting locked in the locker room before the game, also added an assist. The win set the stage for an all-ACC final between No. 7 seeded Virginia and unseeded Maryland.

The final game took place on a steaming hot Memorial Day at M&T Bank Stadium in Baltimore, Maryland, in front of over 33,000 fans clad in orange, blue, red, and black. All that stood between the Cavaliers and their program's fifth title was the same Maryland team that exposed their flaws just eight weeks earlier. The Terrapins led 1–0 after a slow first quarter, but goals from Colin Briggs, O'Reilly, and White gave Virginia a 5–3 halftime lead.

In the second half, Briggs opened the scoring to push Virginia's lead to three, but Maryland knotted the game at six with just under 12 minutes remaining in the fourth quarter. Back-to-back goals from White and another from Briggs provided the Hoos with a lead they would not relinquish. As time expired in its 9–7 victory, Virginia dogpiled after completing its improbable playoff run.

Briggs, the team's third-leading scorer, did not play in the semifinals due to a violation of team rules. He made the most of his return to the field, scoring five goals and providing the spark Virginia needed in the final. Stanwick had a quiet day with just one assist, but staying off of the stat sheet may have big his biggest contribution. He drew the attention of Maryland's best defender, Brett Schmidt, effectively neutralizing him from the team defense as Schmidt worked tirelessly to neutralize Stanwick. Defensively, Virginia hounded Maryland's potent attack, holding them three goals under their season average.

Virginia became the only seventh-seeded team to win the national championship, as well as the only five-loss team. For the postseason Stanwick scored nine goals and dished 12 assists, helping him secure the Tewaaraton Trophy. Five Cavaliers— Stanwick, Briggs, Bocklet, Ghitelman, and Chris LaPierre—were named All-Americans.

62 2001 and 2002 Wins over Duke

When third-ranked Duke visited Charlottesville on Valentine's Day in 2001, the Blue Devils probably weren't expecting too much of a fight from No. 12 Virginia. The Cavaliers hadn't beaten the Blue Devils since 1996 despite there being 12 meetings between the two schools. Head Coach Pete Gillen had never beaten Duke during his tenure at Virginia, and Virginia had lost at Duke earlier that year by a whopping 103–61 margin.

Sporting all orange uniforms, the 16–6 Cavaliers were already considered locks for their first NCAA Tournament berth in four years, though a win over Duke would increase their prospects for a higher seed.

Virginia led 46–42 at halftime after a display of the run-and-gun style basketball that was a key part of Gillen's tenure. A couple minutes into the second half, Virginia found a breakthrough of sorts when an errant shot from Duke landed in the hands of Travis Watson. Watson fed the ball to Donald Hand, who spotted a streaking Adam Hall down the right side. Hall called for the alley-oop pass, and Hand delivered a beautiful lob up to Hall, whose head nearly went above the rim as he dunked over Duke's Shane Battier. Few calls are as ingrained in the minds of Wahoo fans as the reaction from ESPN's Brad Daugherty: "You don't need the peanut butter, 'cause there's a lot of jam!"

The play put UVA up 52–46, though Duke would go on a long run of their own to gain a 61–55 lead with 13:48 left. Virginia would regain the lead, and the teams exchanged buckets throughout the rest of the game. With the Cavaliers up 81–80 with roughly four minutes left, Hall grabbed the spotlight again with another highlight-reel slam. Hall took a feed from Chris Williams and delivered a one-handed tomahawk dunk to send U-Hall into the rafters. This time even Battier backed up out of Hall's way to simply let the play happen.

Two Battier free throws tied the game with 14 seconds left. It took UVA almost half that time just to get the ball past midcourt and when the Cavaliers did it looked as though there were few options available to get a winning shot. Heavily guarded by Chris Duhon, Roger Mason Jr. drove into the lane and put up a layup with less than two seconds left.

The shot missed, but Hall had the presence of mind to come in through the back door from the left corner when the Duke defense collapsed onto the basket as Hall drove. The 6'5" Hall smoothly picked up the rebound and seemingly dropped the ball into the basket for a 91–89 Cavaliers lead. Hall intercepted an ensuing inbound pass from Duke and launched the ball toward the heavens. In seconds the entire playing surface was covered with Virginia fans as Hall and Hand sought refuge on press row in front of Daugherty and Mike Patrick.

The next year's game in Charlottesville on February 28, 2002 had a different air to it. After 9–0 and 14–2 starts to the season, UVA had faltered to 16–9 and just 6–8 in the ACC. The preseason No. 11 Cavaliers, who had risen up to No. 4 after their perfect start, had plummeted out of the Top 25 after losing three in a row and seven out of nine.

No. 3 Duke led 77–65 with 6:53 remaining, and with that game and the one the following Sunday at Maryland key to salvaging Virginia's NCAA Tournament hopes, it appeared that the Cavaliers were destined to continue their free fall. A putback from Watson with 6:26 left, however, started a 17–0 Virginia run which made the loud UVA fanbase delirious with anticipation.

Point guard Keith Jenifer knocked down a runner to give Virginia the lead for good with 1:13 left, and after Mason Jr. missed what would have been a game-sealing free throw with four seconds left, a desperation heave from Duke fell well short. The stands once again emptied onto the floor, and though UVA would miss the NCAA Tournament, it was a moment that Cavaliers fans would not soon forget.

63 Jeff Jones

As a player Jeff Jones never really had the spotlight shining on him. That's what happens when you play on a team with the likes of Ralph Sampson, Jeff Lamp, and Othell Wilson. But you don't get to be a starting guard for the top-ranked team in the country without the talent to back it up.

Though Jones only averaged 8.2 points per game by his senior year in 1982, he made his presence on the court known in other ways. He finished his playing career at Virginia with a program-record 598 assists, which was 231 more than Barry Parkhill, who had established that record in 1973. He also established the record for the most assists in a season at 200. Both of these records would eventually fall to John Crotty, who played for Virginia from 1988 to 1991. Jones led the team in assists for each of his four seasons, including ACC-leading performances his freshman and sophomore years.

During Jones' four years as a player, the Cavaliers won the NIT in 1980, reached the Final Four in 1981, and reached the Elite Eight in 1982, ranking third in the country during his junior and senior seasons. Though he was never an All-ACC player, that didn't make him any less of a fan favorite. For Jones' Senior Night, an easy 84–66 win against Wake Forest, Virginia fans were not shy to proclaim their support for Jones. Though head coach Terry Holland had already taken Jones out of the game in the blowout, Virginia fans began chanting for his return in the final minute. "In a way I didn't know how to react," Jones later said. "I was mostly embarrassed. I didn't know what to do…Everybody on the bench was laughing. Coach looked down to see what my reaction was, and I just sort of shrugged."

Jones would return to the game and bury a 20-footer from the corner to send the fans at U-Hall into euphoria. "No player I've ever had has been more fun to be around," Holland said.

Senior Night, however, wouldn't be the last game for Jones at U-Hall. Though he was picked in the fourth round of the 1982 NBA Draft by the Indiana Pacers, Jones never played a minute in the league. Instead he was hired as an assistant under Holland in 1982, where he would serve until 1990, when he became the head coach of the Cavaliers at the age of 29, the youngest head coach in ACC history. His team would go 21–12 that season, making him then the winningest first-year head coach in ACC history.

During Jones' eight-year head coaching tenure at Virginia, the Cavaliers made the NCAA Tournament five times, reaching the Elite Eight in 1995, and the NIT once, winning that title in 1992. Jones became the first person to win the NIT championship as both a player and a coach. Off-the-court troubles for Jones' players plagued his teams toward the end of his Virginia coaching career, giving Virginia two losing seasons (1996, 1998) in three years for the first time since the mid-1970s. "Jeff has done about as good a job as anybody in the league with his team," Duke coach Mike Krzyzewski said in 1998. "So many times we measure a guy who has one loss or no losses and say that team's playing great. But sometimes we look throughout the league and find people who maybe have less experience or numbers and are making the most of it. Those guys are doing a great job. Jeff has done a terrific job with his team."

Following the 1998 season, Jones, 37, stepped down from the helm after spending more than half of his life in the cozy confines of University Hall. He would later become head coach at American University and then Old Dominion.

64 Be Part of the Country's Best Student Section

When the Collegiate Licensing Company and the Atlanta Tipoff Club announced the winner of the 2014 Naismith Student Section of the Year Award, some may have found the recipient to be a bit surprising. It wasn't Kansas (though it won in 2012). It wasn't Duke. And it wasn't Indiana, Arizona, or Kentucky. It was the University of Virginia's 'Hoo Crew, and at the time of the award, the 'Hoo Crew hadn't even been around for 10 years.

Originally founded in 2005, the 'Hoo Crew was established as a way to increase student attendance at all basketball games—not just the marquee matchups—as well as drive attendance toward traditional non-revenue sports such as baseball, lacrosse, and soccer. The organization, completely student-run, though with the blessing and support of the athletics department, was originally founded by members of a different group by the same name. The original 'Hoo Crew was the moniker for the group that helped to organize groups who wanted to camp out days to weeks in advance for the best men's basketball seats in University Hall. As the team's performance declined in the early 2000s, the numbers at Hooville—the concourse between U-Hall and Onesty Hall that served as the designated campsite—began to dwindle, particularly for unranked, non-rival opponents.

As the university switched over to an online ticketing system, the need for physically camping out before basketball games dissipated, freeing up the name for the new student fan group. Developing an official student fan group is not an easy task, especially for a school that's never found the need to formalize the process. The founders compared student fan groups from other institutions—both in the ACC and elsewhere—such as Wake Forest's Screamin' Demons,

Michigan State's Izzone, Stanford's Cardinal Sixth Man Club, and Arizona's Zona Zoo. Each fan group has its own regulations and requirements. Some required a membership fee for the prime seats; others required minimum levels of attendance, etc. The newly created 'Hoo Crew was designed such that students neither needed to pay a membership fee nor needed to attend a minimum percentage of games. Anyone who wanted to be a member simply needed to sign up and pick up a free T-shirt. Priority seating within the group, however, was determined based on attendance, thereby rewarding those who attended the most basketball games and designated non-revenue events with the best seats in the house.

Though initially met with pushback from students who felt the new system was unfair, the 'Hoo Crew withstood the criticism and has continued to grow in size and presence. The 'Hoo Crew helps organize cheers for basketball games in addition to distributing blue and orange streamers and helping to create giant cardboard heads to be held up to distract opposing free throw shooters. The group also organizes tailgates and similar events to encourage attendance at other fall and spring sports.

In 2014 the group was awarded the third ever Naismith Student Section of the Year Award over 250 other student sections across the country. The award was given based on a video submission, fan voting, and the board of selectors' observations of the group's creativity, organized efforts, and philanthropic endeavors.

Virginia head coach Tony Bennett says that his team has noticed. "They have done a great job creating a home-court advantage for us at John Paul Jones Arena. Our players feed off their energy and enthusiasm, and it makes for a great gameday experience for everyone at JPJ." The 2015–16 Cavaliers finished undefeated at home (15–0) for the first time since the 1981–82 team posted a 12–0 home record.

When Virginia clinched the ACC regular season title in 2014—its first outright since 1981—with a 75–56 win against No.

4 Syracuse, Bennett remarked on the electric atmosphere the 'Hoo Crew had created. "I knew it was going to be electric, but that gives you something defensively. It was special how intense it was and the passion we got from it. The last time it got that loud, I was at the Taylor Swift concert, and I sat there, and there's like 14,000 teenage girls screaming. I remember sitting there like, *I wonder if we can get it like this for a game.* And I have to tell you, it either rivaled it or surpassed it. Sorry, Taylor."

65 The Game of the Decade

On December 11, 1982, senior Ralph Sampson and the Virginia Cavaliers met sophomore Patrick Ewing and the Georgetown Hoyas at the Capital Centre outside of Washington, D.C., for the most hyped regular season college basketball game in 25 years. Several networks sought the rights to broadcast the game between teams separated by 120 miles of Route 29. Ted Turner's TBS eventually won those rights and thus became the first cable television station to exclusively broadcast a college basketball game. A *Sports Illustrated* cover featured Sampson and Ewing laying down and smiling at the camera; of course, both of their figures extended to the back cover out of necessity. About 200 members of the media were in attendance, and roughly that many more applied for credentials but were denied. One radio station even applied for a seat for its photographer.

As it was a unique made-for-television game—and it was promoted as such—the two coaches took the unusual step of agreeing beforehand that the game would be played the old-fashioned way, which meant that there would be no shot clock or three-point

In a clash of the titans, Georgetown's Patrick Ewing tries to box out Virginia's Ralph Sampson, but Sampson would get the better of him, outscoring the Hoyas center 23 to 16 in the Cavaliers' victory.

bucket. At 8:38 PM in front of 19,035 people in the arena and millions more on television, the top two teams in the national preseason rankings tipped off with the Hoyas winning the first possession. But it was Virginia that drew first blood off a jumper from Othell Wilson.

UVA led at halftime 33–23 and extended the lead to as many as 14 points in the second half. Georgetown, however, came back, tying the game twice and as late as 3:19 remaining in the game. Despite battling the flu in the days leading up to the game and an injured left knee from practice the previous week, Sampson nonetheless won the individual matchup between Ewing, outscoring him 23 to 16, outrebounding him 16 to eight, and blocking more shots (seven to five). Georgetown featured three starting freshmen who had struggled all night getting the ball into Ewing's hands in the paint. Although Ewing dunked over Sampson, it was the veteran Cavaliers who prevailed in the end 68–63. As Sampson told the *Daily Press* in 2001, "You probably aren't going to ever have it happen again—not until two more seven-footers who can play the game are born."

66 Terry Kirby

Tabb High School product Terry Kirby was one of the finest high school athletes the state of Virginia had ever seen. Kirby was the top running back in the country, and his recruitment during the 1988 season was perhaps the most heated process the Virginia Cavaliers had been a part of since recruiting Ralph Sampson, the nation's top center in 1979.

Terry Kirby, a dual football and basketball star, runs for yardage against North Carolina State in 1992. (*USA TODAY* Sports Images)

For his football prowess, he was named to both the *Parade* All-American team and the *USA Today* All-USA team following his senior year in 1988, having set multiple Virginia High School League records that would continue to stand for decades to come. In addition to being the top running back, Kirby was also one of the top 50 basketball players in the country.

Over football offers from Georgia, Alabama, Clemson, and Notre Dame, Kirby, 6'2" and 215 pounds, chose Virginia. Kirby's college career occurred when Virginia was at its peak. His 1989 freshman class, which included linebacker Chris Slade (Slade was a fourth cousin of Kirby, and the two of them grew up on parallel athletic tracks), saw the historic rise of Virginia football as the Cavaliers captured their first ever 10-win season and ACC co-championship. By 1990 Virginia, with significant contributions from both Kirby and Slade, had achieved the program's first and only No. 1 ranking in the AP poll.

By the time Kirby finished his career at Virginia, he had set the school's all-time record in career rushing yards at 3,348 and had led the ACC in rushing in both 1990 as a sophomore and 1992 as a senior. At the same time, Kirby didn't let his basketball talent go to waste either. During his high school senior year, his basketball coach said that Kirby "is one of very few players who I think could step right into basketball after football season." And that's exactly what he did.

With both football head coach George Welsh's and basketball head coach Terry Holland's permission, Kirby was a dual-sport athlete. "Kirby was recruited for both sports because that's what he wanted to do and he's good enough to play both sports," Welsh said during Kirby's recruitment. "Kirby's just an exceptional athlete, a 6'3" guard. That's not too bad. He's a big tailback and he's going to be a nice-sized guard."

Holland had no objections to allowing Kirby to play both sports. "I work for the athletic department and I want all our programs to do well," Holland said at the time. "The rule of thumb is whoever needs the player the most has priority."

After his 1991 junior football season, however, Kirby decided it was time to hang up the basketball shorts in favor of the football pads. Because of the length of the football season, Kirby had a late start to the basketball season his sophomore year and, as a result, played in only 12 games, averaging just 2.1 points per game despite having been named the state of Virginia's Player of the Year in high school, averaging 27 points per game.

Kirby fractured his shoulder blade his senior season in 1992 at the game against Clemson, a 29–28 losing effort to the No. 25 Tigers when the Cavaliers were ranked No. 10. He missed the following three games, which included losses to North Carolina and No. 6 Florida State, and the Cavaliers fell from the rankings. Though Kirby would return and play in the ensuing game against No. 17 North Carolina State, Kirby, not yet full recovered, was unable to lead the Hoos to victory. Finally, Kirby returned into top-notch shape in time to participate in a 41–38 win against in-state rival Virginia Tech.

Kirby was drafted in the third round by the Miami Dolphins, where he would spend the first three seasons of his 10-year NFL career. he also played for the San Francisco 49ers for three years, the Cleveland Browns for one, and the Oakland Raiders for the remaining three. During his career he carried the ball 761 times for 2,875 yards (a 3.8 yards-per-carry average) and scored 27 touchdowns.

67 The 2006–07 Basketball Season

With an experienced backcourt, brand new arena, and a roller-coaster season with electrifying wins and disheartening losses, there might not be a Virginia basketball season quite like the one that took place in 2006–07.

It began on November 12, 2006, when No. 10 Arizona entered a 14,593-seat arena with nearly that many people wearing commemorative shirts to celebrate the opening of the new arena. The mascot, Cavman, rappelled down from the rafters to greet university president John Casteen and athletic director Craig Littlepage, as well as to present them with the final basketball used at nearby University Hall, which had been the Hoos' home for four decades. Simulated fire was on the new Jumbotron above center court and the ribbon boards around the arena, green lasers were displayed around the stands, and iconic boxing announcer Michael Buffer introduced the Virginia starting five with his signature, "Let's get ready to rumble!"

Mamadi Diane scored the first points at John Paul Jones Arena with a left-corner three, but things turned sour in a hurry for Virginia. The Hoos trailed by as many as 16 in the first half and were down 49–36 at the break. Diane cut the Wildcats' lead to single digits 1:15 into the second half with a three-pointer from the right wing, and the Hoos would rarely trail by double digits after that. A few key defensive stops plus three long balls from Diane in the second half helped Virginia keep chipping away at the deficit, and two Sean Singletary free throws knotted the score at 68-all with 11:07 remaining. A 9–2 Arizona run took the air back out of the arena, but Diane made another huge three with 5:43 left to give UVA an 80–79 lead, its first since the early going. Free throws and layups helped guide Virginia the rest of the way, and a potentially game-tying three from Arizona's J.P. Prince with less than 10 seconds to go was short, and Virginia won the game 93–90. Diane and Singletary led all scorers with 25 points apiece, the perfect way to open a brand new arena.

The year also included a shocking win at No. 19 Clemson on January 28. Virginia trailed by 16 with 8:48 left and by 14 with four minutes left. But UVA held Clemson without a field goal for the final 8:48 and scored 15 points in the last four minutes—nine of which came from beyond the three-point line—to shock the Tigers. Up by one with 30 seconds left, Clemson turned the ball over, which set Virginia up for a chance to hold for the last shot. Singletary rebounded an errant Diane three-pointer, and after Adrian Joseph missed a layup, Jason Cain tipped it in with 15 seconds left, and that stood as the game-winner in the 64–63 victory.

Perhaps the most memorable moment of that season came on February 1, when "the Shot," a teardrop from Singletary with a second left while he was falling backward, sank No. 8 Duke in Charlottesville, the Hoos' first win over the Blue Devils in five years. Senior night for Cain and J.R. Reynolds came against Virginia Tech on March 1, and they beat their in-state rivals 69–56, combining for 21 points and 13 rebounds.

Starting the season 16–6, UVA arguably never got its due from the voters as the Cavaliers were ranked for just two weeks—No. 25 on November 28 with a 4–0 record and No. 24 on February 20 with an 18–7 record. A 78–72 loss at Wake Forest on March 3 cost the Cavaliers their first outright regular season ACC championship in 26 years, though they did walk away with a share of the regular season title. A loss to longtime ACC Tournament foil North Carolina State in the quarterfinals meant that for the 12th consecutive year Virginia failed to make the semifinals of the ACC Tournament, a drought that would extend to 2014.

Virginia earned a No. 4 seed in the South Region for the NCAA Tournament. The Hoos beat Albany 84–57 to set up a date with Chris Lofton and Tennessee. Though Virginia led 38–35 at halftime, a twisted ankle for Reynolds slowed his production. At the final buzzer, Reynolds and Singletary combined for 45 points, but 22 of Reynolds' 26 points had come in the first half. Virginia led for the final 8:17 of the first and the first 3:48 of the second but was unable to overcome 13 second-half points from Tennessee's JaJuan Smith. Lofton made six free throws in a row down the stretch, but nine points in the final minute from Singletary kept Virginia in it. Lofton made two free throws with five seconds left to push the Volunteers' lead to 77–74, and Singletary had one last look from three. It was just off the mark.

Singletary dropped to the floor, put his head in his hands with his forehead on the hardwood, and was immediately consoled by head coach Dave Leitao and his teammates.

Although the season ended in heartbreak, Virginia finished at 21–11 overall and 11–5 in the ACC for its best conference record in 12 years and a remarkable turnaround after going 4–12 in league play just two years prior. It was a bright spot in an otherwise dark 15-year period for Virginia basketball.

68 Hook and Ladder

Virginia fans were hard-pressed to believe they'd witness something special when No. 20 Georgia Tech rolled into Scott Stadium on November 10, 2001. Al Groh's first season as head coach had reached its lowest point. After finishing September with a 3–1 record, Groh's Cavaliers had lost five straight. Most embarrassingly, Virginia had just lost 34–30 at home against Wake Forest in its first loss to the Demon Deacons since 1983.

Georgia Tech, in contrast, came to Charlottesville at 6–2 overall and 3–2 in the ACC. George O'Leary's squad had just beaten North Carolina and North Carolina State, two teams Virginia had lost to. Tech was ranked as high as ninth earlier in the year and was squarely in the mix for the ACC title.

Sophomore quarterback Bryson Spinner led the Virginia attack that afternoon. In the most heavily discussed storyline of the year, Spinner had shared starting duties throughout the season with fellow sophomore Matt Schaub. Neither quarterback had played well enough to earn the starting job consistently. Georgia Tech, meanwhile, was led by George Godsey, a senior gunslinger who would go on to throw for 3,085 yards during the 2001 season. Still, Virginia had one thing going for it: a serious home-field advantage. The Cavaliers hadn't lost to Georgia Tech in Scott Stadium since 1990, when the Jackets ended UVA's reign as the No. 1 team in the country.

The first half unfolded much like one would have predicted for two teams seemingly headed in opposite directions. Virginia lost a pair of turnovers, and Georgia Tech took a 20–7 lead into halftime. The Cavaliers, however, pulled within 20–14 by the end of the third quarter. After a Georgia Tech punt, Virginia took over at its own 21-yard line with 14:44 left to play.

Over the next hour, Scott Stadium turned into the OK Corral as the Cavaliers and Yellow Jackets produced a shootout for the ages. A seven-play drive in just 90 seconds ended with a Spinner touchdown pass to junior receiver Billy McMullen and gave UVA its first lead at 21–20. Georgia Tech followed with a nine-play touchdown drive to jump ahead 26–21. Georgia Tech's upper-hand was short-lived. Virginia receiver Tavon Mason returned the ensuing kickoff 100 yards to give UVA a 27–26 advantage. Undeterred, Godsey took the lead right back with an eight-play drive that included three straight completions to receiver Will

Glover, who would finish with 13 catches and 172 receiving yards on the day.

But if Godsey wasn't done, neither was Spinner. And after an 11-play march, a Spinner pass to running back Tyree Foreman put Virginia up 33–32 and marked the fifth lead change of the quarter. But Godsey needed only six plays and 1:06 to put Georgia Tech back up 38–33. With only 1:45 left on the clock, it seemed like the Jackets had grabbed the lead for good.

What happened next will likely never be forgotten by anyone who watched it live. After a touchback Spinner completed a pass to freshman running back Alvin Pearman for nine yards. A three-yard run from Spinner gave Virginia a first down at its own 32. A pass interference penalty on a third-down incompletion kept UVA's drive alive. Two completions to McMullen later, Spinner had Virginia at the Georgia Tech 37. Then in one of the most famous plays in Virginia history, Spinner found McMullen on a curl at the Georgia Tech 27-yard line. McMullen, while being tackled, threw a chest pass with two hands to Pearman. The freshman scooped the ball off the turf and scampered untouched into the end zone with 22 seconds remaining. To the amazement of the fans in Scott Stadium, Virginia had completed a successful hook and ladder.

Pearman's score gave Virginia the lead for good. Following the kickoff UVA stopped Georgia Tech's last-gasp drive to win the game 39–38. Spinner finished the game with 327 passing yards, and the Cavaliers won despite allowing an eye-popping 486 passing yards by Godsey. "This was a magnificent college football game," Groh told the press after the game. "It showed everything college football is all about, tremendous will and heart by both teams."

Virginia would finish the season 5–7, but the hook and ladder gave Cavalier fans a highlight to remember. Ironically, the play happened so quickly that it wasn't completely clear what had happened at the time. From some angles inside the stadium, it looked like McMullen had fumbled. But the play design became clearer in postgame interviews. "I knew it would work," senior running back Antoine Womack told the *Daily Press*. "Defenses key on [McMullen] so hard. When he got the ball, three guys were on him like, 'Boom!' They were bringing him down. When Alvin got the ball, I knew we had a touchdown."

Almost 15 years later, memories of the hook and ladder play still live on within the hearts and minds of the Virginia faithful. "That was easily one of the craziest finishes of my career," Spinner told the *Daily Progress* in 2015. "We had faith in the call and in each other and we got it done."

69 Mike Scott

When Virginia forward Mike Scott was deciding between schools in 2007, he wasn't exactly short of offers and interests from the big players: Oklahoma, Clemson, Wake Forest, and North Carolina State, for starters. But Virginia was trending in the right direction. The Cavaliers under head coach Dave Leitao went from going 4–12 in the ACC in 2005 to 7–9 in 2006. By 2007 they were 11–5 and were regular season co-champions with North Carolina. When committing to Virginia, Scott also touted the university's academic reputation despite his father's preference. "UVA wasn't my first pick," said Michael Scott, Mike's father, who felt a stronger connection with Wake Forest's head coach, Skip Prosser.

As it would turn out, Scott's decision to go to Virginia paid off as he made an immediate impact on the team, starting his freshman season and playing in 32 of Virginia's 33 games that season. He averaged 5.7 points and 5.3 rebounds per game. Though the Cavaliers during Scott's freshman, sophomore, and junior seasons were not quite the same as the 2006–07 program that won a share of the regular-season conference title and made the program's first appearance in the NCAA Tournament since 2001, Scott continued to improve his numbers and presence in each game.

He produced an average of 10.3 points and 7.4 rebounds per game during his sophomore season. Virginia finished with a mere 10–18 record and just 4–12 in the ACC that season. By his junior season, and first under new head coach Tony Bennett, Scott realized he needed to change parts of his game if he wanted to succeed under the defense-oriented Bennett and if he wanted to be able eventually to showcase his talent to NBA scouts. "Sometimes I had that selfish mentality in that I wasn't a good team defender; I just worried about my man not scoring," Scott told ESPN. "I didn't know that being a good team defender was helping on ball screens or helping get in the gaps. That's really evolved into my game this last year. My dad always told me, 'Show them all aspects of your game,'" Scott said. "It took me so long to realize that. Now, I'm starting to do it."

Virginia's most consistent scorer, Scott increased his production to an average of 12 points per game his junior year. His rebounding dropped slightly to 7.2 rebounds per game, largely by design under Bennett's system. With three years under his belt, Scott was primed for a big 2010–11 senior season. Through the first 10 games, he was averaging 15.9 points and 10.2 rebounds per game until an ankle injury forced him to undergo a series of season-ending surgeries. Scott was granted a medical redshirt to play a fifth year. During his injury season, he had grown to be somewhat of a coach and mentor for the younger players on the team and was Virginia's No. 1 cheerleader all season. As a result, Scott came back a better leader for his (second) senior year.

When practice began for the 2011–12 season, Bennett said he noticed a difference.

"He's become more versatile—putting it on the floor better, and his ability to pass, score, rebound, defend, just becoming a complete player," Bennet said. "He's also become more mobile and really has gone to work on his body. What I've also liked is how he's matured his game and his mind each year, his leadership and mental approach."

Scott led the Cavaliers to a 22–10, 9–7 ACC season, the first time the Cavaliers reached the 20-win mark or had a winning conference record since making the NCAA Tournament in 2007. Virginia made their return to the NCAA Tournament, bowing out in the first round to an underrated Florida Gators team. Scott finished second in first-team All-ACC voting, just two points behind North Carolina's Tyler Zeller. He led the conference in true shooting percentage (accounting for both field goals and free throws) and for much of the season shot better than 60 percent from the field. Scott completed his career third in Virginia's annals for career rebounds, at 944, and remains 17th on the career points list at 1,538. Scott made a career-high 35 points against Miami his senior season.

Drafted in the second round of the 2012 NBA Draft by the Atlanta Hawks with the 43rd overall pick, Scott remains a viable bench contributor for the team that made the Eastern Conference Finals in 2015. For those who watched him and followed him on social media while in college, Scott's greatest legacy to the fanbase may not have been his points per game his senior year (18) or rebounds (8.3). Instead, few can think of the Scott without thinking of the term "tragical," a completely made up word by Scott that spread like wildfire throughout Twitter and other social media. This whimsical side of Scott was reinforced throughout his career at Virginia as he hid his teammates' belongings as pranks, and well into his NBA career, where Scott became known as the guy with emoji tattoos across his body. With more than 15 different emoji tattoos, Scott explained, "Sometimes they say what you can't say. They can express the words that you can't say about how you feel."

70 Closing out the Orange Bowl

To say the Miami Orange Bowl gave the Hurricanes a home-field advantage would be an understatement. For 58 straight games, the Miami Hurricanes defeated every opponent who came to the Orange Bowl between 1985 and 1994.

Notwithstanding the distinct home-field advantage in 2007, Miami president Donna Shalala and athletic director Paul Dee announced a deal that would move the Hurricanes' home games to the Miami Dolphins' Sun Life Stadium. The Miami Orange Bowl would be demolished, and a new baseball stadium for the Miami Marlins would be built in its place.

When the 2007 ACC football schedule was released, the Virginia Cavaliers discovered that they would have the honor of being the Hurricanes' opponent for the Orange Bowl's last hurrah on November 10, 2007. Coming into the game, Virginia was in the midst of a surprising campaign, sitting at 8–2 on the season and squarely in the race for the ACC's Coastal Division title. On the flip side, the Hurricanes were 5–4 on the year, enduring a difficult season under first-year head coach Randy Shannon.

The night was a who's who of college football legends as a plethora of former Hurricanes turned out for the event. The best of Miami, including stars such as Michael Irvin, Russell Maryland, and Gino Torretta, wanted to support the team in closing out the Orange Bowl strong. It was a night that was supposed to punctuate the Hurricanes' "70 years of dominance," as announced in pep rally fashion right before kickoff by Dwayne "the Rock" Johnson.

The only dominance on display that night, however, came from the Cavaliers. The Hoos started the game with a 96-yard touchdown drive that took only seven plays, and the rout was on.

The score stayed 7–0 until late in the first quarter when Virginia blocked a punt deep in Hurricane territory and then scored two plays later on Keith Payne's five-yard scamper. Following Miami quarterback Kyle Wright's third interception of the first half, a Virginia field goal made the score 17–0. Virginia would add two more rushing touchdowns, one by Virginia quarterback Jameel Sewell, the other by running back Mikell Simpson, to take a 31–0 halftime lead in front of a speechless Miami crowd.

The second half picked up right where the first half had left off. Simpson scored from one yard out, capping a 10-play, 67-yard drive. The night would come to a fitting conclusion when Chris Cook picked up a Miami fumble and rumbled 44 yards for the touchdown that would make the final score 48–0, embarrassing the Miami fans among a crowd of 62,106.

Virginia's defense was tremendous, holding Wright to 94 yards through the air in addition to the three interceptions. Miami as a team only managed 189 yards of total offense and lost two fumbles. The Cavaliers offense was just as good, amassing 418 yards of offense including 288 passing by Sewell. Simpson led the way on the ground with 93 yards and two scores. In the receiving game, the tight ends took center stage with John Philips, Tom Santi, and Jonathan Stupar combining for 10 catches and 154 yards.

When all was said and done, Virginia spoiled the evening with a 48–0 victory, the likes of which had not been seen in the Orange Bowl since the Hurricanes fell 44–0 to Notre Dame in 1973. Beyond that, you'd have to go back to 1958, a 41–0 loss to LSU. Although the night was a sour end to an historically great chapter in Miami Hurricanes football, it was also a high point in an already remarkable 2007 season for Virginia. The game itself marked Virginia's ninth win on the season and, remarkably, the program's first win in the state of Florida in 16 tries.

71 Norman Nolan

When Virginia received a commitment from the 6'8" Norman Nolan, rated the 15th best player in the country and a top four power forward, recruiting experts predicted that the Cavaliers now had the pieces they needed to maintain their status as one of top teams in the country. "The beautiful campus, the great kids, players I met there, and the academics" were all reasons the 1994 McDonald's All-American cited for choosing Virginia over his other offers.

Following a knee injury after graduating from high school, Nolan struggled his freshman season at Virginia, averaging only 2.6 points and only eight minutes per game. Nolan's performance improved his sophomore season, earning a spot as a starter after Junior Burrough's graduation, but still Nolan only managed to pull down 9.5 points per game, a far cry from the 18.1 points that Burrough, for whom many thought Nolan would be the heir apparent, had produced.

With 11.3 points per game his junior year, Nolan began to live up to his touted potential, but it was Nolan's senior 1997–98 season in which he truly broke through. That year, he averaged a whopping 21 points per game, the highest average by a Cavalier since Jeff Lamp had averaged 22.9, leading the ACC in 1978–79. With a 52.4 field goal percentage and scoring 20 or more points in 17 games and 10 or more rebounds in 17 games, Nolan was indispensable to the Cavaliers that season.

The accolades and recognition began to pile up for Nolan, who remains 10th in the Virginia record book for most points in a season at 630 and eighth among season scoring average leaders. He began buying into a potential NBA career after his time at Virginia. The NBA dream began to take over all aspects of his life. Despite citing academics as one of the reasons for choosing Virginia, Nolan had either withdrawn or had a failing grade in every class by the second semester of his senior season. "I thought I could just do enough to get by, which wasn't enough," Nolan later recalled in a 2010 *Daily Progress* article. "I didn't put forth a lot of effort."

Despite spending four years at Virginia, Nolan would be 25 credits shy of a degree at graduation. When the NBA draft came around in June, Nolan's name wasn't called. It certainly didn't help Nolan's cause that, despite his scoring barrage in the 1997–98 season coupled with Curtis Staples' own 18.1 points per game that year, Virginia had a paltry 11–19 record, going 3–13 in the conference to finish dead last.

Nolan bounced around from team to team for some time, working out in several NBA teams' training camps without making a team. Eventually giving up on his NBA dream, he focused his professional career internationally, playing in Italy, Spain, France, Greece, Lebanon, Kuwait, Iran, Venezuela, and Argentina.

Finally, after over a decade of playing professional basketball, Nolan stepped back.

In 2010 Nolan returned to Virginia to work toward earning the sociology degree that he had begun 16 years prior. "It's always been a goal," Nolan told the *Daily Progress*. "It's just been finding the time to do it and wanting to do it. The importance of getting a degree from the University of Virginia is top tier; it's probably the best public university in the country. I didn't want to come here and walk away with nothing."

72 Pete Gillen

When Pete Gillen arrived in Charlottesville to replace Jeff Jones as head coach for the 1998–99 season, the Virginia basketball fanbase was more reminiscent of the Bill Gibson days in the late 1960s and early 1970s than it was of the Terry Holland days with Ralph Sampson. That is to say, fan support was indifferent at best. In the three seasons prior to Gillen's arrival, Virginia finished 12–15, 18–13, and 11–19, respectively, with no winning ACC seasons during that time. In 1997–98 the Cavaliers only had three conference wins, two of which required an overtime effort.

Gillen, who came to Virginia after four years as the head coach at Providence, taking the Friars as far as the Elite Eight in the NCAA Tournament, performed about as expected out of a head coach's first year at a new school. The Cavaliers finished 14–16 overall with a 4–12 ACC record. It wouldn't take long, however, for Gillen to bring the program around.

Virginia's first recruiting class under Gillen was tremendous, as he signed McDonald's All-American point guard Majestic Mapp; *Parade* All-American Travis Watson; and Powerade Mr. Basketball, awarded to the best player in the Washington, D.C., area, Roger Mason Jr. All three players were ranked among the top 50 recruits in the country. With the first of his guys on board, the 1999–00 season shaped up nicely, as Gillen led Virginia to a record of 19–12, (9–7 ACC) and an invitation to the NIT. He followed this up with a record of 20–9, (9–7 ACC) in 2000–01, making his first and only NCAA Tournament appearance with the Cavaliers.

With back-to-back winning seasons for the first time since 1995, Virginia fans had reason to be excited about basketball again. Crowds began to form outside of U-Hall not just hours before games, but also days and sometimes even weeks. Under Gillen's leadership "Hooville," the concourse between U-Hall and Onesty Hall where students would camp out in tents to get better seats at the game, increased its population year after year. It was throughout this time that Virginia students and fans got to

Known for being entertaining, energetic, and emotional, coach Pete Gillen reacts to a call during a 2005 game at Wake Forest.

see just how charismatic the Brooklyn Irishman was. On multiple occasions Gillen and his staff went out to Hooville, particularly when temperatures were below freezing, to deliver nourishment for the students in the form of Buffalo Wild Wings, Domino's Pizza, or Krispy Kreme donuts. Players like Jason Rogers or Majestic Mapp came out to serve food to the campers, thanking them for their support.

But, just as quickly as Gillen turned the program back on track, it seemed Virginia basketball would start heading in the wrong direction. Mason, who at one point was projected to go as high as the teens in the NBA draft, declared early to pursue the professional dream. Mapp tore his ACL and was never able to recover his knee fully. The 2001 class, consisting of Elton Brown, Jason Clark, Jermaine Harper, and Keith Jenifer, would never reach its full potential due to academic issues and off-court discipline issues that led to arrests. The program was plagued with reports of poor team chemistry, an inability to finish the season as strong as it had started, and continued off-court troubles.

Virginia would fail to make another NCAA Tournament with Gillen as the head coach, though the Cavaliers made three straight NIT appearances. After Gillen's first season at Virginia, he wouldn't have another losing season until 2004–05. Gillen resigned following that season, his seventh at UVA.

The final few years were tough for Virginia fans, who remember the team seemingly running out of timeouts just minutes into each half. Gillen himself told the *Richmond Times-Dispatch* that his health wasn't in good shape. Virginia fans and alumni, though, were left with a positive impression of Gillen. They'll remember the sweat-soaked suits that were a signature of the always enthusiastic and energetic Gillen. They'll remember the zippy one-liners and witty quips that Gillen always had in interviews, regardless of wins or losses. "There is not a classier person in the coaching profession anywhere than Pete Gillen," athletic director Craig Littlepage said in a statement announcing Gillen's departure. "He's always handled the coaching responsibilities here with professionalism and humility."

"How many coaches would go through a double-overtime win in December and then stand outside in the cold at a mall and ring the Salvation Army bell for three hours?" asked Mac McDonald, the voice of the Cavaliers for years on the radio. For better or worse, Gillen was "down to earth" and "player friendly," recalled guard Todd Billet who seemingly won countless games for Virginia on buzzer-beater threes. "You didn't feel like you were just being used for your playing time and then pushed out the door," he said. "Coach cared about what your future goals would be."

In his seven seasons at Virginia, Gillen amassed a 118–93 overall record and went 45–67 in conference. The Cavaliers made one NCAA appearance, a heartbreaking loss to Gonzaga, and four NIT appearances. After taking some time off, Gillen returned to the college basketball profession as a color commentator.

73 The Origin of the "Wahoos"

The University of Virginia has collected a handful of nicknames over the years. Although their official mascot is the Cavalier, Virginia fans, students, and alumni more frequently refer to themselves as "Wahoos." The true origins of the name may never be ascertained, though the stories told make the mystery worthwhile.

One popular legend surrounding the origin of the association of the Wahoos with the University of Virginia revolves around a tropical fish that shares the same name. A member of the mackerel family, the wahoo is rumored to have the ability to drink twice its weight, appealing to the idea that students at Virginia, an institution already known for its academics, were just as dedicated to their social activities and could throw down with the best of them. However, the wahoo, whose name stems from a variation of the spelling of Oahu, where the fish can be found abundantly, has no clear ties to the university.

Another common—although equally unlikely—myth connected to the terminology revolves around a popular children's author and his supposed rejection from the university. Rumor has it that Dr. Theodore Giesel, more commonly known as "Dr. Seuss," bought a house overlooking Grounds after not gaining admission and that his allusion to the "Whos down in Whoville" from his story *How the Grinch Stole Christmas* actually referenced the students at Virginia. From the UVA bookstore and other parts of central grounds, one can see a house up in the mountains overlooking the university. This house, known more commonly as the Lewis Mountain House, is an estate built in 1909 for Brigadier General John Watts Kearny, son of Philip Kearny, who had served in the Civil War as a Union general. Dr. Seuss had lived all his life in New England, Europe, and California, with no apparent connection to Charlottesville.

Instead, the legend of the Wahoo most likely stems from a long-standing baseball rivalry with Washington & Lee University dating back to the 1890s. The W&L fans would often refer to the rowdy Virginia players as "a bunch of wahoos" during the games, a term that the Virginia fans embraced. In 1893, around the same time frame as the competition on the diamond with W&L, the "Good Ol' Song" was written in order to welcome home the Virginia football team after a win. Legend has it that a group of students collaborated on the lyrics, incorporating the "Wah-hoo-wah" chant that was popular with the student body at the time.

But even the popular chant has mysterious origins. An 1893 performance of "Wherever You Are, There Shall My Love Be" by opera singer Natalie Floyd Otey at the Levy Opera House in Charlottesville could be the beginning of the phrase. The singer allegedly failed to enunciate "where'er you are" in the song, sounding like "wah-hoo-wah" to the students in the crowd, and from there, the legend was born.

Regardless of origin, by the 1940s, the term "Wahoos" was widely used around Grounds.

Today University of Virginia fans fully embrace the Wahoo within. Clothing and banners are emblazoned with variations of the phrase. The official student fan group, named the 'Hoo Crew, emerged in the fall of 2005. Although the origins of "Wahoo" remain cloaked in mystery and surrounded by legend, the Virginia faithful are happy to be 'Hoos.

74 Matt Schaub

Over the course of two seasons, Virginia quarterback Matt Schaub went from splitting quarterback duties with Bryson Spinner to becoming the ACC Player of the Year and a Heisman Trophy candidate. Few quarterbacks have a career trajectory quite this steep, but that's part of what made Schaub one of the greatest quarterbacks to ever play at Virginia.

Coming out of high school, Schaub was named to multiple All-American high school teams and listed as one of the top 10 quarterbacks in the country by *SuperPrep*. After redshirting his true freshman year in 1999, Schaub had a shot at some significant playing time in 2000 after starter Dan Ellis, who still holds the record for the most number of touchdown passes in a single game with six, missed several games due to a hamstring injury. However, then-head coach George Welsh awarded most of the playing time to fellow redshirt freshman Bryson Spinner.

Welsh retired following the end of the 2000 season, leading to the arrival of Al Groh. For the 2001 season, Groh named Schaub the starter in the season opener against No. 22 Wisconsin in the Eddie Robinson Classic, a game the Cavaliers would lose 26–17. Two critical interceptions led to points, and as a result, Spinner started the next four games before Schaub returned as starter, following Spinner's struggles. During that 2001 season, Schaub split time almost evenly with Spinner, starting six games but playing in all 12. He completed 58.3 percent of his attempts (140-of-240) and threw for 1,524 yards despite only starting half the games.

It wasn't until 2002 that Schaub took over as the true starting quarterback at Virginia, becoming one of the most effective quarterbacks in the country. Schaub led the Cavaliers to a 9–5, (6–2 ACC) season that ended with a 48–22 win in the inaugural Continental Tire Bowl in Charlotte, North Carolina, against No. 13 West Virginia. That season Schaub led the conference in at least six different statistical categories and was second in the country in passing completion percentage. He was named both the ACC Offensive Player of the Year and the ACC Player of the Year and received multiple honorable mentions for All-American teams, not to mention ACC All-Academic honors.

Following the successful 2002 season, Virginia launched a Heisman Trophy campaign for the fifth-year senior quarterback. Though he was unable to match his 2002 numbers in 2003 in large part due to a shoulder injury in the first game of the season that caused him to miss several games, Schaub led the Cavaliers to an 8–5 record and another winning trip to the Continental Tire Bowl, which Virginia won 23–16 against Pitt.

The most highly anticipated game of the season? It wasn't UVA–Virginia Tech. Virginia, by the way, won that game over in-state rival Virginia Tech 35–21, nor was it the South's Oldest Rivalry,

UVA-North Carolina, which Virginia won 38–13. Instead, it was UVA-North Carolina State, two schools that, though the programs played each other annually, didn't have much of a rivalry.

Heading into the November 1, 2003, matchup between the two teams, Schaub led the nation in completion percentage at 71 percent, but N.C. State's Philip Rivers was right behind him at No. 2 at 70.8. The two playing styles were nearly identical. Both quarterbacks liked to sit in the pocket, and neither was particularly agile, but both were deadly accurate.

The game delivered exactly as hyped. Both quarterbacks performed exceptionally well with each throwing for four touchdowns in the shootout. Schaub threw for 393 yards on the day while Rivers had 410. Heading into the locker room at the half, Virginia had a one-point lead after N.C. State missed an extra point in the 24–23 game. By the time the teams were tied at 37 well into the fourth quarter, both quarterbacks looked to be performing at their peaks. But with just 23 seconds left, N.C. State's T.A. McLendon made a 35-yard run for a touchdown, giving State the go-ahead score. A rare interception by Matt Schaub with just eight seconds remaining in the game sealed the Cavaliers' fate as it was returned for a touchdown, and the Wolfpack would go on to win 51–37. Years later, in an interview with *TheSabre.com*, Schaub listed the game as one of the toughest losses he had experienced at Virginia.

Schaub finished his career at Virginia holding 23 different school records, including passing yards, touchdown passes, completions, attempts, completion percentage, 300-yard games, and 200-yard games. "He joins an elite group of Virginia football players who, through their performance, have made their teams significantly different over a long span of time than what it otherwise would have been," Groh said. "I can't imagine that there are very many players in the country that have done as much to carry their team over a long period of time as he has with some of the throws that he has made and standards he has set."

The Atlanta Falcons selected Schaub in the third round of the 2004 NFL Draft. He spent three seasons in Georgia before getting traded to the Houston Texans in 2007 for a pair of future second-round picks. During Schaub's seven-year career at Houston, Schaub made two Pro Bowl appearances and was named the Pro Bowl MVP in 2009. He is the franchise's all-time leader in career wins, passing touchdowns, passing yards, and a handful of other categories. In 2014 he was traded to the Oakland Raiders and in 2015 he went to the Baltimore Ravens.

75 Mike London

Go to class, show class, treat people with dignity and respect—those were Virginia head coach Mike London's three rules that he established for the program upon his arrival in Charlottesville following the 2009 season to replace Al Groh. It didn't take long for the principles to take effect.

Almost immediately after London became head coach, it was noticeable among students and the community that the players were no longer autonomous when it came to academics. Class was mandatory, not optional. Coaches and graduate assistants were dropping in on classes to make sure the student-athletes were holding up their end of the bargain academically before being able to play on the field. If not, it would result in lost playing time. When he suspended three starters his first year, the message was clear. "There were some issues I had with guys as far as going to class and being on time," London told the media. "Unfortunately, it affected the playing time of some young men, so hopefully the message will resonate."

In London's first year as head coach, he immediately won over the fanbase with his emphasis on academics. The results on the field, however, would take a season to catch up. Whereas London finished 4–8 overall with a lone conference win against No. 22 Miami his rookie season, he successfully turned the program around in time for the 2011 season, which saw the Cavaliers go 8–5 overall and 5–3 in conference to finish in second place in the ACC Coastal Division. Earning a berth to the Chick-fil-A Bowl, the Cavaliers made the postseason for the first time since 2007, and London was named the ACC Coach of the Year. It was everything Virginia fans needed to see from the head coach who had won a national championship in his first year at Richmond just three years prior.

Over the next four seasons, however, Virginia never had another winning season, including a winless showing in the conference in 2013, and London's tenure at Virginia would prove to be a short one. The Cavaliers found themselves year after year embroiled in quarterback controversies as London cycled through starting quarterbacks in almost every year during his tenure. Over six seasons Virginia saw five different quarterbacks start season openers, often rotating throughout the season as well, an approach that proved unsuccessful.

Resigning following the 2015 season, London finished with a 27–46 record at Virginia. Just 10 days later, London accepted a position as associate head coach and defensive line coach at Maryland. Time will tell as to what Mike London's legacy at Virginia will be. It won't be the losing record, though. Virginia fans will remember London for being the man who is described across the board—by fans, by students, by players, by parents—as a good guy.

A former police detective in Richmond, London had a brief brush with mortality that helped keep everything in perspective. One night after cornering four restaurant robbery suspects, London approached the van, and as the driver revved the engine as though ready to speed away, London jumped through the van window.

The driver pulled a gun and pointed it at London's head. "When he pulled that, it looked like a bazooka," London told *The New York Times*. "It was in slow motion. It seemed like time froze. Everything flashes before you. It's so eerie. I saw myself in a uniform. I saw my kids. I saw my mom and my dad. It's so surreal."

The driver pulled the trigger. The gun clicked. Nothing happened.

Thankful to be alive, London eventually left the police force and began a career in coaching in 1989, a career that wouldn't put his life in physical danger night after night. In 2000, though, London again found himself in a life-or-death situation—this time with his daughter, who was diagnosed with Fanconi anemia, a rare genetic disease that can lead to bone marrow failure. Following her chemotherapy and radiation treatments, it was determined that she would need a bone marrow transplant. Doctors estimated that it was approximately 10,000-to-1 odds that a parent can match their child. Remarkably, Mike London was a perfect match, and his daughter's body didn't reject it. Following the successful operation, the Virginia football players helped organize annual bone marrow drives on Grounds to continue to raise awareness for the need for bone marrow donors.

76 Eat at The White Spot and Bodo's

Going to a college town for a football game means that the pregame meal is already decided for you. In most cases, and Charlottesville is no different, you'll spend the several hours leading up to the kickoff in a parking lot, eating the finest America has to offer by way of hot dogs, burgers, wings, and other grilled delicacies. But what about the other meals during the weekend? Although there is no shortage of good restaurants in Charlottesville, and one really can't go wrong exploring establishments on the Corner or near the Downtown Mall, there is a right way and a less-than-right way of getting your postgame meals in. Two restaurants in particular have withstood the tests of time and make the list: The White Spot and Bodo's.

The White Spot is a converted barbershop. When the place removed the single barber's chair, it left behind an untiled part of

Hot Dog Night

If you had to guess which game drew the largest crowd ever at University Hall, what would your guess be? If you said Virginia-North Carolina, you'd be right, assuming you specified that the matchup was in women's basketball. On February 5, 1986, 11,174 people packed the seats at U-Hall to set the all-time attendance record. The secret? Hot dogs.

Heading into the 1985–86 season, Virginia head coach Debbie Ryan and the Virginia women's basketball team had come off back-to-back seasons of making the NCAA Tournament and a regular season ACC championship title in the 1983–84 season. The 1985–86 season started off red hot for the Cavaliers, who rattled off 20 straight wins to open the campaign, including wins against No. 8 Auburn, No. 13 Old Dominion, No. 5 North Carolina, No. 18 Duke, and numerous other ranked opponents. Virginia rose to No. 3 and was looking to host then-No. 15 North Carolina.

Unfortunately, few people were in U-Hall to witness the greatness. At the time the women's games were averaging only around 1,000 attendees per game. In an effort to boost numbers, Kim Record, director of promotions, came up with a clever idea to try to draw in the crowds: offer a free hot dog and soda to everyone in attendance. Whether the promotion would be successful, no one really knew. "If you get 5,000 people, I'll dance naked at halftime," said then-associate athletics director Todd Turner.

In addition to the usual channels of promotion, Virginia organized a halftime basketball game between members of the media, including David Teel, Doug Doughty, and Jerry Ratcliffe, in a successful attempt to get the media to write about the game. "At 10:00 that morning," the floor that was ultimately painted over in white. The resulting "white spot" gave the small and narrow quick-serve diner its name. Though the menu is fairly extensive with its all-day breakfast options coupled with sandwiches, subs, hot dogs, and other specials, two menu items steal the spotlight and draw in the television cameras for game day B-roll footage.

Record later recalled, "we were all running around here [at U-Hall], and people are lined up down to Emmet Street."

Despite a maximum capacity of just over 9,000, Virginia let in everyone who wanted to see the game and collect on their hot dog promise. "It was the craziest thing you'd ever seen. You couldn't get into the parking lot," Ryan said. "I was just amazed. You walked into the gym and there was just deafening noise from the minute you walked in. There were people in every single aisle. There were people hanging over the sidelines. They were in every nook and cranny you could think of."

Among the 11,174 people in attendance, unfortunately for Virginia, was the local fire marshal, who, when submitting his report, decreased the maximum capacity of the arena down to 8,392. "I guess you could say it was the *costliest* promotion ever done," Record recalled.

"So the promotion was a huge success in that we set a women's record at that time for attendance, but it cost us about 1,800 seats for future years in University Hall," recalled Terry Holland, who was the head coach of the men's team at the time and later the athletics director at Virginia. "That means we gave away free hot dogs and free admission to that game to lose 1,800 seats times at least 300 games since then at an average of $20 per game. That comes to well over $10 million in lost revenue over the last 20 years for UVA—what a great promotion!"

Despite the record-setting crowd and a double-double effort from freshman Dawn Bryant, Virginia would lose that game at the buzzer 60–58. It would be the Cavaliers' only ACC loss of the season, as they finished first once again in conference play.

The "Gus Burger" is perhaps the single most well-known food item in Charlottesville. Its description is unassuming and doesn't compare to today's triple-fried, double-decker, single-heart bypass monstrosities that garner all the attention. Instead, a Gus Burger is nothing more than a single patty cheeseburger with a fried egg on top. The burger includes ketchup, mayonnaise, lettuce, tomato, onions, and pickles. On its face, it's nothing to write home about, but the Gus Burger has been as much a part of university tradition as any other. Admittedly, the most popular time to order the Gus Burger is between the hours of 1:30 AM and 3:30 AM, coinciding with nearby bars closing at 2:00 AM. The no-frills Gus Burger has inspired recurring eating competitions around the university throughout the years, though it's yet to hit the professional competitive eating circuit.

If you're looking for something a little more decadent, The White Spot has you covered with its Grillswith. Originally written on the menu board as "Grills With Ice Cream," it's not clear whether one can get a "Grillswithout." A Grillswith, though, is two Krispy Kreme doughnuts grilled on the flattop over butter and served side by side with a healthy container—a container!—of vanilla ice cream over the middle. A bite of this slightly crisped, intensely sweet donut coupled with the creamy, cool ice cream is enough to send one over the edge and is really the only proper way to end an evening of postgame victory drinks and indulgences.

The next morning, you may find yourself in a tired state and in search of something to settle your stomach as you drive out of town. Although there are plenty of wonderful breakfast places in Charlottesville, for those on the go, there's none other than Bodo's Bagels. Bodo's is often cited by Virginia students and alumni as hands down the best bagel shop in the country. Yes, that includes you, New York.

Bodo's uses the authentic New York style of making their bagels—boiling them prior to baking them. The shop is constantly baking bagels all day long in small batches, so that no matter what time of day you get there, chances are that you'll get a perfectly crispy bagel on the outside that's soft and bready on the inside. The options are almost endless. A cream cheese bagel is great, but ask a hundred people about their favorite bagel, and you're likely to get a hundred different, unique responses. This author almost always gets a sausage, egg, and melted American on sesame for breakfast, and for any other time of day, he goes for a more unique butter and chicken salad on garlic. For dessert try the cinnamon sugar and butter on a cinnamon-raisin bagel. Bodo's founder Brian Fox prefers a pastrami on everything bagel with kalamata olive spread, tomato, and onions. No matter what the combination, you can't go wrong.

With more restaurants per capita than any other city in Virginia, ranking 14th in the country with approximately 22.8 restaurants for every 10,000 people as of 2013, there's no shortage of options for an out-of-town guest. But for the sports fan looking to complement a decked-out tailgate with a host of local staples, look no further than The White Spot and Bodo's Bagels.

77 2001–02 Virginia Basketball Season

The 2001–02 basketball season started with promise and ended with a mind-boggling thud. Virginia, at one time ranked fourth in the country, collapsed spectacularly during ACC play and failed to make the NCAA Tournament. The collapse revealed serious flaws within Pete Gillen's program and marked the turning point in his tenure as Virginia's head coach.

Virginia entered the year with reasons for optimism. The Wahoos had completed a 20–9 NCAA Tournament season in

2001 and had racked up wins against three top 10 opponents: Duke, North Carolina, and Maryland. Gillen's press-and-run style had brought an exciting brand of basketball to University Hall, and his affable personality had endeared him to the Cavaliers fans. The Wahoos returned four starters: seniors Chris Williams and Adam Hall and juniors Travis Watson and Roger Mason Jr.

Point guard, however, remained a question mark. Majestic Mapp, a former McDonald's All-American, was supposed to be Gillen's starter and program centerpiece. But after a successful freshman campaign, Mapp tore his ACL playing pickup ball in the summer of 2000. What happened next is up for debate, but it didn't end well. According to *The New York Times*, famed UVA surgeon Dr. Frank McCue operated on Mapp's knee. The injury, however, didn't heal, and an infection required a second operation. Mapp eventually sought a second opinion from Dr. Arthur Ting in San Francisco. Though McCue stood by his work, Ting argued that the first surgery had failed. Mapp's family would eventually consider filing a lawsuit against UVA over McCue's procedure.

Mapp wouldn't return to action until midway through the 2002–03 season. That left Gillen with two options. He could slide Mason Jr. over from his natural two-guard position to play the point or he could insert true freshman point guard Keith Jenifer. Gillen would try both tactics throughout the season.

Virginia got off to a 9–0 start that featured a win against No. 15 Georgetown. UVA missed out on a chance for a second marquee victory when its ACC-Big 10 Challenge game against Michigan State was canceled for safety reasons. The Virginia-MSU game was played at the Richmond Coliseum, home to a local minor league hockey team. The game was on an unseasonably warm November day, which caused moisture to appear on the hardwood floor. Players from both sides slipped on the moisture throughout the first half. The game was canceled shortly after halftime. Virginia would end up bemoaning the lost opportunity for a key win.

UVA's troubles started with ACC play. The Cavaliers dropped their conference home opener against North Carolina State and lost a clunker against hapless Clemson on the road. The team bounced back, reeled off four straight conference wins, and appeared to steady the ship. But the Cavaliers lost a road game to Duke and suffered a heartbreaker at home to Maryland on January 31. In retrospect, the Maryland loss appeared to be the season's turning point. There had been palpable excitement in Charlottesville leading up to the game, and students camped out for over a week. The Terps were ranked third in the country, and Virginia was ranked eighth. The Wahoos led 83–74 with 3:22 left, which turned University Hall into a deafening den of support. But Maryland finished the game on a 13–2 run. The Terps ended up with a 91–87 win, and UVA never recovered. In the postgame press conference, Maryland guard Juan Dixon mentioned that Watson and Jenifer had drawn the ire of the Terp players by trash-talking Maryland coach Gary Williams during a late timeout. "I guess they wanted to show off a little bit," Dixon said. "We wanted to protect our coach and we allowed that to motivate us and took it from there."

The month and a half following Virginia's loss to Maryland was disheartening. Virginia limped to a 3–6 finish in the regular season and dropped an ACC Tournament quarterfinal game to N.C. State by 20 points. Many had felt that Virginia needed to beat N.C. State to make the NCAA Tournament. The fact that the Cavaliers got blown out led to a number of questions about the team's commitment to winning.

Virginia's fall from grace was complete when it was left out of the NCAA Tournament and relegated to the NIT. In just six weeks, UVA had fallen from a No. 7 ranking and 14–2 record to 17–11 and on the wrong side of the bubble. For the first time in his tenure, questions arose about Gillen's leadership.

In a season of weird moments, Gillen provided one last head-scratcher after Virginia's NIT loss to South Carolina. The Gamecocks overcame a first-half deficit, outscoring Virginia 47–34 in the second half en route to a 74–67 win. Afterward, Gillen picked up the U-Hall microphone to thank fans for their support during the season. He promised that Virginia would be "even better" next year. It was an off-key message from the soon-to-be-embattled head coach. Gillen coached three more seasons before resigning.

78 2014 Victory Against Pitt

When the Virginia basketball team traveled to the University of Pittsburgh on Super Bowl Sunday in 2014, it was its first trip there since December 5, 1976. Additionally, it was the first matchup between the two teams as conference foes in the expanded ACC. Pittsburgh, along with Syracuse and Notre Dame, joined the conference in the summer of 2013. The Cavaliers, unranked at the time, were 7–1 in the ACC and riding a five-game win streak. All seven of their conference victories were by at least 10 points, and their lone blemish was a close, four-point loss to Duke at Cameron Indoor Stadium. Jamie Dixon's Pitt squad came into the game ranked 18th and just one spot behind Virginia with a 6–2 ACC record.

Pitt's home venue, the Petersen Events Center, is located in the Oakland, Pennsylvania, neighborhood and was a safe haven for the Panthers. In 24 seasons Pittsburgh had only lost a total of 12 times in their arena. Dubbed the Oakland Zoo, the student section has a reputation of being loud and rowdy. A sold-out crowd of 12,508 was on hand for the 12:30 game, which was also broadcast nationally on ESPNU. Spectators expected a defensive matchup as Virginia entered the game ranked No. 1 in the country in limiting opponents to just 56 points per game. Defense is exactly what they got.

Both teams struggled offensively in the first half, and the score was tied at just eight points apiece until Virginia's Joe Harris hit a three pointer with 8:41 left to give the Hoos an 11–8 lead. Virginia trailed Pittsburgh by just two points 23–21 at the half. Sophomore Malcolm Brogdon scored seven points, and the Cavaliers got another six points from junior Akil Mitchell in the first half while limiting Pitt's leading scorer, Lamar Patterson, to just four points. Although the Cavaliers were struggling offensively, Virginia head coach Tony Bennett was happy with his team's defensive performance. "I love this," Bennett told his team at halftime.

The second half was more of the same defensive rock fight between the two teams. With 18:47 left two free throws by Pitt's Jamel Artis would give the Panthers a 25–21 lead, matching their largest lead in the game. Both teams battled back and forth in a half that featured nine ties and three lead changes. At one point with the score tied at 41 and 6:54 remaining, Pitt's Cameron Wright dribbled the ball around the top of the three-point arc as Harris hounded him mercilessly. Seeing the shot clock dwindle, Wright heaved the ball toward the basket, banking in the three-pointer that gave his team a three-point lead and sent the fans into a frenzy.

Free throws from each team over the next six minutes knotted the score at 45. Pitt's James Robinson attempted a three-pointer with 18 seconds remaining in the game, but he missed off the rim. His teammate, Jamel Artis, was able to corral the rebound, but his putback attempt rimmed out, and Virginia's Anthony Gill grabbed the defensive rebound. Bennett called timeout with 9.1 seconds left to draw up a play to give Virginia a shot at the win on the road.

Freshman point guard London Perrantes brought the ball down court as the seconds slowly ticked down. A series of screens

Malcolm Brogdon's teammates swarm him to celebrate his last-second three-pointer to defeat Pitt on the road in 2014.

released Harris, Virginia's leading scorer and best three-point shooter, but Perrantes instead found Brogdon on the arc. With just one tenth of a second left on the clock, Brogdon buried the shot, shocking and silencing the stunned crowd. Virginia's bench and small contingent of fans celebrated as Brogdon, grinning ear to ear, backpedaled down the court with his knees high to his chest and arms outstretched.

Brogdon led all scorers with 16 points, none more memorable than the last three. Following the game, as Brogdon spoke to reporters in the underbelly of the Petersen Event Center, Perrantes decided to give his teammate a hard time about the moments following his big shot. "Tell them what you said," Perrantes told Brogdon. "Tell them what you said when you ran back after you made it." Brogdon flashed another of his broad smiles, looking slightly embarrassed: "What'd I say? I said a couple things."

"You said, 'I've never done this before!'" Perrantes replied.

As Brogdon laughed at his teammate, he nodded, saying, "I did. It was shocking."

The game-winner was Brogdon's first on any level, and he achieved it in a game where points were hard to come by due to two hard-nosed defenses. "It was tough," Mitchell said after the game. "That's what we wanted. That was a lot of fun. It was fun to see a team defend us the way that we would probably defend ourselves. That's Coach Bennett. That's Jamie Dixon."

79 Al Groh

Al Groh had a tall order when he arrived in Charlottesville in 2001 to lead the Cavaliers. Unlike the previous football coaches before him, Groh wasn't hired to turn a program around. Instead, he was following in the footsteps of George Welsh, who had taken Virginia to heights never before matched. Groh's job was to bring Virginia football to the next level.

Groh, who had played for Virginia as a defensive end from 1963–65, certainly had the pedigree for it, having been the head coach for the New York Jets in 2000 and an assistant coach for various NFL teams since 1987. In that year he had made the move from college football, where he was head coach of Wake Forest, to the pros. As head coach of the Jets, Groh had a 9–7 record.

Upon Groh's arrival in Virginia, the Cavaliers were coming off what was considered to be a down year under Welsh, a 6–6 season that had resulted in an Oahu Bowl loss to No. 24 Georgia. Though he failed to reach a bowl game in his first year, Groh's 5–7 rookie campaign as Virginia head coach saw wins against ranked Clemson and Georgia Tech teams that gave Virginia fans reason for hope in the future.

Groh's second year featured a schedule ranked as the 11th toughest in the nation by *USA TODAY*'s Sagarin rating. Behind the hands of wide receiver Billy McMullen and the split quarterbacking duties of Matt Schaub and Bryson Spinner, Virginia marched their way to a 9–5, (6–2 ACC) record with a Continental Tire Bowl win against No. 15 West Virginia and a final AP poll ranking of 22. Groh was named the ACC Coach of the Year for the first time.

For a while Groh continued his success in Charlottesville, recording an 8–5 season in 2003, 8–4 in 2004, and 7–5 in 2005, reaching a bowl game each year. During this stretch the Cavaliers were ranked as high as No. 6 in the country and in 2005 defeated No. 4 Florida State as an unranked team. Performance dropped the following year with a 5–7 finish, causing Groh's coaching seat to begin warming up. Behind All-American Chris Long in 2007, Groh led the Cavaliers to a 9–4, (5–2 ACC) campaign that had the Cavaliers playing for a Coastal Division title and a trip to the Gator Bowl. That year Virginia won an NCAA-record five games by just two points or less, earning Groh his second ACC Coach of the Year honor.

The program took a steep decline in Groh's final two seasons. In 2008 Virginia fell to 5–7, including a 31–3 loss to Duke, a program that had just snapped a 22-game losing streak one year prior. Throughout the 2008 season, and to some degree even during the 2007 season, which many viewed as "lucky," the students were not shy in expressing their displeasure over the state of the school's football program. Signs and chants became commonplace in Scott Stadium on gameday with a common message: "Groh must go."

The negativity became so rampant that the athletics administration banned all signs and posters from the stadium for a period in an attempt to create a more enjoyable game experience. The irony of banning signs at the university founded by Thomas Jefferson was not lost on the students, and protests led to the ban being removed at midseason.

In 2009 the Cavaliers plummeted even further, falling to 3–9 overall with a last-place finish in the ACC's Coastal Division. Following a loss to William & Mary to open the season and his eighth loss to rival Virginia Tech over his nine-year run, Groh was dismissed.

Behind only legendary George Welsh, Groh's nine years at the helm were the second-longest tenure of any Virginia head coach, matching Frank Murray, who went 41–34 (.544) during his nine years. Groh finished with a 59–53 (.528) record at Virginia, making him the fourth winningest coach in Virginia history, among those who coached for more than two years.

Groh's legacy at Virginia, however, extends well beyond just the coaching wins and losses. Groh, whose vision for the university's football program was to bring it to the national championship, believed that in order to be a big-time football program Virginia needed to act like a big-time state school as the flagship of the Commonwealth. As part of this vision, Groh instituted the "Sea of Orange," replacing Virginia's tradition of dressing up formally for football games with wearing unified school colors.

Having coached in the NFL for 13 years for five different teams, Groh had developed a reputation of having a strong NFL pipeline, opening his practices to scouts and NFL executives while closing them off to media. His connections with the pros meant that, despite mediocre team performances at Virginia, a player who excelled in his position could still have an opportunity to get selected in the NFL draft, and nearly 70 players who had played under Groh went on to join an NFL team, including multiple first-round selections.

Following his final game against Virginia Tech in 2009, Groh, knowing his fate, opened his postgame press conference with a version of the poem titled "The Guy in the Glass." The poem's message—that at the end of the day, the only verdict that matters is the one of the person staring back at you in the mirror—resonated with Groh, who said that, "When I visited the guy in the glass, I saw that he's a guy of commitment, of integrity, of dependability, and accountability. He's loyal. His spirit is indomitable. And he is caring and loving. I'm sure I will always call the guy in the glass a friend."

80 Jim Dombrowski

Virginia's greatest offensive tackle, a 6'5", 295-pound native of Williamsville, New York, never really had aspirations of a career in athletics. Jim Dombrowski, a 1986 graduate, played hockey first and foremost, calling it his first love. At some point he realized he was actually pretty good at football, too. By the time he was a senior, he was playing all aspects of the game as a member of both the offensive and defensive lines as well as the team's kicker and punter. He was named an Adidas All-American in football his senior year.

Recruited by then-head coach Dick Bestwick, Dombrowski came to Virginia with the intent of playing football but ultimately becoming an orthopedic surgeon. It wasn't until his junior year, he recalled to *Virginia Magazine*, after seeing some of his opponents get drafted fairly high in the NFL draft, that he realized, "Maybe I can do this as a career."

Though Bestwick recruited Dombrowski, George Welsh had been hired as head coach when the star lineman came on board. Dombroski, together with Welsh, quarterback Don Majkowski, and others, helped turn around a program that had spent decades at the bottom of the ACC standings. During his four years at Virginia from 1982 to 1985, Dombrowski, whose background in hockey as a goalie gave him the skillset he needed to excel on the offensive line due to the knee-bending positions and quick footwork required, became one of the best tackles Virginia ever had.

For his efforts Dombrowski received the Jacobs Blocking Trophy in 1984 and again in 1985 for being the ACC's best blocker. He was a two-time, first-team All-ACC selection and was also the university's first ever unanimous first-team All-American in 1985. For all of his athletic accolades, Dombrowski, a biology major, didn't let his academics drop. He was the first recipient of the university's Ralph Sampson Award, annually given to the third-year athlete best exhibiting academic excellence combined with superior athletic performance.

In 1986 the New Orleans Saints selected Dombrowski as the sixth overall pick in the draft, and he spent the entirety of his 11-year professional career with the Saints. Though he played in only three games his rookie season, he became a starter for them in 1987 and appeared in a Saints-record 147 consecutive games before retiring in 1996.

His No. 73 jersey was just the fifth number to be retired at Virginia. In 2002 he was selected to the ACC's 50th Anniversary Team. In 2008 Dombrowski was elected to the College Football Hall of Fame as part of the class that included Troy Aikman, Wilber Marshall, and Jay Novacek. "You look at the list of names on that, and it's like, 'Geez, those guys are good,'" Dombrowski told *Virginia Magazine*. "Probably the least recognizable is the offensive tackle from Virginia."

Of his many memories at Virginia, one that stands out in particular was Virginia's 1984 Peach Bowl win, the first bowl Virginia had ever appeared in. "That was a big part of my career in helping take the school to its first bowl game," he told the *Daily Progress* in 2002. "I still have vivid memories of returning to the team hotel in Atlanta after the game, and there were people on the balconies all the way up inside the hotel. It was one big party."

81 Join the Sea of Orange

"Guys in ties, girls in pearls." That was the old adage used to describe the football game attire of UVA undergrads. Virginia, a school of southern belles and gentlemen, had a tradition of fans, students, and alumni alike, dressing up for football games, similar to Southeastern Conference counterparts Ole Miss and Vanderbilt.

Until the 2003 season, that is. Following a surprisingly successful year in 2002, the expectations for the 2003 team were high and with the expectations came increased excitement from the Cavaliers fanbase. There was also an underlying feeling that Virginia could be turning into a football school, and the idea of creating a "Sea of Orange" among the 60,000 fans in Scott Stadium was something head coach Al Groh was pushing hard. The thought was that the Sea of Orange would be a visibly imposing sight to visiting teams.

Many fans embraced the change, but much like most things at a tradition-rich institution like UVA, there was significant resistance. Opponents to the Sea of Orange hung on to tradition and pointed to rabid fanbases in the SEC where many of their students still wear shirts and ties to games. Proponents of the Sea of Orange argue that the tradition of wearing a coat and tie to football games was rooted in the fact that up until the arrival of George Welsh in 1982, Virginia's football was so terrible that football games were social events where dressing up would be appropriate. Those proponents thought dressing up for a football game was indicative of overall apathy toward what was happening on the field.

Many Virginia fans found a happy medium that has allowed the Sea of Orange to be embraced by the fanbase at large. Today, women oftentimes seek out orange sundresses while men will opt for a bright orange dress shirt or even an orange blazer so they can sport the best of both worlds, though the majority of male students have embraced their orange T-shirt mentality. As attendance in Scott Stadium soared under the peak years of the Groh era, the program looked to be on the verge of becoming the flagship program that the athletics administration under Groh had envisioned.

82 Virginia Stuns South Carolina

Six years into play at University Hall, the Virginia basketball team had a chance to do something special on January 11, 1971. Against No. 2 South Carolina and legendary coach Frank McGuire, the unranked Wahoos looked to take down a team that was the class of the Atlantic Coast Conference at the time. During a season that would see South Carolina advance to the Sweet 16 of the NCAA Tournament, the Gamecocks went to University Hall that chilly night with a record of 10–2, and their two losses had come on the road to North Carolina and Maryland.

Trailing 49–48 with a couple of minutes left, then-Virginia head coach Bill Gibson decided to take a page out of Dean Smith's playbook and hold on to the ball. In the days before the shot clock, teams could hold the ball for the last shot for a very long time or just run out the clock as long as they wished. Guard Barry Parkhill had yet to be named to an All-ACC or All-American team and was actually in the first of his three years on the varsity team at UVA, as NCAA rules at the time required freshmen to play on freshman-only teams. Gibson placed his trust in his young star, and Parkhill dribbled out the clock for several minutes. With less than 10 seconds to go, Parkhill drove inside from the right elbow and hit a running jumper from the baseline to give the Cavaliers a 50–49 lead. "Based on the rules at the time, there was no five-second clock," Parkhill said in 2006. "We shortened the game over the period of 40 minutes; over one stretch I dribbled six minutes off the clock. We got the ball back with, I want to say, two minutes to go or a minute and a half. Coach just decided, 'Let's go for the last shot,' and it went in."

Four seconds remained on the clock, and the Gamecocks had one last chance to steal the win away. After a Hail Mary-style inbounds pass, a long-range shot for the win was too strong and bounced harmlessly into the hands of a Virginia player to end the game. Pandemonium erupted as students and fans rushed the court in celebration of the first historically significant win at U-Hall.

The win represented more than just an isolated upset over a highly ranked conference foe. It lifted the Cavaliers to an overall 9–2 record (3–1 ACC), and with wins against Wake Forest and Georgia Tech over the course of that week, it helped set the stage for something unprecedented. For the first time in the 23-year history of the Associated Press poll, the Cavaliers were ranked. In the January 19 edition of what was then known as the Top 20, UVA was ranked No. 19. A week off saw Virginia rise to No. 15 before dropping out on February 2 after losses at Clemson and in the rematch against South Carolina.

Even though Virginia finished the 1970–71 regular season on a six-game losing streak, a win against North Carolina State in early February ensured the first winning season for the Cavaliers basketball program since 1954. Although none of Gibson's teams reached the NCAA Tournament in his 11 seasons, the latter part of his tenure helped set the stage for the first glory days of UVA basketball.

83 Pop Lannigan Founds UVA Basketball

Virginia basketball is undefeated against the Charlottesville YMCA, winning by a combined score of 142–51 for a perfect 5–0 record. There's no significance to this, of course, but it shows that when Virginia basketball was founded as one of the first basketball programs among major universities in the South in the fall of 1905 that the pickings were slim in terms of creating a formidable schedule.

Henry "Pop" Lannigan was hired by the university in 1905 as an associate athletics director and full-time trainer. Though he was initially the first coach for the University's track and field team, there weren't very many sports then that Lannigan *didn't* play a role in. In addition to coaching track and field and baseball, Lannigan, described as "the life and spirit of University of Virginia athletics," also started boxing and basketball programs for the university.

In its inaugural season, the Cavaliers, as they would eventually be called, went 8–2. Six of the 10 games were against YMCA squads, and in fact, Virginia played the Charlottesville YMCA team three times that season. Virginia's first basketball game was January

18, 1906, a 30–9 victory against Charlottesville YMCA at the Monticello Guard Armory, though most of the Virginia basketball games would be played in the university's first basketball arena, Fayerweather Gymnasium. The first season included wins against Washington & Lee and William & Mary as well.

During his 24-season tenure at the university, Lannigan amassed an impressive 254–95–1 record, a .726 winning record. Lannigan remains the university's longest tenured basketball coach and still holds the highest win percentage, though the record books still await current head coach Tony Bennett's contributions. In fact, Lannigan accomplished what no other Virginia head coach has been able to replicate: a perfect, undefeated season. Lannigan's 1915 team featured what the university refers to as the "Famous Five"—Wellington Stickley, Bill Nickels Jr., John Luck, Bill Strickling, and Andrew Dittrich. The season included pairs of wins against George Washington, North Carolina, Duke, and Virginia Tech, among others. Only twice—North Carolina (30–29 in overtime) at home and Catholic (29–28) on the road—did the opposing team finish within five points of the Cavaliers. Virginia finished 16–0 on the season in an era without any national champion designations.

84 Visit Lambeth Field

Behind a set of upperclassmen dorms at the university lies a field with amphitheater-style seating and beautiful colonnades adorning the background. Known as Lambeth Field, this field was named after Dr. William Lambeth, the "Father of Athletics" at Virginia. In addition to playing a monumental role in reforming the game of football to improve player safety and increase parity across programs, Lambeth, the university's first athletic director, oversaw the establishment of a football program at Virginia that became an elite powerhouse not just in the South—but nationally as well.

Supporting the powerhouse football program—and a successful overall athletics program—would require strong facilities. In 1901 on a 21-acre plot of land, construction began on what would become known as "Lambeth Field," which was previously part of the Rugby Dairy Farm. Lambeth Field would become home to the university's football, baseball, and track and field programs. The facility itself was built in multiple phases and was ultimately completed in 1913.

Though not fully finished, Lambeth Field opened in 1902 for its first athletic competition. By its completion in 1913, Lambeth had replaced the stadium's original wooden bleachers with what stands today—a classically designed, 8,000-seat stadium arcing around the field with Virginia's signature colonnades overhead. In all the facility cost about $50,000. In 2015 dollars this comes out to approximately $1.25 million. Fans were encouraged to attend the games in wagons and horse-and-buggies to enjoy the sport.

The first game in the fully completed stadium in 1913 featured the "Football Classic of the South," a contest between Virginia and Vanderbilt that resulted in a commanding 34–0 win for Virginia. Tickets were $7.50 for students and $9.50 for alumni. Virginia went 7–1 in 1913, outscoring its opponents by an aggregate score of 265–28 with its only loss coming to Georgetown 8–7.

By 1930 with all three sports playing or practicing simultaneously at Lambeth, it became clear that the university had outgrown the space. When football players complained that errant javelin and discus throws were getting dangerously close to them, plans were put in place to build a new stadium. By the fall of 1931, Scott Stadium opened with a capacity of 25,000.

Today, Lambeth Field is still behind Lambeth Housing for upper-class students and is used as an open playing field for recreational and intramural sports. To commemorate the 100th anniversary of the completion of Lambeth Stadium and its grand opening, a plaque was dedicated at Lambeth Field in 2013 in memory of Dr. William Lambeth. The plaque was unanimously approved by the university's Board of Visitors and was largely funded by Kevin Edds, a 1995 graduate of the university and writer and director of the film *Wahoowa: The History of Virginia Football.*

85 Yusef Jackson

He is Yusef Jackson, the son of the Jesse Jackson, the reverend who ran for president of the United States in 1988. But he wanted to be Yusef Jackson, standout football player.

A bit of a late bloomer, Jackson went from being 5'8" and 140 pounds as a high school freshman to 6'3" and 215 pounds by the time he was a senior making decisions about college. Though, like many other high school players bound for college football, he played on both sides of the ball, he excelled at linebacker, registering an average of 12 tackles per game during his senior season at St. Albans in Washington, D.C. His college recruitment included offers from Virginia, Richmond, Rutgers, and William & Mary, among others, declining offers to visit major programs like Wake Forest, Duke, and Syracuse, according to his high school coach.

When Jackson arrived on Grounds in August of 1988, he made his intentions known from the beginning that he only wanted to be known as a freshman linebacker for the university—not a distraction for the team because of his father's political ambitions. At media day Virginia promised reporters an hour of Yusef Jackson's time, and in an article by the *Chicago Tribune*, it was reported that as many as a dozen reporters showed up at his interview tent, though it was unlikely that Jackson would see any playing time that year. Indeed, under guidance from his father and coaches, he ended up taking a redshirt year as a freshman to learn the system.

Instead of the hour, Jackson informed the reporters that he would only answer questions for 10 minutes. In hindsight, the reporters did not use their time wisely. They asked questions about Rev. Jackson's "Keep Hope Alive" speech. They asked questions about riding the Rainbow Express from Chicago to Atlanta, a parade of seven chartered buses representing Jackson's presidential campaign. They asked questions about his father making history. The younger Jackson declined these questions. "I'm very proud of my father," the *Chicago Tribune* quoted Jackson, "but I'm going to have to make my own way here and on the football field. That's the way it should be."

Immediately following the limited interview, he spent the rest of the hour in the bleachers with the rest of the freshmen, eager to show his teammates—and the upperclassmen—that he had no interest in displaying an ego based on his last name. And so began Jackson's collegiate football career. Virginia assistant coach Ken Mack had complimented his game, describing him as "very intense, very physical." By the time he was a sophomore, Jackson had gone from playing on the fourth team his redshirt year to starting linebacker for the No. 1 Virginia Cavaliers.

Through seven games heading into that fateful 1990 contest with 6–1 Georgia Tech, Jackson was fifth on the team with 26 tackles despite missing two games that season. Jackson's father was proudly in the stands that day rooting for his son, though he wasn't the only famous father that night. Several of Jackson's teammates had familiar last names: receiver Derek Dooley was the son of Georgia coach Vince Dooley; center Bill Curry Jr. was the son of Kentucky coach Bill Curry, defensive back Scott Griese was the son of Hall of Famer Bob Griese, and Rickie Peete was the son of golfer Calvin Peete. Interestingly, Jackson was the only one of the group on scholarship at Virginia; the remaining members of the star-studded lineage were walk-ons.

Jackson would go on to graduate from the University of Virginia School of Law in 1996.

86 Virginia's First Scholarship

In today's world of corporate bowl game sponsorships, media rights, College Football Playoffs, and other influxes of cash that remind us just how much of a golden goose college football is, it can be hard to think of a time when the major football programs, including Virginia, were unwilling or unable to award scholarships for football players. Just as today's debates revolve around the question of whether schools should be permitted to pay collegiate student-athletes, the same was true in the early to mid-1900s.

With Virginia coming off of a 4–3–2 season in 1929 and a 4–6 season in 1930, the athletics program, particularly football, looked abysmal. Virginia's first official athletic director, Jim Driver, described Virginia's athletes as lacking "the will to win and the will to give and take punishment." In 1930 Driver hired Fred Dawson, the former Nebraska coach who brought relevancy to Nebraska with a 23–7–2 record from 1921 to 1924, to turn the Virginia program around.

Despite Scott Stadium opening on October 15, 1931, with a reenergized crowd at hand, Dawson was unable to bring the attention to Virginia that everyone had hoped, finishing with just one winning season in three years, leading to his resignation. "I am convinced that at Virginia," he said when seeking to resign, "where there are no athletic scholarships that bring in football players, the football coach is under a great handicap; so great, in fact, that I am content to step aside and see what someone else can do." His successor, Gus Tebell, was equally unsuccessful, going 6–18–4 over the next three seasons.

Virginia brought in Norton G. Pritchett to take over as athletic director in 1935. Pritchett, full of enthusiasm and determination, refused to allow Virginia to dwell at the bottom of the Southern Conference. Many placed the blame for the football program's failures on the fact that Virginia did not award scholarships. Although students were generally in favor of awarding athletic scholarships to football players, the university's Board of Visitors resisted. Finally, a group of alumni out of Richmond proposed a plan for athletic scholarships to the board, a plan that would require Virginia to leave the Southern Conference, which did not permit academic scholarships at the time.

Pritchett knew that with a stunning football facility, a strong academic foundation, and a potential among the fanbase for passion, he would need the ability for a coach to hand out scholarships if he was to attract the best available coach. In 1937 Pritchett

First Woman on Athletic Scholarship

Though the first scholarship was awarded to football tackle Lee McLaughlin in 1937, it wouldn't be until 1977 that Virginia would award its first scholarship to a female recipient, Margaret Groos, a standout cross country runner. During Groos's time at Virginia, she won the cross country national championship in 1979. In 1981 she set the world record for indoor 5,000-meter run with a time of 15:34.71, a time that still stands atop Virginia's records.

Groos also holds the current Virginia record for the outdoor 5,000-meter run at 15:51.24. She was named a two-time All-American in cross country (1978, 1979) and an All-American in the 1,500-meter outdoor run.

convinced the Board of Visitors to leave the Southern Conference, and the Cavaliers were in business.

Pritchett then hired the "Pigskin Magician," Frank Murray, who had coached Marquette for 15 years and accumulated a 90–32–6 record during his time there. The two of them offered the university's first scholarship to Lee McLaughlin at tackle, who certainly earned the right.

At Virginia, McLaughlin would ultimately serve as captain not only of the football team, but also the track team. He would go on to be drafted by the Green Bay Packers, where he played for a year, starting all eight games, before leaving to fight in World War II. Eventually, McLaughlin would become the head coach at Washington & Lee University, where he coached a team to the National Small-College Championship and was named the National College Coach of the Year in the same season.

Bill Dudley, McLaughlin's teammate while at Virginia, said of McLaughlin, "Lee was one of the finest guys I have ever known and one heck of a football player." McLaughlin was inducted in the Virginia Sports Hall of Fame in 1987 and received the *Sports Illustrated* Silver Anniversary Award.

87 Beta and Seal

While not on the level of Georgia's Uga or Texas A&M's Reveille, two dogs became well-known around Grounds to the point of legend status in the mid-20th century. Their names were Beta and Seal. Beta was a black-and-white mongrel named after the Beta Theta Pi fraternity house where he lived after showing up on its front porch one day in the 1920s.

The stories say that while sitting in on a course on Plato at Cabell Hall, his name was even called out in the roll, and he barked in response. However, the most famous story related to Beta came after a football game on the road at Georgia. Inexplicably, Beta was left behind in Athens. Presumed lost, Beta was never expected to return to Grounds. Instead, two weeks later the brothers of Beta Theta Pi allegedly heard a scratching at the door and opened it to find none other than the school dog, cold and haggard. To this day it is not known how Beta returned to Charlottesville.

After being involved in a car accident on April 6, 1939, Beta was euthanized. He left Beta House in a hearse to the University Cemetery, not far from the corner of Alderman and McCormick Roads, where he was laid to rest with 1,000 people in attendance.

Seal was a black mutt known for being cross-eyed. Like his predecessor, Seal was routinely allowed to attend lectures on Grounds, during which he was known to take a nap and was the only dog allowed in many restaurants around town. Perhaps the single most famous moment for any of the UVA dogs came from Seal in 1949 during a football game at Pennsylvania. He walked from the 50-yard line, wearing an orange-and-blue-blanket, over to the section where the Penn cheerleaders were. As *The Cavalier Daily* put it at the time, "Slowly he walked from midfield to the Quaker side. Indifferently he inspected their cheerleading appurtenances. Eighty thousand people watched with bated breath. Coolly, insolently, Seal lifted a leg—the rest is history."

That episode garnered him the nickname "Caninus Megaphonus Pennsylvanus." Longtime football team physician Dr. Charles Frankel often took care of Seal, as did several fraternities and the university cafeteria.

Old age and injury weakened "the Great Seal of Virginia," who was put to sleep in December 1953 at the University Hospital. An estimated crowd of 2,000 attended his funeral, held at the University Cemetery. Frankel gave the eulogy. "I know of no other individual at the university or animal who could attract as many mourners to his funeral. Of course, none of us had ever had the same opportunity with a megaphone," Frankel said.

88 Roger Mason Jr.

It seemed as though the heyday of Virginia basketball had all but passed by the time that shooting guard Roger Mason Jr., a top-50 basketball recruit coming out of high school, came on Grounds as a freshman in 1999. The final three years of Jeff Jones' coaching career at Virginia were met with a 12–15 record in 1995–96 and an even worse 11–19 record in 1997–98. Head coach Pete Gillen was brought in for the 1998 season and had taken the Cavaliers to a 14–16 record in his first rebuilding year.

Still, Mason joined a strong 1999 recruiting class of Majestic Mapp, who was a McDonald's All-American and ranked as a top 25 high school recruit, and Travis Watson, who was a *Parade* All-American and a top 30 high school recruit. Virginia appeared to be set up for the near future with a deep bench that could withstand the natural turnovers of college basketball.

In Mason's first season in 1999–00, the Cavaliers finished with a 19–12, (9–7 ACC) record that left them just shy of an NCAA Tournament bid. Instead, Virginia fell in the first round of the NIT, losing to Georgetown 115–111 in triple overtime. During his freshman year, Mason averaged 7.6 points per game, played in all 31 games, and started in 11 of them.

Excitement for Virginia basketball grew again for the 2000–01 season. Virginia went 20–9, (9–7 ACC) locking up an NCAA Tournament bid as the No. 16 team in the country. Again,

Virginia would have a first-round postseason exit, falling 86–85 in a heartbreaker to Gonzaga despite Mason's career-high 30 points that game. Spending time at both shooting guard and point guard after teammate Mapp went down with a torn ACL, Mason had a

Roger Mason Jr., who led the Cavaliers in scoring during 2000–01, drives past Georgia Tech guard B.J. Elder during that season.

breakthrough sophomore season, starting in 28 of the 29 games and averaging a team-high 15.7 points per game. Notably, Mason shot 88.4 percent from the free-throw line, leading the conference and setting a Virginia record that still stands today. He earned third-team All-ACC honors that year.

Though Virginia would fall to a 17–12, 7–9 ACC record his junior year, Mason continued to improve, picking up an average of 18.6 points and 4.1 assists per game, and many advised him that he would be a top 15 NBA draft pick that year if he declared early. Unfortunately for Mason, a late-season shoulder injury that was re-aggravated during his first workout after declaring for the 2002 NBA Draft caused him to slip into the second round. Mason was drafted 31st overall by the Chicago Bulls.

Mason's time with Chicago was short-lived as he was traded to the Toronto Raptors a year later and waived by the Raptors a year after that. Mason spent a few years playing internationally before returning to the NBA in 2006 to play for the Washington Wizards.

During his 10-year NBA career, Mason played for seven different teams. He retired in 2014 and now serves as deputy executive director of the National Basketball Players Association.

89 Super Bowl Sunday Against Ohio State

Ralph Sampson had plenty of individual highlights over his four years in Charlottesville from 1979 to 1983, but one of his finest came on January 25, 1981. It was Super Bowl Sunday, and in the days before eight-hour-long pregame shows for the big game, there was a regular lead-in for the game. Ahead of Super Bowl XV, the

Cavaliers played against Ohio State in front of a national audience on NBC, their first game played on live national television.

With a sellout crowd on hand at University Hall on a relatively warm Central Virginia day, Sampson outright dominated the Clark Kellogg-led Buckeyes, scoring 40 points while picking up three blocks and 16 rebounds in 35 minutes of action as UVA led 44–29 at halftime and won 89–73. The win moved Virginia to 16–0 on the season, the latest win in what would end up as a 23-game winning streak to start that remarkable year.

A mild ankle injury sidelined Sampson for three-and-a-half minutes in the first half, but that didn't stop him from establishing a career-high mark for points, one that would stand throughout his entire career. And he still scored 14 points in the first half despite missing time with the injury. "That's as well as I've seen him play in the first half. He has shown a remarkable ability to play on that ankle," Virginia coach Terry Holland said. "He realizes a player who's as important to us as he is has to be ready to play."

Sampson was a rebound shy of earning a double-double before halftime. "It was one of my better games, I'd say. I felt like I could be devastating from the beginning," Sampson said.

Sampson's 40 points would stand as the second most scored by one player at University Hall until Donald Hand scored 41 in 1999. Jeff Lamp also scored in double figures for Virginia with 11 points on 4-of-9 shooting and 3-of-8 from the line against Ohio State that night. Two days after the game, Virginia would achieve a No. 1 ranking in the polls for the first time in program history.

90 Thomas Jones

When running back Thomas Jones committed to play football for the University of Virginia beginning the fall of 1996, it was a good time to be a Cavalier. Under head coach George Welsh's leadership, Virginia was at the peak of its program, winning an ACC co-championship and the Peach Bowl in 1995. Prior to Jones' arrival, Virginia had just made three consecutive bowl games and six in the previous seven years. Jones looked to build on this.

In his freshman season, Jones witnessed and learned from fellow running back Tiki Barber, who was then in his senior season and en route to set the Virginia career rushing record at 3,389 yards that season. Where Barber left off upon graduation, though, Jones picked up. Barber had 1,397 rushing yards his junior year in 1995 and an ACC-best 1,360 yards his senior year. Jones followed suit. In 1998, his junior season, Jones led the team and the ACC with 1,303 yards and in 1999 he again led the team and conference with a whopping 1,798 rushing yards, good for third in the nation, while setting the school record for most rushing yards in a single season. That record still stands today.

Jones would go on to earn first-team All-American honors from the Associated Press, Football News, Football Writers Association of America, Walter Camp Foundation, and *The Sporting News*. He finished eighth in the 1999 Heisman Trophy voting and was just the third ACC running back ever to become a consensus All-American. Jones eclipsed Barber's career rushing record, putting up a total of 3,998 yards, which still stands atop Virginia's annals today.

Whereas some athletes coming out of high school say that they picked Virginia not just because of its athletics program, but also for its academics, Jones delivered on this, graduating in only three years with a psychology degree. "UVA is a very special place and a very special school," he said in a *UVA Today* piece. "There's a lot of positive energy there. It's one of those schools where you can think and grow freely. You can be yourself. I think a lot of other universities are more structured, but UVA says, 'Hey, be you and be great.'"

The Arizona Cardinals selected Jones in the first round as the seventh overall pick of the 2000 NFL Draft. He spent three years in Arizona before being traded to the Tampa Bay Buccaneers for a year. He eventually signed a contract with the Chicago Bears as a featured back in 2004 until 2006 and played in Super Bowl XLI. He then spent three seasons with the New York Jets and another two with the Kansas City Chiefs before retiring in 2011. While with Kansas City, he became only the 25th player in NFL history to reach the 10,000-yard rushing club.

His retirement didn't mean, however, that Jones would fade into the background. Instead, Jones transitioned to being an actor, playing a role in the hit BET show *Being Mary Jane* and later playing a bodyguard in *Straight Outta Compton*, among other shows along the way. He is also producing a multi-part series titled *The NFL: The Gift or the Curse?* which places the spotlight on concussions in the league, something that has long been an area of interest for Jones. In 2012 Jones announced that he would be donating his own brain to the Sports Legacy Institute upon his death in hopes that would help the institute's research on sports and brain trauma.

Even after his 12 years in the NFL and ongoing acting career, Jones looks back most fondly on his time at Virginia. "I have more fond memories of Charlottesville than from anywhere, whether it be the NFL, where my acting has taken me, etc.," Jones said in an article in *Virginia Magazine*. "UVA was the start of the evolution process for me. There's something special about Charlottesville."

91 Travis Watson

Virginia head coach Pete Gillen's first recruiting class at Virginia, the 1999 class, was a monster. It featured three top 50 recruits in McDonald's All-American Majestic Mapp, shooting guard Roger Mason Jr., who had averaged 22 points as a high school senior, and *Parade* third-team All-American Travis Watson.

The 6'7" power forward who largely played as a center, Watson had made an immediate impact on a Cavaliers squad that had just finished 14–16, (4–12 ACC) the year before. Of the three prime recruits, Watson was the only one to be a consistent starter as a freshman, starting 30 of the 31 games that season despite being the shortest center in the ACC. As a freshman Watson averaged 11.4 points and 8.3 rebounds per game and for his efforts he was named to the ACC All-Freshman team. Virginia finished 19–12 that season with a 9–7 ACC record and ended up losing in triple overtime to Georgetown in the first round of the NIT.

Starting in all but one game due to a strained right hamstring, Watson's numbers continued to improve as a sophomore. He started 28 of 29 games, missing the start to Missouri on account of a strained right hamstring. Still, Watson provided 16 points and 10 rebounds in 27 minutes in his only game coming off the bench. He points and rebounds continued to improve his junior and senior years. By his senior season, he was averaging double-double figures with 14.3 points and 10.4 rebounds per game. By the time he graduated from Virginia, Watson had pulled in 54 double-doubles, the 12th most in ACC history.

Watson was named second-team All-ACC in each of his sophomore, junior, and senior seasons. He pulled down 1,115 rebounds over the course of his career behind only Ralph Sampson in the Virginia record book. He still holds the Virginia record for most career offensive rebounds at 381 and remains fourth on Virginia's all-time career rebounding average list. In both 2002 and 2003, Watson led the ACC in rebounds. He is also third among Virginia's all-time career blocked shots leaders at 130.

During Watson's time at Virginia, the Cavaliers were ranked as high as No. 7 his junior year and No. 4 his senior year—a far cry from the 14–16 record when he had first arrived in Charlottesville. After graduating from Virginia, Watson played in Europe and Israel for nine years, leading the Euroleague in—what else?—rebounding in 2007 and the Greek League in both 2004 and 2005.

92 The Father of Athletics at Virginia

It's not easy to try to pinpoint the single most important accomplishment of Dr. William Alexander Lambeth during his time at Virginia. As a student he earned both his MD and PhD from the university. He served on the faculty for *40 years*. He headed up the department of physical education, served as the superintendent of buildings and grounds, and was the university's first athletics director. Oh, and he completely revolutionized the game of college football.

Lambeth had dreams of building up a major college football powerhouse at a time when Virginia was already one of the strongest programs in the South—with a claim to being one of the elite nationwide. Lambeth became the driving force—and chief fund-raiser—for a new, 8,000-seat facility that would house Virginia football, baseball, and track and field, a facility known today as Lambeth Field.

His contributions to the world of athletics, however, extend well beyond the cozy confines of Charlottesville. He was active in the national athletics community, including serving as a member of the American Olympic Committee for the 1908 Games in Stockholm and as the treasurer of the NCAA. Lambeth also was a leader in establishing intercollegiate track rules, including eligibility guidelines later adopted by the NCAA. He was a driving force behind the creation of the Southern Conference, which Virginia, together with many of the modern-day ACC and SEC schools, joined.

These contributions alone are likely enough to last a lifetime for even the most influential athletics administrators today. But for Lambeth it's just the tip of the iceberg. In 1909 Virginia football player Archer Christian suffered severe head injuries as a result of getting trampled in a game against Georgetown that ultimately led to his death. Christian's death was one of dozens each year directly related to football, a game growing in violence without advancements in player safety. The incident made the front page of *The New York Times*, and public opinion began swaying towards the disbanding of football. West Virginia and at least five others had dismantled their programs.

This wasn't the first death for Virginia. In 1895 George Phelan, a law student, died in a game between "the Laws and the Meds." In 1897 a Georgia player died in a game against Virginia in Athens, Georgia. "I love football and believe in it and am not afraid to get up in public and say so," said Virginia president Edwin Alderman. "When played in the right way, it is a noble game."

Alderman appealed to the Inter-Collegiate Athletic Association—predecessor to the NCAA—to explore rules changes that could lead to a safer, more enjoyable game for all. Lambeth, who had been appointed to the ICAA's football rules committee in 1908, supported Alderman's appeals and led the charge from inside the committee. Opposing Lambeth was Walter Camp, effectively the head of the committee and known as the "Father of American Football" who had devised both the scoring system and the line of scrimmage instead of the rugby-style scrum. Camp was dedicated to the game he had helped to create and was reluctant to make drastic changes.

Eventually, through Alderman's well-documented and well-received appeals to the ICAA and Lambeth's intense research on the football-related deaths and his political savvy with Camp, changes were accepted and approved by the ICAA. Lambeth proposed a set of rules that would change the game from one of brute strength and dominance by the winning team to one of strategy, allowing smaller teams to outplay larger opponents. Instead of soccer-style player substitutions, where a player could not return to the game once substituted, Lambeth proposed to change the rules to permit multiple substitutions, allowing players to rest and recover between plays. He also proposed to require at least seven players along the line of scrimmage to prevent "mass momentum plays," banned players from pushing and pulling a ball carrier, and allowed forward passes to reach beyond the line of scrimmage. Notably, he also changed the game from two halves to four 15-minute quarters, which increased the amount of actual playing time while allowing more breaks for players to rest.

Camp took Lambeth's proposed rules under advisement and suggested to Lambeth that he test these proposed changes at the University of Virginia first. So, in 1910 during springtime scrimmages, the first games of modern football were played by Virginia at Lambeth Field.

Lambeth's reforms promoted parity among the nation's football teams, and the rules spread throughout both high school and professional football. The reforms were approved by the rules committee and put into place for the 1910 season. Lambeth complimented his fellow committee members for "preserving to the youth of America one of the most powerful and useful auxiliary [sic] forces in the educational system."

93 Dave Leitao

When University of Virginia athletic director Craig Littlepage announced Dave Leitao as the new Virginia basketball head coach for the 2005 to 2006 season, it wasn't difficult for fans to follow the line of thinking behind the hire. Whereas his predecessor, Pete Gillen, was compassionate, witty, and affable, Leitao, who coached under the legendary Jim Calhoun at Connecticut, had more of a reputation for being business-oriented, short-tempered, and stern. Whereas Gillen's teams had earned a reputation for being unruly with known issues off the court such as a DUI arrest, assault and battery charge, failure to meet Virginia's academic standards, and so forth, the Leitao regime held promises of discipline and structure above all else. "It's so important to do things in the proper way," he said. "You're not just representing yourself or the people around you or the basketball program. You're representing a university; you're representing a state."

Just prior to Leitao's arrival, the Cavaliers had finished the 2004–05 season at 14–15 overall and just 4–12 in the conference. In his first year, Leitao led the team behind captains J.R. Reynolds and Sean Singletary to a 15–15 overall record and a much-improved 7–9 ACC record, including wins against No. 24 North Carolina and No. 11 Boston College. Though they were picked to finish last in the league during the preseason, Virginia finished seventh. The Cavaliers fell 65–49 in the first round of the NIT to Stanford.

Leitao had his strongest season his second year. Reynolds, a senior, and Singletary, a junior, were captains of the team. Virginia basketball had moved to its new home across the street at John Paul Jones Arena. The season opened with Michael Buffer's signature "Let's get ready to rumble" to tip off a 93–90 Virginia upset of

No. 10 Arizona and set the tone of the season and the new arena on the right foot. John Paul Jones Arena became such an attraction for students and fans that Virginia enjoyed an overall 16–1 home record, going a perfect 8–0 at home against ACC opponents. Their lone home loss came in a one-point defeat to Stanford.

Virginia finished the ACC regular season at 11–5 to clinch a share of the regular season title alongside North Carolina, who had beaten Virginia 79–69 earlier in the season as the No. 1 ranked team in the country. Virginia would fall in the first round of the ACC Tournament but would make the NCAA Tournament for the first time since 2001 under Gillen. Virginia defeated Albany 84–57 but fell to Tennessee in the second round 77–74. Leitao was named the ACC Coach of the Year as a result of his 2006–07 campaign.

Though only his sophomore season as head coach, that would be the peak of Leitao's career at Virginia. Over the next two years, Virginia fell back below mediocrity in the ACC, finishing the 2007–08 season at 17–16, (5–11 ACC) and falling even further in 2008–09 with only a 10–18, (4–12 ACC) record despite having the ACC Rookie of the Year in Sylven Landesberg. After only four seasons—just one of which finished with a losing overall record— Leitao was forced to resign his position, a move that came as a surprise for most fans. After all, four years is a short leash for a head coach even within the big business paradigm of college basketball. Leitao, the university's first African American head coach, had led Virginia to its first NCAA Tournament win since an Elite Eight run in 1995.

For many alumni, however, Leitao's rigid approach to the team didn't settle well with the type of partnership that they expected from a head coach and his players. Leitao's short temper—visible on the court as he yelled at players and officials alike and sat players on the bench at the first sign of a mistake—didn't fit the Virginia mold.

Leitao finished with a 63–60 record at Virginia. After taking some time away from coaching altogether, he became the head coach of the Miami Red Claws, an NBA Development League team, in 2011. He served as an assistant coach at Missouri and then Tulsa before getting rehired by DePaul in 2015, which happened to be where Leitao was coaching just before Virginia had signed him. During his first term at DePaul from 2002–05, Leitao's team made two NIT appearances and one trip to the NCAA Tournament.

94 A Soccer Dynasty

What does it take to be called a dynasty? A period of unprecedented dominance in the sport? A star player who commands every aspect of the game? A Hall of Fame coach leading the way? In the early 1990s, Virginia men's soccer had all of these. There was no team more dominant in men's soccer than Virginia.

When Bruce Arena first arrived at Virginia in 1978 as the head coach of Virginia men's soccer (and also as an assistant lacrosse coach until 1985), the Cavaliers were in decent, but not great shape. Though Virginia consistently had winning records, it had only made the NCAA Tournament, also known as the College Cup, once, and that occurred in 1969. It wouldn't take long for Arena to change this, making the tournament in his second season in 1979. A losing campaign in 1980 with an 8–9–1, (2–3–1 ACC) record would be the only such blemish under Arena's 18-year tenure. Beginning in 1981 Virginia made the NCAA Tournament and wouldn't miss another one under Arena.

Virginia nabbed its first national championship in 1989, a shared title with Santa Clara. The Cavaliers scored the match's first goal at 26:48 and would hold on to the lead until Santa Clara scored the equalizer with only 6:23 remaining in regulation. After two 15-minute overtime periods and two 15-minute sudden death overtime periods, neither team was able to find the back of the goal, as the weather deteriorated to below zero-degree wind chill. The game ended as the second longest in NCAA Tournament history, and both teams were awarded a piece of the championship. It wouldn't take long before Virginia would be back in the spotlight after missing the College Cup finals in 1990.

In 1991, after winning the ACC championship, Virginia again faced Santa Clara in the national championship, but this time after a scoreless regulation and four overtime periods, Virginia emerged victorious with a 3–1 advantage in the decisive penalty kicks. Virginia's Claudio Reyna was named the tournament's offensive MVP. In 1992 Virginia did it again. This time Virginia set an ACC record of 32 straight unbeaten games en route to another ACC championship before defeating San Diego 2–0 in the College Cup finals, the first time the Hoos didn't need any overtime periods to clinch the Cup. Again, Reyna was named the offensive MVP.

In 1993 the Cavaliers again took home both the ACC Championship with a 2–1 win against Clemson and the College Cup with a 2–0 win against South Carolina. After scoring all five goals in the Cavaliers' final two games of the tournament, Nate Friends was named the offensive MVP, and Brian Bates was named the defensive MVP of the tournament. Goalkeeper Jeff Causey finished his career at Virginia with three straight shutouts in the NCAA finals.

In front of a record crowd of over 12,000 fans, Virginia won an unprecedented fourth straight national championship in 1994 with a 1–0 win against perennial powerhouse Indiana. The Cavaliers' lone goal came from A.J. Wood in the 21st minute after a team display of fundamental passing, speed, and ballhandling. "I'm extremely proud of our team today and our program and I'm very

Morgan Brian

Morgan Brian wrote on her goal sheet in grade school: "Play college soccer in at least Division I and start!" Or at least—that's what she wrote at first until her coach told her that he wasn't satisfied with this goal and she needed to revise it. "Play on the national team," Brian skeptically wrote off to the side.

In grade school Brian played with teammates four years older, which meant that as she was just starting to hit her pre-teen and teenage years everyone else had already experienced growth spurts and muscular advancement with which she was unable to keep up, earning her the nickname "Plankton," the smallest main character of the popular cartoon series *SpongeBob SquarePants*.

Largely because of her size, she was not picked to join the Olympic Development Program, a U.S. Youth Soccer initiative to identify and develop a pool of youth players in an effort to increase the success of the U.S. National Teams in the international arena. Brian was the only one of her teammates not selected. Disappointed and frustrated as to whether she had peaked in grade school and was perhaps not good enough to compete at the collegiate or international level, Brian began to wonder if she would have a career in soccer after all. Thanks to guidance from her coach, she stuck with the sport and continued to play. It wouldn't take too long before whatever doubts she had about competing at the Division I level would subside as she was named the 2010–11 Gatorade National Girls Soccer Player of the Year—just another in what would become a seemingly endless series of accolades.

At Virginia, Brian's career was nothing short of remarkable. A multiple-time first-team All-American across various publications and a multiple Player of the Year recipient, Brian became only the fourth women's player in history to win the MAC Hermann Trophy, soccer's

happy for the senior class of A.J. Wood, Nate Friends, Clint Peay, and Tain Nix," Arena said. "They have accomplished something that may never be accomplished again in Division I athletics."

Since then, no team has won more than two national championships in a row, and only Indiana has won the title in back-to-back years. After Arena left Virginia to coach D.C. United in the MLS, most prestigious award, in consecutive years. Only North Carolina's Mia Hamm and Cindy Parlow and Portland's Christine Sinclair have been able to complete such a feat. (Notre Dame's Kerri Hanks won the trophy twice in non-consecutive years.)

Successful as it was, Morgan Brian's time at Virginia is only the beginning of her story. Throughout her collegiate career, Brian had the privilege and challenging task of juggling between playing for Virginia and playing for the U.S. Women's National Team. She earned her first cap with USWNT in a 4–1 victory against South Korea on June 15, 2013, in Foxboro, Massachusetts, and scored her first goal with the USWNT in a 7–0 win against Mexico on September 3, 2013, in Washington, D.C. She was the only current collegiate player on the USWNT roster during the 2014 World Cup qualifying tournament. Brian became the youngest player on the USWNT roster for the 2015 FIFA Women's World Cup. "Whether I play a minute or start or I don't play at all, I'm happy to be here and play the role I need to play," Brian said in an interview during the World Cup qualifying tournament.

What Brian didn't really expect, though, was that not only would she play minutes in the World Cup and not only would she start, but she also would became a national hero en route to a World Cup Championship for the United States. Due to a little bit of luck for Brian, she was able to start in central midfield in the final three matches of the World Cup as fellow midfielders Megan Rapinoe and Lauren Holiday each drew their second yellow card of the tournament. The suspensions gave way for Brian to start against China, Germany, and Japan, and she played in every minute of all three matches. With the instincts of a defensive midfielder, Brian didn't have any goals or assists to her credit in any of the three final matches, but her success in the role she played for the Women's National Team was unquestioned.

George Gelnovatch, who played for Virginia from 1983 to 1986 and coached as an assistant under Arena, took over at the helm in 1996. Virginia has still not missed an NCAA Tournament since 1980, a nation-best 35 straight appearances.

Virginia has since won two additional College Cups—in 2009 and 2014. Those who played at Virginia in the early 1990s have become some of the most recognizable United States soccer names, most notably Reyna, who was a member of the U.S. Men's National Team for four straight FIFA World Cups from 1994 to 2006, captaining both the 2002 and 2006 teams.

Arena was inducted into the National Soccer Hall of Fame in 2010.

95 Origins of the Blue and Orange

Virginia's colors are blue and orange, but it wasn't always that way. A 1904 article from *College Topics*—later renamed *The Cavalier Daily*—describes the story of a town hall-style meeting in 1888 in order to change the university's colors. "Up to that time," the *College Topics* article stated, "the colors had been silver grey and cardinal red, intending to represent the gray of the Confederacy, dyed in blood."

As the uniforms endured countless laundry cycles, it became clear that the gray and red could not withstand fading and would not stand out on a muddy playing field. Plus, the sight of a team sporting gray and a faded red—otherwise known as pink—was never particularly intimidating.

On his way to practice that day was Allen Potts, wrote Kevin Edds, the man behind the documentary *Wahoowa: The History of Virginia Cavalier Football*, in an article on *TheSabre.com*. Potts, a member of Virginia's first football team in 1888, was wearing his football uniform and a navy blue and orange scarf that he had obtained one summer at Oxford University while on its rowing club. Though Oxford's school colors were blue and white, it's rumored that Potts had traded his blue and white scarf for an orange and blue scarf from the Grosvenor Rowing Club after a race.

In addition to being a star on the football team, Potts would also become a star for Virginia's baseball and track and field teams. Suffice it to say, he was a popular man on campus.

"[Potts] had rolled about his neck a very large silk handkerchief, striped navy blue and orange," the *College Topics* article further stated. "Some student sitting behind him reached over and pulled the handkerchief from his neck and waving it yelled, 'How will these colors do?' This seemed to take the fancy of the crowd, and orange and blue were chosen without opposition."

It wasn't until Edds followed the Potts family tree, as part of his research for the *Wahoowa* documentary, that he was able to track down the legendary scarf. Potts' great-granddaughter Jane Potts told Edds that the part of the scarf that she owned had been framed but destroyed in a fire. However, the scarf had been cut in half. Edds was able to locate the other half of the scarf in the Virginia Historical Society's catalog, and it was labeled "Fragment of silk boating scarf" with a description of, "One half of silk boating scarf from which the colors of UVA were selected." And so finally, Edds had found the closest piece of concrete evidence to confirm the urban myth that had been passed down for more than a century.

According to Edds, Virginia's blue and orange also served as the foundation for establishing the colors of the University of Florida. "Years later," Edds wrote, "a sundry store owner on the University of Florida campus would come to visit his son who was attending UVA. When looking in a Charlottesville store for a pennant to sell to Florida fans back home, his son came up with the idea of the gator, a native Floridian reptile, as the mascot. When the Charlottesville factory delivered the Gator-clad pennants to Florida that fall, they consisted of an orange alligator over a navy blue background, as those were the only colors the factory had in stock... used for the hometown UVA pennants."

96 Mark Bernardino

He spent 41 years of his life at the University of Virginia building the men's and women's swimming and diving program into the powerhouse of the ACC. During that time Mark Bernardino and his swimmers have captured championships, Olympic medals, and countless accolades. "It's the hard work and devotion of the swimmers, the athletes willing to make sacrifices to achieve the highest levels of the sport," Bernardino said in a *Virgina Magazine* article. "It's the dedication of the assistant coaches instilling our philosophy that hard work pays off."

When Bernardino graduated from Virginia's McIntire School of Commerce in 1974, he had already made a name for himself as one of the program's top swimmers. During his time he set six program records, qualified for three NCAA Championships, and qualified for the 1972 U.S. Olympic Trials. In 1974 he received the UVA Male Athlete of the Year Award. That's not too bad for someone who had begun swimming around the age of 10 at a local community pool outside of Philadelphia. Bernardino described swimming as "just one of a handful of sports I played as a kid," not placing any particular emphasis on it.

Two years after graduation, he returned to Virginia as an assistant coach, earning his master's degree from the Curry School of Education in 1978, at which time he was appointed as head coach of both the men's and women's swimming and diving teams. Thirty-five years later, Bernardino would step away from the program having been the longest tenured coach ever at Virginia, earning a combined 27 ACC championships—16 on the men's side and 11 on the women's—and being named the ACC Coach of the Year 26 times—18 with the men's team and 13 with the women's. No other ACC head coach has won as many men's titles as Bernardino, and only North Carolina's Frank Comfort won more women's titles with 15. Under Bernardino, 18 swimmers received ACC Swimmer of the Year honors for a total of 26 times, and 16 earned ACC Freshman of the Year honors.

At the national level, Bernardino coached 98 individual All-Americans (with a combined 205 honors), 124 All-American relays, and four NCAA champions who won six individual national titles. Internationally, Bernardino has coached 12 student-athletes who went on to compete at the Olympic level. Four of them captured gold medals—Melanie Valerio (1996 Atlanta 4x100 free relay), Ed Moses (2000 Athens 4x100m medley relay), Matt McLean (2012 London 4x200m freestyle relay), and Lauren Perdue (2012 London 4x200m freestyle relay) for the United States.

Somewhat abruptly, Bernardino resigned in 2013. "It is a difficult day filled with mixed emotions, and I have not come to this decision lightly," he said in a release. "This job and this university, along with my family, have been my life and my passion for nearly as long as I can remember. But I come to this decision with confidence in the future." Though Virginia swimming alumni sought answers, they weren't going to receive them publicly, as Bernardino and the university entered into mutual non-disparagement agreements. The following year, Bernardino was named the associate head coach at South Carolina.

Outside of the pool, Bernardino has also received recognition as the 2010 recipient of both the Raven Society's Raven Award, the society's highest honor given to an individual for excellence in service and contribution to the University of Virginia, and the university's Algernon Sydney Sullivan Award, presented to individuals for excellence of character and service to humanity. "A son of the university...Mark Bernardino's accomplishments and contributions to our community are legend. Yet, one would be hard pressed to meet a man of such marked modesty and compassion for others. When you encounter Coach B, you find yourself reassured, encouraged, and esteemed," said associate dean of students Aaron Laushway, a member of the Sullivan Award Selection Committee.

97 Visit Scott Stadium

The Carl Smith Center, home of David A. Harrison III Field at Scott Stadium, is quite the mouthful. So, the Wahoo faithful just call their beloved stadium "Scott Stadium." Originally built in 1931 to replace the 8,000-seat Lambeth Field, Scott Stadium's construction began in 1930 and was completed in 1931. Paid for by university rector Frederic W. Scott and dedicated to the memory of his parents, Frederic Robert Scott and Francis Branch Scott, Scott Stadium boasted an initial capacity crowd of 22,000. In its dedication game on October 15, 1931, a capacity crowd showed up, though Virginia would lose to Virginia Military Institute.

The stadium represented a major upgrade from Lambeth Field, which at the time of its construction was among the best facilities in the South, and was shared between the university's football, baseball, and track and field programs. A decision was made to upgrade the football program's facility when a Virginia football player complained that javelins and discuses were being thrown dangerously close to the players during practice. The new stadium had concrete bleachers built right into the hillside of the sunken field, as well as parking for 5,000 cars. Previously, spectators were simply encouraged to pull up to Lambeth Field in wagons and horse-and-buggies to enjoy the games.

Though Scott Stadium is now more than 80 years old, you wouldn't be able to tell today, as the stadium has undergone several major renovations. University president Edgar Shannon decided to upgrade the facilities in 1974, and after nearly $800,000 (about $3.75 million in 2015 dollars), the stadium received new aluminum seating, an Astroturf playing surface, and general restoration work.

By 1980 the university had installed upper decks on the east and west sides of the stadium, increasing the maximum capacity to 40,000. Two years later, with the installation of portable lights, Virginia played its first ever night game at Scott Stadium, which turned out to be a whopping 48–0 loss to defending national champion Clemson. Virginia was coming off a 1–10, (0–6 ACC) season and finished 1982 with just a 2–9, (1–5 ACC) record.

Scott Stadium's artificial playing surface was replaced in 1995 with natural grass and named David A Harrison III Field, which is still used today. In 1999 the south end zone was closed off for additional seats, and in 2000 an upper deck was added to the south side to increase capacity to 61,500, which includes approximately 5,000 for "the Hill," the north side of the stadium typically filled by students. The completed project in 2000 was named The Carl Smith Center, home of David A Harrison III Field at Scott Stadium.

Scott Stadium has produced some incredible memories for the Cavaliers fanbase, including Virginia's first ever Thursday night game, which saw the Hoos take down second-ranked Florida State to deliver the Seminoles their first ACC loss since joining the conference. It's also brought some less-fond memories, such as the 1990 loss as No. 1 Virginia fell to Georgia Tech at the last minute, ending any chance of a national championship that year.

Carl W. Smith

Emblazoned underneath the massive 1,824-square-foot video board at Scott Stadium known as Hoo Vision are the words "CARL SMITH CENTER." Just about every other weekend in the fall, tens of thousands of Virginia fans pass through the stadium's turnstiles, rooting for the blue and orange without as much as a passing thought as to the man and family behind one of the facility's namesakes.

A native of Wise, Virginia, and member the football team from 1947–51, starting at offensive guard in 1949 and 1951, Carl W. Smith was a 1951 graduate whose heart never left the Grounds of Mr. Jefferson's university. In 1960 Smith founded Amvest Corp., a coal and natural gas corporation based in Albemarle County that eventually grew to be worth more than $575 million. Through Amvest and other investments, Smith and his wife, Hunter, contributed more than $60 million during Smith's lifetime, including what was at the time the single largest monetary contribution in the history of the university, an unrestricted $25 million gift made in 1997.

Of the $25 million gift, $2 million went to the University of Virginia's College at Wise to build the Carl Smith Stadium, a $7 million project. The remaining $23 million was dedicated to the renovation and expansion of the existing Scott Stadium, a three-year project that added the upper deck and 15,000 seats, taking the stadium from one of the bottom third to top third among ACC schools in terms of size. In 2003 the Smith family donated $1.5 million to the university to help fund the Cavalier Marching Band to replace the Virginia Pep Band following a controversial halftime show at the 2003 Continental Tire Bowl against West Virginia.

The Smith family's contributions to the university reach well beyond the confines of Virginia athletics. In addition to the football stadium and marching band, Hunter Smith pledged $10.7 million in 2009 for the construction of a band rehearsal hall. The facility, named the Hunter Smith Band Building, was completed in 2011 for a total construction cost of $12.7 million. In addition to the music facility, the Smith family also made significant contributions to the schools of medicine, law, architecture, and business; the Jefferson Scholars Foundation; and the Children's Medical Center.

> Carl Smith also served both as a member of the university's Board of Visitors from 1980–88, where he chaired the Finance Committee, and as a two-term trustee of the Darden Graduate School of Business Administration Foundation. He also served as chair of the Jefferson Restoration Advisory Board, where he sought to preserve the historical buildings on Grounds.
>
> Smith passed away on December 8, 2005, at the age of 78. "Of all the people who have touched Virginia athletics—from student-athletes to coaches, administrators, and alumni, none had a greater love for the university than Carl Smith," athletics director Craig Littlepage said following Smith's passing. "His impact on our programs will be felt forever, and the Carl Smith Center will be a lasting legacy of the good he did for the university and Virginia football. The collective thoughts of those associated with the department of athletics will be with Hunter and the family."

The Rolling Stones and Dave Matthews have both performed at the stadium.

Good times or not, Scott Stadium is consistently ranked as one of the most beautiful college football stadiums in the country with the Blue Ridge Mountains in the background set against the traditional Jeffersonian-style architecture with the pergola plaza on the open north end.

98 Chris Slade

By the time Michigan State upset then-No. 1 Michigan on October 13, 1990, the No. 2-ranked Virginia Cavaliers had already beaten North Carolina State 31–0. The television camera focused on Michigan State players celebrating the big win. "They showed a camera shot of the Michigan State players and they were saying,

'We're No 1,'" Virginia sophomore defensive end Chris Slade said at the time. "I said, 'No, uh-uh, we're No. 1.'"

It's not surprising that Slade would point that out. Not one to hold back on what was on his mind, Slade had been confident and vocal since his first year on Grounds. In the first start of his collegiate career at Clemson in 1989, Slade led the charge of a handful of Virginia football players to taunt the Clemson players running down The Hill at Death Valley, one of the most well-known—and most intimidating—college football entrances. "I had a personal vendetta against Clemson," said Slade at the time.

During his senior year of high school, Slade had narrowed his choices to Virginia, North Carolina, Alabama, Georgia, Ohio State, and Clemson. The Tigers were the most aggressive of the group, as "they made some bad statements about some of the schools I wanted to go to." But Slade's vocal confidence wasn't confined to just the Clemson games. "Down the road," Slade said as a freshman, "I can see myself being a captain, leading the team to some more bowl games. I think I have the feel, the knock to be a leader out there."

Good thing for Slade, he also had the talent to back up his words. By the time he had started only four games, he had already accumulated two sacks, 38 tackles, and two forced fumbles.

During Slade's four-year career at Virginia, in addition to achieving a No. 1 ranking in the AP poll for three weeks in 1990—something previously thought impossible—the Cavaliers made a bowl game in each of Slade's first three years. They reached the 1990 Florida Citrus Bowl (Slade was named the Defensive MVP), the 1991 Sugar Bowl, and the December 29, 1991 Gator Bowl. Virginia finished 7–4 overall during Slade's senior year but did not make it to a bowl game. As he had predicted his freshman year, Slade did in fact become a captain of the 1992 team.

In spearheading Virginia's potent defense during his four years, Slade was named a consensus All-American during his junior and senior years, becoming the school's first ever back-to-back consensus All-American. In 1992 he was also named the National Defensive Player of the Year by the *Football News*. While wreaking havoc on opposing teams' quarterbacks, Slade set both Virginia and ACC records for career sacks at 40, a number that has remained untouched since. In Virginia's annals the next closest player is linebacker Clint Sintim, who from 2005 to 2007 collected 29 sacks. Since the NCAA began tracking sacks as an official statistic in 2000, only one player has recorded 40 or more sacks: Arizona State's Terrell Suggs with 44. Slade also continues to lead the Virginia record books for career tackles for loss at 56.

After a tremendously successful collegiate career that resulted in his jersey's retirement at Virginia, Slade was drafted in the second round of the 1993 NFL Draft as the 31st overall selection to the New England Patriots. Slade played eight fruitful seasons there in a career that included an AFC Championship in 1996 and Pro Bowl and All-Pro honors for Slade in 1997. He played his final professional season with the Carolina Panthers in 2001. Slade started in 108 of the 142 games he played over his nine years in the NFL, recording 665 tackles and 53.5 quarterback sacks.

Among Slade's greatest memories at Virginia was his time when the Cavaliers were the top team in the nation. "You almost felt like a rock star," he said in a 2011 interview. "Everybody on Grounds knew you—and they—were a part of history. It made me realize why I had come to school there. Whenever I walk around today in Atlanta, I walk with my chest out. People always want to talk about that 1990 game."

99 Virginia's Statistically Impossible Loss

When a team loses on a buzzer-beater, it's a heartbreaker. When a team loses after holding what seemed to be an insurmountable lead, it's frustrating. When a team loses a game that statistically speaking was a guaranteed win, that's a whole other level.

In head coach Tony Bennett's second year at Virginia in 2011, the Cavaliers were 16–14, (7–9 ACC), heading into the ACC Tournament with no realistic chance of making the NCAA Tournament short of winning the ACC Tournament. The Hoos were seeded eighth and slated to face ninth-seeded Miami, a team Virginia had lost to 70–68 in the regular season in overtime.

Miami used an 11–2 run to close out the first half with a 31–25 lead against Virginia. Down by as much as 37–30 midway through the second half, Virginia launched a tremendous comeback, scoring 20 of the next 22 points of the game to take a commanding 50–39 lead with just 2:14 to play. When senior guard Mustapha Farrakhan made one of two free throws with under 42 seconds to go and a 10-point lead, the game looked all but finished. After all, Miami had only scored eight points in the first 18 minutes of the second half. Miami used just under eight seconds before Durand Scott took the shot that would launch an improbable series, hitting his first three-point bucket of the game with 35.2 seconds remaining.

Renowned baseball statistician Bill James developed a formula in 2008 to determine when a game can be said to be over with 100 percent statistical confidence. His formula, tested both by him by his editors at StatSheet.com, was only defied once, in 1974, when North Carolina came back from eight points down with 17 seconds remaining against Duke.

The formula looked like this:

- Take the number of points one team is ahead.
- Subtract three.
- Add a half point if the team that is ahead has the ball; subtract a half point if the other team has the ball. Numbers less than zero become zero.
- Square that.
- If the result is greater than the number of seconds left in the game, the lead is safe.

Applied to the Virginia-Miami game, the Cavaliers were up by 10 points. Subtract three, and you're left with seven. Miami had the ball, so subtract half a point, making the number 6.5. Square that figure, and you're left with 42.25. The number of seconds left in the game? Thirty-five. By all accounts, even if tested at the start of Miami's possession with 42 seconds remaining, Virginia's lead was 100 percent statistically safe. "For us [to lose], everything that could go wrong had to go wrong, and they had to finish," Bennett said following the game.

Virginia guard Sammy Zeglinski would miss both of his ensuing free throws. Miami's Malcolm Grant would hit another three-pointer. Zeglinski would turn the ball over on the inbounds, and Miami's Julian Gamble would dunk the ball on the inbounds. Suddenly, Virginia fans could not believe what was happening in front of them. The 10-point lead, built upon a dazzling performance by the Hoos in the second half, had dwindled down to two.

Virginia point guard Jontel Evans, who had been sharp all night, misjudged a pass to Farrakhan, and was picked off by Miami's Scott instead, who tied the game with 13.9 seconds remaining. Neither team was able to score the winning bucket in regulation, and the game was sent into overtime. Miami was able to complete the comeback, coming away with a 69–62 win. "This was tough," freshman forward Joe Harris said. "I've never been part of anything like this. It feels horrible. I've never lost a game like this before in my life. I don't even know how to explain it."

"I've never been a part of anything like this," Evans echoed. "It's a shock to me. I'm still amazed that we're sitting here with an 'L.'"

As rare of an occurrence as this may be, five years later, Virginia found themselves in a similar situation at Wake Forest, but this time the Cavaliers came out victorious. On January 26, 2016, No. 11 Virginia was down seven points with just 20 seconds remaining. As time was expiring, Virginia sophomore Darius Thompson hit a buzzer-beating three—his only three of the night—to seal a 72–71 win for Virginia.

100 Bronco Mendenhall

Only five days after the resignation of football head coach Mike London, Virginia had found its man. It wasn't Mark Richt. It wasn't Rhett Lashlee. It wasn't Scott Frost. It wasn't Kirby Smart. In fact, it wasn't a name that anyone had been talking about as a candidate.

Instead, it was Brigham Young University's Bronco Mendenhall, an established head coach of a major program and someone, who for the most part, nobody even knew was on the market.

When Mendenhall first arrived at BYU in 2005, the Cougars had suffered three consecutive losing seasons, each of which included a loss to in-state rival Utah. The similarities to Virginia are not lost on the Wahoo faithful, as the Cavaliers suffered four consecutive losing seasons just prior to Mendenhall's arrival in Charlottesville.

In Mendenhall's first year at BYU, the Cougars finished the regular season with a 6–5 record and a trip to the Las Vegas Bowl. In the 10 years that followed during Mendenhall's tenure at BYU, the Cougars never had a losing season. By the time Mendenhall left BYU, he had taken the Cougars to a bowl game in each of his 11 years at the helm, one of only 11 programs to advance to a bowl game each season during that period. The Cougars won six of the 11. The only team to have a better bowl record during this time was Florida State with seven wins, including a national championship in 2014.

Mendenhall made an impression during the press conference announcing his hire. "Just from what I've seen already, certainly change has got to be made here," Mendenhall said. "Change is good. In fact there was a great book called *Change or Die*, and I don't intend to die."

One thing that won't change is Virginia's rigorous academic standards. Mendenhall, whose BYU teams averaged nine wins per season, made comparisons between the two schools, noting that BYU's academic standards and restrictive honor code, which, among other things, prevented alcohol consumption, made it challenging to recruit top players to play for him. Without BYU's honor code, Mendenhall said, his entire staff felt that the options of good players to recruit seem endless.

Virginia's incoming class of 2016, almost exclusively recruited by London, remained largely intact despite the turnover at the helm. On National Signing Day in early February 2016, Mendenhall and company generated newfound excitement among the Virginia fanbase, taking to social media and viral videos to reinvigorate a fanbase that had grown accustomed to losing seasons.

Though Mendenhall has not yet coached a game at Virginia at the time of this publication, he has already begun to make his

Virginia athletic director Craig Littlepage (left) poses with Bronco Mendenhall during the 2015 press conference announcing Mendenhall's hiring as head coach.

mark on the school. During the summer of 2015, it was reported that Virginia was considering a new $50 million football operations facility, one that would be used as an important recruiting tool for top players, and improved facilities for weightlifting and practice. The project stalled during the 2015 football season as the university's Board of Visitors and athletics administration waited to see how the coaching situation would play out. In Mendenhall's opening press conference, he said, "What I do know now after seeing our team and seeing this institution [is that] I'm fiercely committed now to not only change on the field but for the infrastructure and the physical structures. If we are serious—and I am—about not taking a back seat to anybody, then a new facility for football exclusively is paramount as a visible and tangible sign that we are serious."

As Mendenhall begins his rookie campaign in fall of 2016, he knows there are critics out there, but his message is clear. "I see even in this room those already fiercely committed and can't wait to come and support and see how this goes, and others are skeptical. I get it," Mendenhall said. "I will outlast you."

Acknowledgments

For the better part of my adult life—since I first came on the Grounds as an undergraduate at the University of Virginia—there have been times when I feel like I eat, sleep, and breathe Virginia athletics. It's been an evergreen source of great joy for me, though admittedly, the joy has a tendency to come with what seems like more than its fair share of heartbreak as well.

As an undergraduate and as a law student, I attended every home football and basketball game that my schedule allowed. I made time to attend and support Virginia's non-revenue student-athletes, not only because the sports interested me and I thought they didn't get enough attention, but also because they were just really darn good at what they did. When I finally left Charlottesville to get a real job, I didn't stop following the teams. Instead, I founded the site *Streaking the Lawn*, which has since grown beyond my wildest imagination and has a staff that works almost around the clock to cover all aspects of Virginia athletics, something I've continued for nearly a quarter of my life now.

In short, I thought I knew just about everything there was to know about Virginia sports. When Triumph Books approached me to write about Virginia, I saw it as an opportunity to brush up on some history and exercise some of my creative writing skills. What I didn't expect was uncovering entire eras of Virginia sports that would lead to me reading what felt like every sports section of every newspaper in the state. I didn't expect to fall in love all over again with the rich history that is Virginia athletics.

For that, I first want to thank Triumph Books for making this book happen, from start to finish, and for holding my hand throughout the process.

I also want to thank the crew over at the site, *Streaking the Lawn*. Whether or not they knew it, they all played a huge role in my being able to put this together. I want to thank in particular Eric Hobeck, Matt Trogdon, Caroline Darney, Ryan Reese, and Pierce Coughter for their contributions to this book, without which I would probably still be staring at a blank page. Also a big shout-out to Will Campbell, Paul Wiley, and Brian Schwartz for keeping the site afloat while I neglected my duties over there in order to reach the finish line over here.

My friends and family have been tremendously supportive of me in this endeavor for well over a year and kept moving me forward chapter by chapter. You all deserve free signed copies of this book, but I know you'd just as well rather go out and buy a copy and continue supporting my efforts, right?

I have to thank my older (and only) brother, Keith, in particular, for choosing to go to UVA over Duke. If we're going to be honest here, I have to admit that I was most likely going to follow you to whichever school you had picked. So thank you for getting it right.

Thanks to the audience of *Streaking the Lawn*, who unwittingly served as a focus group for many of these chapters.

For me, this book wasn't about finding that one little gem of a story that no one had ever heard of before. It was about taking a stroll through history and finding the 100 things that stood out the most. I think along the way, you'll probably find a gem or two that you've probably never heard, but for the older fans, I hope this serves as a refreshing walk down memory lane that evokes the feelings you felt when you first lived it. For the younger fans, I hope this gives you a glimpse at just how rich the history at Virginia is and that it inspires you to become a part of the history going forward.

Sources

Books

Graham, Chris and Patrick Hite. *Mad About U: Four Decades of Basketball at University Hall.* Augusta Free Press Publishing Division, 2006.

Ratcliffe, Jerry. *The University of Virginia Football Vault: The History of the Cavaliers.* Whitman Publishing, LLC, 2008.

Videos

Edds, Kevin. *Wahoowa: The History of Virginia Cavaliers Football.* Daedalus Creative LLC, 2010.

Newspapers

The Cavalier Daily (Charlottesville, Virginia)

Chicago Tribune

Daily Press (Newport News, Virginia)

The Daily Progress (Charlottesville, Virginia)

The New York Times

The Roanoke Times (Roanoke, Virginia)

The Sunday Morning Star (Wilmington, Delaware)

The Virginian-Pilot (Norfolk, Virginia)

The Washington Post

Magazines

Sports Illustrated

Websites

NCAA.org

RaycomSports.com

Richmond.com

StreakingtheLawn.com

TheSabre.com

UVAmagazine.org

VirginiaSports.com